Black Women Navigating the Doctoral Journey

With the increasing focus on the critical importance of mentoring in advancing Black women students from graduation to careers in academia, this book identifies and considers the peer mentoring contexts and conditions that support Black women student success in higher education. This edited collection focuses on Black women students primarily at the doctoral level and how they have retained each other through their educational journey, emphasizing how they navigated this season of educational changes given COVID and racial unrest. Chapters illuminate what minoritized women students have done to mentor each other to navigate unwelcome campus environments laden with identity politics and other structural barriers. Shining a light on systemic structures in place that contribute to Black women's alienation in the academy, this book unpacks implications for interactions and engagement with faculty as advisors and mentors. An important resource for faculty and graduate students at colleges and universities, ultimately this work is critical to helping the academy fortify Black women's sense of belonging and connection early in their academic career and foster their success.

Sharon Fries-Britt is Professor of Higher Education at the University of Maryland, College Park, USA.

Bridget Turner Kelly is Associate Professor of Student Affairs at the University of Maryland, College Park, USA.

Black Women Navigating the Doctoral Journey

Student Peer Support, Mentorship, and Success in the Academy

Edited by Sharon Fries-Britt and Bridget Turner Kelly

Routledge
Taylor & Francis Group

NEW YORK AND LONDON

Designed cover image: © Getty Images

First published 2024
by Routledge
605 Third Avenue, New York, NY 10158

and by Routledge
4 Park Square, Milton Park, Abingdon, Oxon, OX14 4RN

Routledge is an imprint of the Taylor & Francis Group, an informa business

© 2024 selection and editorial matter, Sharon Fries-Britt and Bridget Turner Kelly; individual chapters, the contributors

The right of Sharon Fries-Britt and Bridget Turner Kelly to be identified as the authors of the editorial material, and of the authors for their individual chapters, has been asserted in accordance with sections 77 and 78 of the Copyright, Designs and Patents Act 1988.

Library of Congress Cataloging-in-Publication Data
Names: Fries-Britt, Sharon, 1959– editor. | Kelly, Bridget Turner, 1973– editor.
Title: Black women navigating the doctoral journey: student peer support, mentorship, and success in the academy / edited by Sharon Fries-Britt and Bridget Turner Kelly.
Description: New York: Routledge, 2024. |
Includes bibliographical references. |
Identifiers: LCCN 2023011839 | ISBN 9781032496177 (hbk) |
ISBN 9781032484853 (pbk) | ISBN 9781003394648 (ebk)
Subjects: LCSH: Doctoral students—African Americans. | African American women—Education (Graduate)—United States. | African American women—Education (Higher)—United States. | Mentoring in education—United States. | Peer teaching—United States. | Universities and colleges—United States—Sociological aspects. | Discrimination in higher education—United States.
Classification: LCC LC2781 .B4755 2024 | DDC 378.1/982996073—dc23
LC record available at https://lccn.loc.gov/2023011839

ISBN: 978-1-032-49617-7 (hbk)
ISBN: 978-1-032-48485-3 (pbk)
ISBN: 978-1-003-39464-8 (ebk)

DOI: 10.4324/9781003394648

Typeset in Perpetua Std
by codeMantra

This book is dedicated to our former and current Black women doctoral and master's students. Know that your support of each other serves as a light for us all!

Contents

CONTENTS

Acknowledgments

We were so blessed to have the administrative brainpower of Tyanna A.E. Clayton-Mallett, a PhD student at the University of Maryland, on this book project. In addition to co-authoring Chapter 1 with us, Tyanna provided administrative leadership at every stage keeping us organized, motivated, and on top of deadlines! Tyanna, you made this project seamless and enjoyable at every turn. Your infectious smile and laughter were just what we needed when we had to dig deep to complete our work. We appreciate you and recognize all that you gave to make this a success. We also want to thank our wonderful editor, Heather Jarrow, for her excellent guidance and feedback through each of the stages of development. It has been a joy to work with you on this, our second book project with Routledge. Thank you for advancing this important topic.

Our deepest appreciation goes to all the chapter authors for the work that you have contributed. To a person, each of you stayed the course over the past two years to bring your experiences to light. Your tenacity and dedication to work during the height of the COVID global pandemic and stay focused on your research and this book are beyond admirable. Individually and collectively, your chapters offer an enormous gift to the field. Thank you for being on this journey with us and for sharing your network experiences with peers. The insights that you offered provide leaders with important homework to shift the burden from students to institutional systems of support. Last, but certainly not least, we want to thank our dear sister colleague and friend Dr. Christine Stanley for dropping the intellectual and personal mic in the foreword! We deeply appreciate the time that you gave to carefully read each chapter and to connect the critical insights offered by the authors while recognizing the complexities in their work of the intersecting identities of Black women. Your willingness to share your own journey and the key individuals who have poured into you deepen our understanding of your brilliance and mother wit. You are the embodiment of so many aspects of the Network Mentorship model. Thank you for mentoring me (Sharon) and supporting my advancement to full professor and so many other colleagues in the field!

To readers of this book, thank you for your support and for advancing the success of Black women on the doctoral journey!

Black Women Navigating the Doctoral Journey: Student Peer Support, Mentorship, and Success in the Academy

Building Communities of Support, Mentorship, and Success

Christine A. Stanley

The professional success of Black women in academia matters. Centering Black women students' experiences on their PhD journey matters. Communities of support for Black women in academia matter. Black women in the academy, regardless of whether they identify as faculty or student, remain disproportionately low in numbers. The PhD journey for scholars of color is an academic pathway filled with hierarchical experiences associated with sexism, racism, homophobia, transphobia, Islamophobia, anti-Semitism, and xenophobia and often undertaken in isolation.

The co-editors of this book, *Black Women Navigating the Doctoral Journey: Student Peer Support, Mentorship, and Success in the Academy*, examine this journey through the unique experiences of Black women undergraduate and graduate students across a range of institutions who mentor and support each other through a community process of obtaining a PhD degree.

The literature on mentoring in academia is filled with formal and informal models and frameworks that are often assumptive, prescriptive, and based on relationships that fail to account for social inequalities, the intersection of race and gender, and persistent patriarchal systemic structures that impact successful recruitment and retention policies, practices, and processes. What we see in this book is a nuanced and transparent window into understanding how powerful and successful Black women mentor each other in an organizational and cultural landscape that was neither built for their access nor success. For example, if we look at some of the sections within each of the ten chapters, we first see the **"A Case for Mentoring"** where co-editors, Fries-Britt and Turney Kelly, share the need and rationale for peer mentoring including graduate and undergraduate students at historically white institutions. In Section II, **"Intersectional Peer Mentoring,"** we see the experiences with mentoring through the intersectional lens of race, ethnicity, gender, sexuality, nationality, and culture. Section III, **"Peer Mentoring During a Global Pandemic,"** provides us with an understanding of Black women at different stages of the journey who persist with each other, working part and full time, while raising families. Finally, in Section IV, **"Centering Healing in Peer Mentoring,"** we see the importance of how Black women build communities of healing and wellness to strengthen the "mind, heart, body, and soul."

I am a Black, cisgender woman who grew up in Jamaica, West Indies. The contents of this book speak to me personally. As a postcolonial scholar in the academy who held institutional and national positions of titled leadership, these experiences taught me the value of people and being among Black women who embody my existence in a world that catalogs me to fit mentally oppressive models of how I should profess, lead, look, act, think, or simply be. I have been given a lot, and I try to give back to others through my mentoring. Furthermore, my experiences illuminated social and political contexts that shape identity and endemic disparities in our institutions, society, and world. Undoubtedly, this book should speak to many stakeholders in higher education – current and prospective graduate students, tenure-track faculty, senior-level administrators, philanthropists, and legislators. However, regardless of positionality and audience, I agree with the co-editors that ultimately, this work "is critical to helping the academy fortify Black women's sense of belonging and connection early in their academic career." Colleges and universities espouse diversity and inclusion and claim that these concepts matter. However, if the diversity of the professoriate matters, then it is high time we look beyond traditional hierarchical mentoring relationship practices to more alternative and inclusive possibilities that center the experiences of others who still remain on the margins in academia. The place to begin is understanding Black women, our history, and the power within and among us. There is much to learn from our experiences for individual and institutional transformation. However, as the co-editors titled Chapter 10, "There Is Only So Much a Peer Can Do." Therefore, I'm compelled to ask the question, "Are we ready to listen, learn, and take action, to make the academy more just and inclusive?" The journey to attaining a more inclusive professoriate community first begins with a step toward understanding what it takes for Black women to succeed in academia. When Black women matter, we *all* matter. As the late poet Maya Angelou shared, "If you have the privilege of being born a black woman, it is my belief, that it is a part of your divine mission to liberate yourself from all external and internalized oppression and thereby liberate the world (Douglas, 2019)." And as the Black Feminist Visionaries of the Combahee River Collective (1983) (Beverly Smith, Demetia Frazer, Cheryl Clarke, Akasha Hull, Margo Okazawa-Rey, Chirlane McCray) and Barbara Smith and Audre Lorde taught us, "until Black women are free, none of use will be free." The contributors in this book are liberating humanity and the academy.

REFERENCES

Collective, C. R. (1983). The Combahee river collective statement. *Home girls: A Black Feminist Anthology, 1*, 264–274.

Douglas, A. A. (2019). 928 *Maya Angelou Quotes* (Vol. 5). UB Tech.

Preface

Bridget Turner Kelly and Sharon Fries-Britt

With the increasing focus on the critical importance of mentoring in advancing Black women students from graduation to careers in academia, the purpose of this book is to identify and consider the peer mentoring contexts and conditions that support Black women student success. Specifically, this book focuses on Black women students primarily at the doctoral level and how they have retained each other through their educational journey, emphasizing how they navigated a season of educational changes given COVID and racial unrest. This book is directly connected to our work of *Building Mentorship Networks to Support Black Women: A Guide to Succeeding in the Academy* (Routledge, 2022). It provides examples of how Black women retain each other for success in the academy. This second book probes more deeply the peer mentoring aspect of the framework we introduced in the faculty book (Kelly & Fries-Britt, 2022) examining how peers stand in the gap (especially during this COVID and racial unrest season when the pressures were more intense) and how the connections sustained them and allowed them to accomplish key academic benchmarks as they navigated two critical pandemics. We also address many of the key issues and concerns in the literature on Black women students and their experiences in the academy. The unique focus of this second book on Black women students navigating the journey to and through the PhD allows us to shine a light on systemic structures in place that make it necessary for peers to support one another through mentoring.

Mentoring in higher education is established as an important factor in professional success (Behar-Horenstein et al., 2012; Merriam et al., 1987; Rowe, 1981), particularly for minoritized students (Blackwell, 1989; Turner & González, 2014). Due to the intersections of gender and race, Black women students, in particular, are further implicated by adverse academic climates. Patton (2009) argued that mentoring relationships are vital in assisting minoritized women in overcoming "the dual-edge burdens of race and gender ... in 'old boy'" networks (p. 511). Stanley and Lincoln (2005) asserted that successful mentoring relationships are "characterized by trust, honesty, a willingness to learn about self and others and the ability to share power and privilege" (p. 46). Similarly, Fries-Britt and Snider (2015) submitted that trust and transparency are essential but difficult to achieve.

Traditionally, mentoring relationships are often hierarchical and flow unidirectional, mentor to protégé. This form of mentorship has been ineffective at supporting Black graduate students (Borum & Walker, 2012; Davis et al., 2012; Esnard & Cobb-Roberts, 2018; Gregory, 2001; Lewis et al., 2013, 2016; Minnett et al., 2019; Patton, 2003, Patton 2009; Tillman, 2012). Researchers point out the need to recognize models such as reciprocal mentoring relationships, co-mentoring, and alternative forms of mentoring for Women of Color, especially among Black women (Davis et al., 2012; Esnard & Cobb-Roberts, 2018; Gregory, 2001; Minnett et al., 2019; Tillman, 2012). Black women experience gendered racial microaggressions in college, leading to marginalization and alienation, causing them to cope by leaning on support networks (Borum & Walker, 2012; Lewis et al., 2013, 2016). Consequently, peer mentoring is utilized as a form of resistance to systems of oppression and institutional barriers for Black women in academia from faculty to students (Henderson et al., 2010; Patton, 2003). According to Minnett et al.'s (2019) recent piece, ArCasia, and Devean's (JAD) framework on peer mentoring for Black women doctoral students, this act of resistance consists of radical coping, communal sista scholarship, and the cultivation of an authentic holistic self.

In this book, we learn how a high school student who identifies as a queer Black woman has to think now about her pathway to the doctorate because of systemic oppression, how undergraduate students building supportive networks with peers will have to strategically learn how to do this to get into and be successful in their doctoral studies, and we hear firsthand how Black women in different stages and from different parts of the world journeyed in the doctoral degree.

While this book centers students, there are significant implications for interactions and engagement with faculty as advisors and mentors embedded in this work. This work is critical to helping the academy fortify Black women's sense of belonging and connection early in their academic career. We also believe this work will bring understanding to what contributes to Black women's alienation in the academy. We set the context by identifying how to create and sustain effective peer mentorship as it directly connects to how we, the editors, see ourselves utilizing our mentoring practices.

ORGANIZATION OF THE BOOK

This book is organized into four sections to reflect an array of mentoring experiences for Black women doctoral experiences. Each section touches on and considers the ways Black women doctoral students assume the labor and support of their peers during their PhD journey. At the end of each chapter, the authors have included implications for administrators, faculty, and others working on supporting Black women doctoral students. Specifically, the authors assigned "homework" to provide detailed steps institutional agents may take to spur change.

Section I-A Case for Mentoring describes the need and rationale for peer mentoring of Black women students, particularly at historically white institutions (HWIs). Along with a current Black woman doctoral student, we as editors of this book discuss our own experiences finding peer mentors during our doctoral journey and role modeling the continued importance of peer mentoring beyond the doctoral degree. This section also makes a case for peer mentoring pertaining to high-achieving Black women students in science, technology, engineering, and mathematics (STEM) and the strong implications for graduate school and needing peer mentoring at their next academic stage.

Section II-Intersectional Peer Mentoring brings awareness to how peer mentorships can affirm the multiple social identities Black women doctoral students hold while navigating higher education. There is a contribution from a Black queer woman, who, as a high school student, writes about her college search and finding peers who also identify as Black queer women. Another chapter within this section discusses three Afro-Caribbean women's experiences with triple invisibility within their doctoral journey and how they created a sense of belonging to retain each other.

As research on the global impact of the pandemic on higher education institutions is ongoing, **Section III-Peer Mentoring During a Global Pandemic** offers narratives from Black women who were part-time students, mothers, in their first year of their doctoral journey and who were in the process of finishing their dissertation. The global pandemic compounded the already stressful experience of the doctoral journey as a Black woman. Thus, the creation of a peer network became essential during a global pandemic. Contributions to this section narrate how peer mentoring relationships were essential to surviving and thriving within their doctoral program.

In **Section IV-Centering Healing in Peer Mentoring**, Black women offer ways peer mentorships have been a sense of healing and spiritual fulfillment. Wellness and wholeness can fall by the wayside for Black women within doctoral programs, and peer mentoring relationships provide a sense of revival for Black women. Contributors within this section not only talk about the collective healing and spiritual fullness of peer mentoring but they also talk about the implications their peer mentoring networks have on institutional change for social justice.

AUDIENCE

The target of this book is higher education, including faculty and graduate students in Education, Sociology, Psychology, African American Studies, Chicana/o Studies, Latin American Studies, and Asian American Studies. The book will be of special interest to graduate students, pre-tenure, and tenured Faculty of Color. Those who lead departments, colleges, and universities will also find interest in the book.

NEED

Due to a gap in mentorship from the lack of Black women faculty in institutions, especially in HWIs, Black women graduate students establish horizontal mentorship consisting of other Black women. The informal bonds created among each other comprise academic, emotional, psychosocial, and professional support, helping to mitigate racial microaggressions from professors, colleagues, and peers (Apugo, 2017). Moreover, Black women experience distinctive racial and gendered marginalization involving microaggressions, stereotyping, and alienation (Borum & Walker, 2012; Lewis et al., 2013, 2016) due to the intersectionality of their social identities. Mentoring for Black women graduate students is more than the traditional definition of mentoring that consists of academic and career guidance (Patton, 2003).

The social inequalities Black women experience due to the intersection of race and gender are validated and acknowledged by Black women faculty. Notably, Black women graduate students identified components such as nurturing, mothering, trust, and culturally relevant counsel that can only be found from Black women's mentorship (Patton, 2003). However, there is a lack of sufficient representation of Black women faculty in graduate programs (Myers, 2002; Thompson & Dey, 1998; Tillman, 2001; Walkington, 2017) which often leads Black women graduate students to find culturally similar peers who can compensate for the lack of formal top-down mentoring (Minnett et al., 2019; Patton, 2003; Walkington, 2017). In these peer mentorships, the concept of mothering found in Black women faculty and graduate students mentorship is transformed into "sistering." Peer mentors serve as a sister and friend who can understand firsthand the microaggressions and other minoritized experiences Black women experience in academia (Minnett et al., 2019; Patton, 2009). The sisterhood cultivated from peer mentorship among Black women graduate students is crucial in navigating the racial climate on college campuses, directly impacting the completion of Black women's terminal degrees.

Women students mentoring women students, especially in minoritized communities, is an important aspect and dimension of mentoring that is often overlooked. Exploring the meaning of peer mentoring in doctoral programs is needed to support minoritized students and advance equity in the academy. Being a Black doctoral student brings its unique challenges. Doctoral programs, acting as microcosms of the social context, are rampant with institutionalized gendered racism that operates through the programs' internal climate, policies, and procedures (Nagbe, 2019). This book examines women student mentors who help other women students navigate unwelcome campus environments laden with identity politics because of their low representation, racism, sexism, and other structural barriers. This book illuminates what minoritized women students have done to mentor each other and provide avenues for institutions to support and foster their success. This timely book is needed since COVID-19 and the racial unrest in 2020 exacerbated inequities among Black women graduate students.

REFERENCES

Apugo, D. L. (2017). "We all we got": Considering peer relationships as multi-purpose sustainability outlets among millennial Black women graduate students attending majority white urban universities. *The Urban Review, 49*(2), 347–367.

Behar-Horenstein, L. S., West-Olatunji, C. A., Moore, T. E., Houchen, D. F., & Roberts, K. W. (2012). Resilience post tenure: The experience of an African American Woman in a PWI. *Florida Journal of Educational Administration & Policy, 5*(2), 68–84.

Blackwell, J. E. (1989). Mentoring: An action strategy for increasing minority faculty. *Academe, 75*, 8–14.

Borum, V., & Walker, E. (2012). What makes the difference? Black women's undergraduate and graduate experiences in mathematics. *The Journal of Negro Education, 81*(4), 366–378.

Davis, D. J., Chaney, C., Edwards, L., Thompson-Rogers, G. K., & Gines, K. T. (2012). Academe as extreme sport: Black women, faculty development, and networking. *Negro Educational Review, 62/63*(1–4), 167–187.

Esnard, T., & Cobb-Roberts, D. (2018). *Black Women, Academe, and the Tenure Process in the United States and the Caribbean.* Springer.

Fries-Britt, S., & Snider, J. (2015). Mentoring outside the line: The importance of authenticity, transparency, and vulnerability in effective mentoring relationships. *New Directions for Higher Education, 2015*(171), 3–11.

Gregory, S. T. (2001). Black faculty women in academy: History, status, and future. The *Journal of Negro Education, 70*(3), 124–138.

Henderson, T. L., Hunter, A. G., & Hildreth, G. J. (2010). Outsiders within the academy: Strategies for resistance and mentoring African American women. *Michigan Family Review, 14*(1), 28–41.

Kelly, B. T., & Fries-Britt, S. (Eds.). (2022). *Building Mentorship Networks to Support Black Women: A Guide to Succeeding in the Academy.* Routledge.

Lewis, J. A., Mendenhall, R., Harwood, S. A., & Browne Huntt, M. (2013). Coping with gendered racial microaggressions among Black women college students. *Journal of African American Studies, 17*(1), 51–73.

Lewis, J. A., Mendenhall, R., Harwood, S. A., & Browne Huntt, M. (2016). "Ain't I a woman?" Perceived gendered racial microaggressions experienced by Black women. *The Counseling Psychologist, 44*(5), 758–780.

Merriam, S. B., Thomas, T. K., & Zeph, C. P. (1987). Mentoring in higher education: What we know now. *The Review of Higher Education, 11*(2), 199–210. https://doi.org/10.1353/rhe.1987.0004

Minnett, J. L., James-Gallaway, A. D., & Owens, D. R. (2019). Help a sista out: Black women doctoral students' use of peer mentorship as an act of resistance. *Mid-Western Educational Researcher, 31*(2), 210–238.

Myers L. (2002). *A Broken Silence: Voices of African American Women in the Academy.* Greenwood Publishing Group.

Nagbe, M. N. (2019). The Black (W) hole: Examining institutional racism in doctoral education, an orgcrit perspective. *Texas Education Review, 8*(1), 6–23.

Patton, L. D. (2009). My sister's keeper: A qualitative examination of mentoring experiences among African American women in graduate and professional schools, *The Journal of Higher Education, 80*(5), 510–537.

Rowe, M. P. (1981). Building mentorship frameworks as part of an equal opportunity ecology. In J. Farley (Ed.), *Sex Discrimination in Higher Education: Strategies for Equality* (pp. 23–33). I.L.R. Pub. Div.

Stanley, C. A., & Lincoln, Y. S. (2005). Cross-race faculty mentoring. *Change, 37*(2), 44–50. Retrieved from http://www.eric.ed.gov/ERICWebPortal/detail?accno=EJ71166

Thompson, C. J., & Dey, E. L. (1998). Pushed to the margins: Sources of stress for African-American college and university faculty. *Journal of Higher Education, 69*(3), 324–345.

Tillman, L. C. (2001). Mentoring African American faculty in predominantly White institutions. *Research in Higher Education, 42*(3), 295–325.

Tillman, L.C. (2012) Inventing ourselves: An informed essay for Black female scholars in educational leadership. *International Journal of Qualitative Studies in Education, 25*(1), 119–126. https://doi.org/10.1080/09518398.2011.647728

Turner, C. S. V., & González, J. C. (Eds.). (2014). *Modeling Mentoring Across Race/Ethnicity and Gender: Practices to Cultivate the Next Generation of Diverse Faculty.* Stylus.

Walkington, L. (2017). How far have we really come? Black women faculty and graduate students' experiences in higher education. *Humboldt Journal of Social Relations, 1*(39), 51–65.

Section I

A Case for Mentoring

Section I of this book introduces the importance of overall mentoring to augment success strategies for Black women in the academy. It specifically identifies the importance of peers but also acknowledges that peer mentoring networks composed of all Black women are not always available. The premise of the *Black Women Networking Model* (BWNM) by Kelly and Fries-Britt (2022) is that Black women should be intentional about building a support network composed of other Black women to fortify and anchor their success. Kelly and Fries-Britt are unapologetic about the need to form these systems of support between and among Black women as they, and other Black women, have often navigated the academy facing blatant opposition to their very existence in the academy. The BWNM certainly does not preclude Black women from actively building other communities of support; in fact, this is what Black women have always done as they have labored on behalf of others' success. Rather, it calls attention to the need to center and support Black women within a community where full membership is unquestioned. The BWNM is a network where unconditional support and critique can be offered from a place of love and respect and with an ethic of care for the growth and development of Black women.

In Chapter 1, authors Sharon Fries-Britt, Bridget Tuner Kelly, and Tyanna A.E. Clayton-Mallett briefly reviewed the BWNM (Kelly & Fries-Britt, 2022) emphasizing the importance and connection of the peer component of the model as it serves as the focus of the chapter and book. Peers are central to the networking model as they share the same positionality and are able to provide support from a place of knowledge in real time. Fries-Britt et al. reflect upon their own peer mentorship experience across three different generational time frames highlighting key factors that shaped their access to peer networks and support. While each author represents a Black woman who has navigated the doctoral process in different decades, their experiences provide important insights into

DOI: 10.4324/9781003394648-1

1

the enduring nature of issues that impact Black women across time. In this chapter, they build upon the connections and themes that undergird their experiences including themes of family being their first mentors, the rarity of having peers in the doctoral program of the same race and gender as them, peers as important but not sufficient to support them through the PhD, and how they have used their experiences to shape how we mentor Black women doctoral students. They highlight critical ways that they were able to construct support systems in spite of the low numbers of Black students enrolled in their respective programs. Additionally, Fries-Britt and Kelly share key insights from their combined 60 plus years in the academy of what undergirds their mentorship philosophy and how they approach relationship building with current and former Black women students.

Focusing on the importance of establishing peer networks early, Joy Gaston Gayles and Chelsea Smith feature the power of community for high-achieving Black undergraduate women in science, technology, engineering, and mathematics (STEM) in Chapter 2. Employing Yosso's (2005) framework of Community Cultural Wealth (CCW) in a case study of six Black undergraduate women in STEM, they examine how the early development of peer mentorship networks aids in the retention of Black women. CCW provided the context for Gayles and Smith to disrupt the dominant narrative of Black women underachieving in STEM and allowed the authors to focus on the experiences of the women to inform strategies for success. Establishing the practice of building peer networks at the undergraduate level for Black women could not be more important as the authors note:

> Focusing on peer mentoring and creating communities of support for Black women undergraduates is an important starting place for a conversation on mentoring and supporting Black women graduate students because what happens at the undergraduate level informs and shapes the graduate school experience.

This chapter offers powerful examples of how these women were impacted by their experiences in and out of the classroom. They make three key observations. First, the women in the study were academically prepared and had many K-12 experiences that also equipped them for studying in STEM, which counters the assumption of academic deficiency in all Black students. Second, the women had to deal with the realities of the "double bind" as their positionality as Black women in STEM meant as they were often the only in their classes or program. In this role, they did not have as much in common with peers in the major and struggled to feel a sense of belonging in the major. Because of these and other experiences, Gayles and Smith observe that the women in the study were intentional about creating a community of mentorship and support. They looked to

2

peers outside of STEM majors for support and were involved in student groups and organizations on campus that gave them access to other peers like them. They also found it important to seek out help and resources from other supportive adults on campus and off campus who could help guide their navigation of the field.

REFERENCES

Kelly, B. T. & Fries-Britt, S. L. (2022). *Building Mentorship Networks to Support Black Women: A Guide to Succeeding in the Academy.* Routledge Press.

Yosso, T. J. (2005). Whose culture has capital? A critical race theory discussion of community cultural wealth. *Race Ethnicity and Education, 8*(1), 69–91.

Chapter 1

Multigenerational Reflections on the Importance of Peer Mentoring in the PhD Journey

Sharon Fries-Britt, Bridget Turner Kelly and Tyanna A.E. Clayton-Mallett

Twenty years ago, Patton and Harper (2003) argued that mentoring was the missing link for Black women in their graduate education. The authors observed that Black women often turn to alternative sources of support outside of higher education including support from parents, extended family, church community, and civic and professional organizations. In our *Black Women Network of Mentoring Model* (see Figure 1.1), we identify four key networks that are essential to the success of Black women in the academy. The power of community mentoring is the fourth area of support that reflects these alternative sources of mentorship described by Patton and Harper. We concur that the power of community mentorship is critical for Black women's success in the academy. In our model, we submit that the community network draws on the African principle of social uplift, strength through the building of networks, and family legacy and histories. The people in this community network matter as does the ability to draw upon the legacy and history of a people who have endured and succeeded against all odds.

Notwithstanding, the power of the extended community without other forms of support is insufficient to ensure success for Black women in the academy. The other components of the *Black Women Network of Mentorship Model* are possibility models (mentoring relationships between Black women of different rank or status), centering self (radical self-care to view oneself as container of knowledge and success), and peer mentoring (mentor/mentee share similar

DOI: 10.4324/9781003394648-2

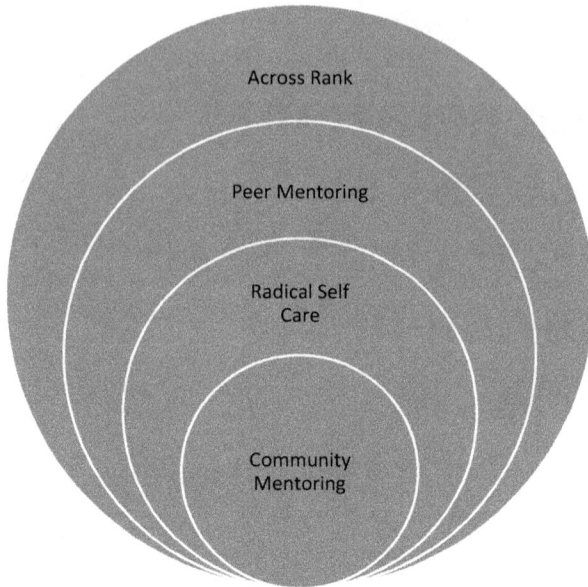

Figure 1.1 Black women networking of mentoring model (BWNM; Kelly & Fries-Britt, 2022)

marginalized identities and status in the academy; Kelly & Fries-Britt, 2022). Many of these components are well established in the literature. The unique aspect of our model is the centering of Black women and the power that comes from utilizing all aspects simultaneously and in support of each other's success. Unfortunately, the ability of Black women to find mentors and support in their graduate education remains an enduring challenge most especially at historically white institutions (HWIs).

In this chapter, we focus on the key network of peers which has increasingly become a source of support identified by Black women as essential to their success (Apugo, 2017; Grant, 2012; Lane et al., 2022; Minnett et al., 2019). Participants in Patton and Harper's study noted the importance of peers, especially when Black women faculty or administrators are not available. In this sense, peers can be viewed as a "substitute" form of support to fill the gap for the lack of faculty and professional staff who are Black women. We argue in our model that every level of support is essential and plays an important role, not as a substitute for something else but as a pillar of strength that provides a foundation for success. Peers have a unique understanding of what you are experiencing in real time. They can be reliable sources of support for current resources and information about the department and the heuristics of the department.

We offer examples from our graduate experience and peer mentor networks. Our narratives reflect a unique opportunity to learn from generational differences and time frames in higher education; yet, there is a familiarity across our stories that transcends time. Each of our experiences is distinct and unique; nonetheless, they are connected as they reflect our shared understanding of what it takes to navigate the academy. This chapter is organized around three key themes that emerged as each of us reflected on our doctoral journey and as Sharon and Bridget reflected on mentoring Black women doctoral students. After we present themes and evidence from our reflections, we close this chapter with key takeaways/homework for those with the power to make a difference in the lives of Black women doctoral students.

KEY THEMES

The first theme that cut across our reflections was that family were our first mentors, and those relationships shaped our philosophy of mentoring. The second theme we uncovered in our reflections was how rare it was to have a full community of peers in our doctoral programs who shared our same racialized gendered identity. The third theme was that once we found some peer mentors, it was not sufficient for the support we needed to get through PhD. The final theme is from Sharon and Bridget's reflections on how their own journey and life experiences shape how they mentor Black women doctoral students today as faculty.

FAMILY WERE OUR FIRST MENTORS

Sharon (Baby Boomer Generation): While my years at Maryland have been edifying, the academy is not the foundation for my commitment to mentoring, giving back, racial justice, and advancing equity. Nor is it where I acquired my courage to fight for opportunities for Black folks and other minoritized communities. These lessons, and many others, I learned from my parents (June Garfield Fries and Mary E. Fries), as well as a host of relatives and others in the Black community. My dad was a career military man in every sense of the word, and my mother worked in educational settings most of her working life. I am first-generation college educated. However, my mom completed her undergraduate degree in her 50s, and my dad's military expertise was built over the course of 30 plus years of service. They were highly successful in their careers demonstrating enormous talent and excellence despite the barriers that they encountered. Their life lessons meant that they parented me with a heavy dose of realism. They were my first teachers and, in every way, prepared me for the realities of life. I grew up listening to thoughtful and passionate conversations about the systems of oppression and injustice in American society and the individual and collective responsibilities we have to make a difference. Conversely, my parents always celebrated the moments of tremendous success that moved our nation forward. Yet, they were clear that we had a long way to go in America to dismantle the deeply embedded threads of racism and white supremacy woven in the fabric of our nation. Thus, years before I enrolled in a doctoral program, I was getting the necessary foundation needed to navigate the academy. The sense of self-worth that every Black family eventually understands is important to convey to their child is ever so necessary in navigating academia!

Bridget (Generation X): How I mentor comes from my parents – John and Clevonne Turner, who both worked in higher education as administrators. I witnessed them consistently pouring into Black students at the historically and majority white colleges where they worked. They hosted barbeques and weekend retreats for Black graduate students, and I saw how my parents mentored the students but also how the students mentored each other and my parents. I grew up knowing that it was important for Black students, in particular, to be there for each other. I also learned that Black administrators needed a community of students who looked like them and who lifted them up because, like my parents, they are often the only or one of few Black administrators on their campuses (Mosley, 1980; Perna et al., 2007). It was a network, a community mentor approach with no hierarchy or power. That network still resounds in my life today with faculty and administrators at the university whom my parents mentored as graduate students. They continue to tell me and my parents how much it meant to have Black administrators looking out for them in an overwhelmingly white, highly selective graduate school experience. Having this example in my life on its own would be enough to instill in me a love for mentoring, but it is amplified by the consistent messages I received from my parents to always do my best, know my Black history, and practice racial uplift to counter the systems of oppression and marginalization.

Tyanna (Millennial): I often reflect on the experiences that ushered me into my doctoral program. One strong memory was seeing my mother obtain her bachelor's degree in communications from a small liberal arts all women's college. I remember when she would pack lunch for my older brother and I, make sure we had enough work, and set us up in a student lounge while she was in class. Throughout her journey, she included us in class assignments. For example, in one class, she was required to take photographs, and of course, she included a photo of me in the project. At the time, I did not know the impact of seeing a single Black woman, mother of two, free-spirited, God-filled person walking across the stage to receive a degree. Fast forward, her desire for me to gain knowledge only strengthened with the experiences she provided me despite whatever monetary challenges were presented. Trips down south to see family, museum experiences, carefully curated TV shows with discussions (e.g., making my brother and I watch the Roots series), and prioritizing Black culture were all experiences that led me to my doctorate degree.

Despite our coming from different generations, for all of us, our parents instilled a love of learning and the importance of doing our best in school and in life. Education was a central part of our early mentoring experiences and ones that we carried with us into our own doctoral journey. The care our parents took to give us examples of making a way out of no way, bucking deficit messages, and education as a central driver in our lives enabled us to have a key pillar of our mentoring network model – radical self-care. We each came into our doctoral programs believing that we were enough, and we were worthy of finding support and mentors.

RARITY OF SAME RACE AND GENDER PEERS IN DOCTORAL PROGRAM

Bridget: I was beaten down and wounded by former advisors during my undergraduate and my master's programs, and I did not have Black peers to accompany me on my journey. I was told by my master's academic advisor that I should not do what he labeled "minority work." He did not think I should do work involving marginalized populations. One of my white male professors in my master's degree told me, "You definitely should not do work on race." Race was the only thing that excited me. My advisor tried to steer me away from the one thing that I was passionate about in graduate school. Without the mentoring I received from Sharon as my doctoral academic advisor or the Black peers I met in my doctoral journey, I would not have gotten my PhD or be a professor today.

When I finally met Sharon, I latched onto her and asked her to advise me because I knew I needed somebody that I could believe in who could believe in me. The rest of what I needed to know as a doctoral student, I thought I could figure out having grown up with parents in higher education. I was wrong. There is more that I needed to survive and thrive as a full-time doctoral student. As wonderful as Sharon is as a mentor, one person cannot meet all of our needs. I needed peers who were in my classes, in the hallways, and in the struggle of trying to earn their graduate degree. There were so few Black and Black women students in my doctoral program that I had to look outside of my area of social foundations to classes in higher education, curriculum and instruction, and student affairs to find Black peers. As a full-time doctoral student, I held several different 20-hour assistantships on campus to pay for my tuition, fees, housing, and food. Those assistantships are where I met my first Black woman supervisor and peer. Other than Sharon and those two individuals, I did not get to work with people who shared my same race and gender identities.

Sharon: I worked full time during my doctoral program and took all my classes in the evening. As a first-generation college student, it was important for me to be gainfully employed, especially after having earned two degrees as a full-time student. In the late 1980s, I didn't have a significant number of diverse non-white peers in my courses. At the time, I was one of a few Black women administrators at a senior level. Having access to a group of peer mentors, especially other Black women, would have been remarkable during my doctoral studies. I started my doctoral studies with a close Black male friend and colleague. He ended up not pursuing the doctorate because he already held a high-level position on campus earning good income. While he valued the PhD, in his own cost–benefit analysis he determined that it would not make a huge difference for him in the long run given the success that he had already achieved. I, on the contrary, was single, had no children, and was only in the second full-time job in my career. As it turns out, he never needed the degree to get to the highest levels of administration at two leading research universities. I certainly needed the PhD to begin the academic journey and climb to full professor, a choice that I would make again given the rewards on the other side.

I had many other colleagues, most of whom were white and taking classes while I was enrolled. There was mutual respect and interactions in the classroom, but we never formed a community of intentional support to share ideas and to encourage each other through the process. The few Black peers that I took classes with were often in different programs. Those who were in my same program were at different stages in their academic process making it even more challenging to connect. I distinctly remember one other Black woman who was in the same program but working with a different advisor. She was at least three years ahead of me. We took a quantitative methods class together. In fact, several other Black women were in that class, and we all bonded to form a community of support to make it through the class together. However, we never talked about intentionally establishing an ongoing community of support.

Tyanna: Peer mentoring has become a lifeline for me, in addition to my relationship with my advisor. As a PhD student, I learned the importance of having a network of people that can affirm your presence, lovingly challenge you, and can match the belief you have for yourself. I have always believed in the power of peers, but that belief was more pronounced starting with my experience pursuing a master's degree. I was a part-time student when I pursued my master's degree, and consequently, I encountered a couple of cohorts of students due to my course schedule. A cohort model in graduate programs provides a shared experience for students, whereby the cohort moves students through their graduate program together. The shared characteristic of going through a graduate program can be a strong source of peer support. Unlike the full-time students in my courses, I did not have a core group of peers that I could call my cohort. My full-time work was a priority. It was also hard to build relationships with students because of the limits on my time. As a full-time employee, I was not involved in many cohort gatherings because I planned my schedule to accommodate my full-time work schedule. While I focused on finishing my master's degree in the shortest time as a full-time employee, I did not pay much attention to establishing a peer network.

I was self-motivated and disciplined; however, I still noticed my singular, brown-skinned body in most of my classes. I still longed to see faces that looked like mine.

In my final two years, two Black women made all the difference in my master's experience. Seeing their face in the classroom, collaborating on projects, and their support of my work was the affirmation I needed to make it across the finish line in my final year of my master's program. As a seasoned professional, these two Black women often sought my advice about their career next steps and just advice on life. I also got to experience their sage advice and seek out their opinion on how to handle personal challenges. So, our relationship morphed into a "sista friend" relationship. During a final class discussion, one of them expressed appreciation for my mentorship of her during the program. As a part-time student, I thought I would not have the time for a peer mentoring network, but I was wrong. Those two Black women came into my life at the right time and made me understand the need for a peer support system outside of an advisor within a graduate program.

We set the context of our doctoral journeys with these stories because navigating the academy for us and for many other Black women has always required that we consider the various contexts within which we engage in our work. Black women still experience being one of a few Black students in a program, cohort, classes, residence hall, and perhaps never having a Black faculty member let alone advisor (Grant & Simmons, 2008; Rasheem et al., 2017). These themes are not new narratives; rather, they reflect enduring narratives that cut across generations and impact Black women's journey in the academy.

PEERS WERE IMPORTANT BUT NOT SUFFICIENT FOR SUPPORT IN THE PHD

Tyanna: When I decided to leave my full-time job to become a full-time PhD student, I was intentional about figuring out the best PhD program to provide me with the necessary support during my PhD journey. After making a list of all the things I wanted in a program, a healthy relationship with an advisor and a supportive peer network were the two traits that rose to the top of my list. After seeing and hearing horror stories of past friends' experiences with their PhD programs, I knew I needed to ask the right questions to gauge which program had a healthy student–faculty atmosphere and supported a peer network among PhD cohorts. I had to choose between two institutions, the University of Maryland (UMD) being one of two. The other university was a reputable institution, giving me a merit scholarship with full tuition and a nice stipend. When I talked with current students, predominantly students of color, at that institution, many spoke about the lack of healthy relationships between faculty and students. From their responses to my questions, they were not in community with each other but alone in their pursuit of a PhD.

My initial conversations with students from the UMD were quite different. Some of the Black women and non-Black women who were current students talked about the supportive environment among faculty but, most of all, among the students. I already built relationships with some current students as a non-degree seeking student taking a study abroad course. In the midst of trying to choose between UMD and the other institutions, I remember Dr. Kelly confidently said the program was ready to create a loving, challenging, and supportive environment that would ensure my success. The majority of current students were other Black women and welcomed me with open arms into the program. Undoubtedly, the UMD was the right choice for me.

Within my journey thus far, the peer mentoring experiences are a source of care, nurturance, challenge, and love. The Black women who are my peer mentors create a sense of joy and healing within me. We take breaks from academic work, seek out new experiences, share life advice, and they do not hoard information. For example, they readily share information about scholarships, research opportunities, how to apply for funding, etc.; we are all invested in the success of each other. We help each other see the light at the end of the tunnel and the rainbow in the sky. I am adamant about ensuring my PhD journey is filled with love and care. My current peer support system includes Black women and Black men across the diaspora. My experiences living and working in Ghana, West Africa, have helped me be a source of support for Black international students within my program. From deciphering U.S. American ways of life to meal fellowships to challenging dialogue in and outside the classroom, we know that our PhD journey is much better in community than in solitude.

Sharon: I had access to a peer group composed of Black colleagues with whom I worked with on campus. Many of these colleagues had earned their PhD, and they understood what I was going through and were always affirming my ability to succeed academically. I also had a Black female mentor on campus who was the highest ranking Black administrator at the time, Dr. Marie Davidson. She operated in excellence and was a tremendous advocate and possibility model for me throughout my career. The tenured faculty in my program were white and predominantly male with one white female tenured faculty member. I was fortunate to have a good relationship with each of them. I felt like they valued the work experiences that students brought to the classroom, and they were genuinely supportive of students. They were outspoken about racial inequity and often studied these issues in their respective work. I never felt like I needed to convince them of the importance of my research interests. In fact, my academic advisor and mentor Dr. Richard Chait is the person that I credit for my career as an academic at UMD, a story I share (Fries-Britt & Kelly, 2005) in an article written with my colleague Dr. Kelly. While I didn't have a steady group of Black women on the journey with me, I was able to find important sources of support all along the way.

I felt like my academic advisor listened to me and worked to understand what was important to me. I didn't always feel like I received this same support from other colleagues who were seeking to mentor me in the early stages of my administrative career. In student affairs, there were very few Black women in leadership positions in the mid-1980s. Navigating the early stages of my career, I felt like there were expected ways to behave and show up as a Black woman that didn't work for me, and I tended to be vocal about it. I challenged issues when they surfaced, and at times, this was appreciated but only to a certain point. I felt like I was supposed to stop when folks started feeling uncomfortable. Having the space to discuss these and other experiences that we are having in academia is important. The role of peer mentors is essential in helping to create this circle of support. These are the colleagues who can identify most with what you are encountering in your academic program. While I didn't consistently have these peer relationships throughout my career, I have worked to help my students build these connections.

Bridget: I found Black peers in my doctoral journey through classes and random encounters throughout the College of Education. Lionel was getting his master's in measurement and statistics, and his peer mentoring saved me throughout my quantitative courses. Richelle was getting her doctorate in Curriculum and our late-night phone calls and weekend study sessions helped me stay strong when relationships, deadlines, and microaggressions became too much. Wallace was getting his doctorate in higher education and watching him advocate for himself as one of a few Black students in his program gave me hope. We eventually came to socialize together and brought in others to form Sankofa. Sankofa (pronounced SAHN-koh-fah) is a word in the Twi language of Ghana meaning "to retrieve." It means "go back and get" or to return. We chose that word for our peer mentoring group because we needed to retrieve lessons from our African ancestry, to go back and get what we missed from our ancestors being forcibly removed from Africa. We needed those lessons and history to survive our present state in an anti-Black and white-dominated college and university.

Our Sankofa group of Black graduate students from all different programs within the College of Education came together monthly for potlucks at one another's homes. The host chose the topic. The monthly gatherings gave me a sense that I was not alone and that I was part of a community of people who believed in me, supported me, but also challenged me when I needed to rethink an issue or do something different in a course. I remember one month we debated the talented tenth idea and got into a heated discussion about our responsibility to the Black community as people pursuing their PhDs. We did not always agree. We argued, laughed, listened, and always ended up committed to the group and coming back together next month. The group had people who identified as women, men, parents, low-income, middle-class, part-time, and full-time students. After we graduated, the group disbanded. During the start of the COVID-19 pandemic, we reconnected online and held Sankofa meetings via Zoom. We got together in person in fall of 2022 and celebrated the 25th year of our Sankofa gathering.

There were Black women doctoral students in Sankofa that I could talk to about the racialized gendered experiences we encountered. But there was also an outlet for all Black women graduate students whom I sought out to heal some of the wounds and violence I encountered in graduate school. Special thanks to a Black woman, Sharon Kirkland, who was there for me and so many others. She offered a Black woman graduate group counseling session that was a lifeline for me. I knew I needed help. I was experiencing depression and turmoil in my personal relationships. I was not getting what I needed from a one-on-one counseling session with the university-assigned white woman therapist. As a skilled and compassionate Black woman therapist, Sharon was someone I trusted, and the group therapy was healing to me as a doctoral student. The peer mentoring I received in Sankofa, the doctoral advising I got from Sharon, and the Black women doctoral student group therapy are central to how I made it to the finish line.

Each of us struggled, to different extents, to find Black woman peers in our doctoral programs, but once we did, it made our journeys more doable and fulfilling. Each of us also discussed how the relationship with our academic advisors was just as important as our peer mentors. Collectively, our experiences of not having the Black woman peers we needed and subsequently finding them made each of us intentional in seeking them out in the doctoral journey (Tyanna) and working to cultivate the support for Black women doctoral students as faculty (Bridget and Sharon).

MENTORING APPROACH FOR BLACK WOMEN DOCTORAL STUDENTS

Sharon: Not surprisingly, all aspects of my life experience, especially my academic career, have been pivotal in developing my mentoring philosophy. Many of the doctoral and master's students whom I have advised have been Black women who reflect a wide range of diversity within their Black identity (e.g., African-American, Black African, Caribbean, and Multiracial). They have been tremendously diverse in other ways including personality type, regions of the country where they were raised, educational generational status, types of undergraduate institutions they attended, socioeconomic status (SES), and so much more. I share a few of these as a reminder of the intricacy of Black women's identity and the complexity and multifaceted nature of our lives. When I establish a mentoring relationship with a Black woman student, it means that I must not make assumptions that we will get along because we share at least one social identity. I start by investing in understanding more about what has shaped and influenced their life. This process takes time and evolves over the course of building a relationship. I think carefully about how we establish a long-term connection with an eye toward learning as much as I can about what each student envisions for their career and life. Just because I am a student's advisor, I don't take for granted that they will consider me a mentor. Even for those women who came to Maryland to work with me because they want me to be their mentor, I recognize that it is more than a label. It requires time to build a relationship to work collaboratively in ways that allow for the exchange of learning, growth, and even disagreement to take place.

Having the opportunity to mentor and work with Black women has fortified me and my experiences in the academy. It has helped me to navigate the academy and has been one of the most gratifying aspects of my career. Many Black women labor alone and feel the need to move through the academy camouflaging many aspects of their talent and ability. Doctoral programs can feel isolating, unempowering, and unnecessarily competitive. I endeavor to build a foundation of support and connection for students to enhance their skills, abilities, and confidence to succeed in the academy. I will highlight two key aspects of my approach as they form the foundation of how I like to establish a relationship.

When I left the division of Student Affairs to become a faculty member, I was invited back the very next year to give a keynote address for the regional Student Affairs conference hosted by the UMD. The theme of the conference that year was leadership. While I can't remember the exact title of my talk, the primary message was that as leaders we need to learn to cultivate people's talents and not clone them into mini versions of ourselves. In today's parlance, it would be fair to say that I was throwing shade at the division. I left the division in part because I felt like my success depended on me "cloning" myself after those who were perceived as succeeding. There was no way that I felt that I could be fully successful and free to be myself by following this strategy. Instead, I took the risk of starting my career over to become a tenured faculty member when the opportunity became available. There were many reasons behind this decision, and by no means was it seamless; however, I determined that in the long run, I would have more control over myself and my professional life with an academic career. It turns out I was right.

I try to remember that my students want the same freedom. That each is distinct and unique, and ultimately, they want the power of their own self-authorship. Honoring this is something I try to always do, but it is not always easy. There are some practical realities of advising all students, and my role in helping them reach key benchmarks (e.g., time to degree, comprehensive exams, proposal defense, and primary career interests) is important to their ultimate success. There are times where I have to balance the degree of support with real challenge to move them along and to help them understand that there are some expectations in the academy that still must be observed. This is not always easy, but it is an important part of preparing all students for success in the academy, especially Black women.

I have always encouraged my students to work to support each other and to form study and social groups to keep each other motivated. I have used my research teams as spaces for cultivated peer connections and encouraging students to write and engage in research together. I often connect new doctoral students with former students in the field who can help them think through research and career decisions. My former students are always willing to give back and help others through the process.

I have often shared that my reason for wanting to create authentic relationships with my students is because I am investing in my future colleague and the type of professional I want to see out in the field who operates with integrity and has a healthy sense of use of power and the building of relationships. I look at the current titles that we have as professor and student as place holders. They are temporary. Yes, there are official responsibilities, and an ethic of care and duties that I have as a professor to guide a student through the academic process. Likewise, students must be committed to their work and success in the academy. My end goal for students is much greater than graduation. I am committed to building a community of colleagues who are not only prepared to serve in major roles but who have a sense of integrity and are committed to helping others gain access and opportunity that will advance this nation.

Bridget: In my over 20-year career, I have mentored, chaired the dissertation of, and served as the academic advisor for five Black women and one Black trans student. I have also mentored, advised, and/or served on the dissertations of five additional Black women doctoral students. Because of how I came into the faculty role, wanting to be a model for other Black students, it meant the world to be a possibility model in the faculty. Not all Black students or Black women that have been in PhD programs while I was faculty have been interested in working with me, but working with the ten Black women students who chose to work with me has been transformational. It has filled my cup to be along for the journey as Black women PhD students complete their degree and embark on a career as faculty or administrators in higher education. While I share two salient identities of race and gender with Black women PhD students, I would like to share a story when this was not the case.

When I was in graduate school and even in my first decade of being a faculty member steeped in equity and inclusion work, I was unfamiliar with the terms people who identify along a gender spectrum used. I met a prospective PhD student who identified as a Black woman. I helped recruit her and she became my first Black woman doctoral advisee. The student took a class with me, served as a teaching assistant with me, and asked me to chair their dissertation. Over the course of the student's time in the doctoral program, the student transitioned and now identifies as trans* genderqueer and uses he/him/his gender pronouns. In a meeting I was facilitating with him and other faculty, I consistently misgendered him and used she and her to refer to him. After the meeting, a colleague took me aside and shared with me what I did.

I was so thankful to the colleague because I mis-gendered the student out of habit and had not realized it. My intent was to honor the student. My intent aligned with my belief that people have a right to identify any way they desire in terms of gender. My intent was to address the student in the way he had expressly asked to be addressed. However, my impact was the exact opposite of my intent. I harmed the student by mis-gendering him and not respecting his gender pronouns. Because this colleague knew my intent and how I wanted to honor people's gender pronouns, they felt comfortable coming to me and telling me what they observed. This was impactful because I was embarrassed, disappointed, and surprised at myself. It was such a misalignment between my stated beliefs and my actions that it served to remind me how I needed to be conscious and intentional when I interacted with people around their gender pronouns. Had the colleague not held me accountable, I might have further damaged a relationship with the student and not been able to repair the harm.

This student and I were able to talk about their gender, my work on honoring their gender, and how we could build our relationship. It was remarkable to have a Black doctoral student that also had high racial salience, and this student was my first opportunity to chair, advise, and mentor a Black PhD student. Beyond the racial salience we shared, we connected over our love of intergroup dialogue, closeness to our families, and love for our partners. We also discussed being Black in the academy and how it impacted our work. When we taught a multiculturalism class together it was instructive for the students to see that race was one of the only identities we shared. Some of the differences that I identify as a cis-gender woman come from an upper-middle-class SES, and both my parents have graduate degrees. This was not the case for the student who not only identifies as genderqueer but comes from a low-income background and is a first-generation college student. We grew close as advisor/advisee and frequently spent time outside of class and off-campus eating meals, hanging out in my home, and connecting at conferences. It was a new experience for me to advise and eventually mentor a student who shared the same melanin brown skin as me and experienced racism as it intersected with other marginalized aspects of our identities. I feel blessed that we still connect and pour love into each other whenever we talk. Our relationship has definitely been reciprocal with both of us learning alongside each other. He retained me at a time when I was the only faculty of color, only Black faculty in my program. Getting him to the finish line of his PhD was fulfilling, yet only a stop along the journey and thankfully not an end to our relationship. The relationship between my first Black doctoral student and myself illustrates that I am a work in progress as a mentor. It takes unlearning white supremacy, patriarchy, classism, among other systems of oppression to fully show up as my best self to mentor students.

How I mentor also comes from the field of student affairs. I have never been a student affairs practitioner. But I love and am loved deeply by people who are in that field. The idea of care for the whole person is central to the student affairs field, and for me, central to mentoring. When I mentor, I think about the whole person, not just the academic or intellectual aspect of them. I ask about mentee's beliefs, wellness, family, friends, fitness, and what they need from our relationship. I am not trying to mold that person into me or even who I think they should be.

I believe one of my purposes in mentoring is to help people see the light that is already inside of them. In order to do this, I have to get to know the whole person. Helping people uncover their light, their gifts, talents, and unique contributions they can make has been something I strive for and try to cultivate with mentees. I view people as already talented and gifted. While I view everyone in this way, I am drawn to marginalized students, partly because that is what I saw as a child watching my parents cultivate peer networks of Black students at Massachusetts Institute of Technology (MIT) and Wellesley where they worked. The other reason I want to instill in marginalized students that they are talented and gifted is because I know how it feels to doubt your worth. I doubted myself as a Black student and as a Black woman professor at a historically white university.

Tyanna: One of the reasons why I am enjoying my PhD journey is because the program created an environment ripe for healthy mentoring relationships between advisors and students and among students – the faculty in my program model peer mentoring. Not only do I see them supporting one another, but they also love and challenge each other. They are also intentional in encouraging students to build support networks among each other and help facilitate valuable community-building activities among students. For example, Dr. Kelly has organized group advising sessions with her advisees. These group sessions allow her advisees to get to know one another, practice their presentations for dissertation proposals and defenses, receive peer feedback, and help each other reach the finish line of their PhD. Even when Dr. Kelly is not present, we still gather to support one another. As an advisee, I have grown closer to other Black women in the program and lean on them as a source of encouragement. We essentially have become a cheering squad for each other, and it feels good to have an investment from other Black women in my success. Faculty and administrators also advocate in academic spaces above students' "pay grade" for better funding and resources, so our PhD journey is not a bitter and resentful experience.

KEY TAKEAWAYS/HOMEWORK

It is impressive to read about the experiences of Black women "holding each other down" but make no mistake that institutions are equally (if not more) responsible for making the changes necessary to prevent the oppression Black women doctoral students face in the academy. Institutions must read the words of the Black women authors in this book and think critically about the experiences they create for Black women doctoral students. Critical reflection must lead to systemic and institutional change. Institutions must not rely solely on the resilience and strength of Black women to figure it out, but they must invest in the resources to create the spaces that allow Black women doctoral students to flourish. Peer mentoring is but one of the many keys needed for Black women doctoral students to thrive, succeed, and finish their doctoral degrees.

REFERENCES

Apugo, D. L. (2017). "We all we got": Considering peer relationships as multi-purpose sustainability outlets among millennial Black women graduate students attending majority white urban universities. *The Urban Review, 49*, 347–367.

Fries-Britt, S., & Kelly, B.T. (2005). Retaining each other: Narratives of two African American women in the academy. *The Urban Review, 37*(3), 221–242.

Grant, C. M. (2012). Advancing our legacy: A Black feminist perspective on the significance of mentoring for African-American women in educational leadership. *International Journal of Qualitative Studies in Education, 25*(1), 101–117.

Grant, C. M., & Simmons, J. C. (2008). Narratives on experiences of African-American women in the academy: Conceptualizing effective mentoring relationships of doctoral student and faculty. *International Journal of Qualitative Studies in Education, 21*(5), 501–517.

Kelly, B. T., & Fries-Britt, S. (Eds.) (2022). *Building Mentorship Networks to Support Black Women: A Guide to Succeeding in the Academy.* Routledge.

Lane, T. B., Patterson-Stephens, S. M., Perez, E. N., & Pierre, D. F. (2022). Examining relationships matter: A qualitative study of black women in doctoral education. *Journal of African American Women and Girls in Education, 2*(1), 27–46.

Minnett, J. L., James-Gallaway, A. D., & Owens, D. R. (2019). Help a sista out: Black women doctoral students' use of peer mentorship as an act of resistance. *Mid-Western Educational Researcher, 31*(2), 210–238.

Mosley, M. H. (1980). Black women administrators in higher education: An endangered species. *Journal of Black Studies, 10*(3), 295–310.

Patton, L. D., & Harper, S. R. (2003). Mentoring relationships among African American women in graduate and professional schools. *New Directions for Student Services, 2003*(104), 67–78.

Perna, L. W., Gerald, D., Baum, E., & Milem, J. (2007). The status of equity for black faculty and administrators in public higher education in the south. *Research in Higher Education, 48*, 193–228.

Rasheem, S., Alleman, A. S., Mushonga, D., Anderson, D., & Ofahengaue Vakalahi, H. F. (2018). Mentor-shape: Exploring the mentoring relationships of Black women in doctoral programs. *Mentoring & Tutoring: Partnership in Learning, 26*(1), 50–69.

Chapter 2

Retaining Each Other
The Power of Community for African American Women Undergraduates in STEM

Joy Gaston Gayles and Chelsea Smith

INTRODUCTION AND CHAPTER OVERVIEW

Black women, from undergraduates to professionals, are underrepresented in critical areas of need, such as science, technology, engineering, and mathematics (STEM). Further, Black women are poised to make significant and innovative contributions in STEM areas and deserve access to high-paying career opportunities. However, this talent pool remains untapped and underserved, as evidenced by the low numbers of Black women who select, persist, earn degrees, and enter STEM careers. Racial and gender gaps are prevalent at each juncture along the pathway to a career in STEM, represented by fewer numbers and a lack of representation for Black women. Sadly, when Black women persist within STEM fields, they often experience a chilly climate and lack of belonging, creating a host of challenges to persistence and thriving. Further, because there are so few Black women in STEM fields, they are less likely to receive mentoring, guidance, and support that we know from the literature can bolster student success (Freeman, 1999). Nonetheless, stories exist, but are often untold, of high-achieving Black women who are resilient and navigate these environments to persist despite the odds.

In this chapter, we share what we learned from high-achieving Black undergraduate women in STEM about the importance of creating communities of support for themselves and others and the critical role of peer mentoring. We intentionally framed the discussion as lessons for institutional leaders to encourage necessary shifts in the institutional environment to support Black women in higher education better. Focusing on peer mentoring and creating communities of support for Black women undergraduates is an important starting place for a

DOI: 10.4324/9781003394648-3

conversation on mentoring and supporting Black women graduate students because what happens at the undergraduate level informs and shapes the graduate school experience.

IMPORTANCE OF MENTORING

In this case, understanding the importance of mentoring for high-achieving Black women undergraduates is essential to facilitating their success (McPherson, 2017). Research supports that the best mentoring relationships challenge and support students to meet and exceed their goals and keep students excited about learning and personal growth (Freeman, 1999; Patton, 2006; Seymour & Ray, 2015). The difficulties for Black women high-achieving students are multifaceted in part because of their intersecting identities within the context of predominantly white environments that inherently overlook and dismiss the intellectual prowess of Black students (Espinosa, 2011; Griffin, 2006; Griffin & Allen, 2006; McGee & Bentley, 2017). Matriculating in such environments makes it difficult for Black women to form connections and relationships with faculty and peers that lead to student success (Freeman, 1999). For example, Fries-Britt and Griffin (2007) found that Black high-achieving students had better mentoring relationships with Black faculty than non-Black faculty because they could understand and identify with their lived experiences. However, Black faculty are underrepresented on predominantly white college campuses, especially in STEM fields (Kelly et al., 2017).

The reality is that most colleges and universities, except historically Black colleges and universities and minority-serving institutions, are overwhelmingly white (Matias et al., 2021). The numbers of Black students, for example, far exceed and are out of proportion to the number of Black faculty and administrative staff. As a result, when Black students enter predominantly white college campuses, they do not see themselves reflected within the environment, which sends a strong message about belonging and environmental culture. Further, this dynamic makes Black students less likely to have access to mentoring and support to navigate such cultural climates (Meeuwisse et al., 2010). If college campuses are serious about attracting and retaining Black students, they must take transformative action to recruit and retain Black faculty (Commodore et al., 2018; Kelly et al., 2017).

We know from the literature that when students of color are mentored and have communities of support on campus, they are also more satisfied with their overall college experience (Meeuwisse et al., 2010; Strayhorn & Saddler, 2009; Strayhorn & Terrell, 2007). Rockinson-Szapkiw and Wendt (2020) found a connection between peer–mentor relationships and increased self-confidence, leadership, professional skills, and persistence. However, Black students, particularly in STEM majors, have difficulty in connecting to peers in their discipline. As a result, they miss out on the benefits of peer mentoring if they do not find ways to create supportive communities for themselves. Retaining each other on predominantly white college campuses often is, but should not be, the sole responsibility of Black students.

MENTORING FOR BLACK WOMEN UNDERGRADUATES IN STEM

Within STEM environments are systems, structures, policies, and practices that privilege white males at the expense of Black women and other underrepresented people of color (Johnson, 2011; Seymour & Hewitt, 1997). Examples include narrow, noninclusive curricula and teaching practices, lack of mentoring and support, gender and race-informed stereotypes, and deficit assumptions about abilities and academic performance across race, gender, and socio-economic status (Fassinger & Asay, 2006; Gayles & Ampaw, 2014; George-Jackson, 2011; Parson, 2016). Such adverse experiences within academic spaces characterize a chilly climate and lack of belonging for Black women. Without a strong sense of belonging, students often experience difficulty in identifying, affiliating, and connecting to the environment in ways that help them thrive and reach their full potential. Studies that center the experiences of Black women, for example, help us learn more about what is problematic within academic spaces and the kinds of support they need to navigate successfully. Moreover, such studies can be instrumental for institutions to make shifts in the college environment aligned with retaining minoritized populations.

Black women within STEM disciplines are among the most vulnerable and underrepresented student subgroups (Fletcher et al., 2017). Lack of representation creates a dynamic that makes it challenging to navigate when microaggressions and other forms of discrimination occur (Charleston et al., 2014; McGee & Bentley, 2017; Morton & Parsons, 2018). Addressing and speaking up about such negative experiences takes a lot of courage and psychological energy, in addition to the intellectual energy required to complete rigorous coursework (Smith et al., 2007). For these reasons and more, Black women are especially in need of mentoring and communities of support to navigate chilly cultural climates and avoid suffering in silence while simultaneously making degree progress. Cultivating ways to enhance Black women's experiences is pivotal in maintaining their engagement and persistence in majors where they are underrepresented. To fill the gap, many Black women students rely on the wealth from their cultural backgrounds to navigate chilly climates. Yet, doing so does not dismiss the need for mentoring and support within the college environment. Understanding Black women's experiences from a critical lens can enhance our knowledge of how best to support them within college environments.

CONSIDERING COMMUNITY CULTURAL WEALTH

Community cultural wealth (CCW) is a framework that centers communities of color, including Black women, bringing attention to the range of cultural knowledge, skill, and abilities that communities of color possess (Yosso, 2005). Further, CCW is a critical theory that disrupts the dominant narrative about what counts as capital. CCW offers a counternarrative that is anti-deficit in nature and centers communities of color as places and spaces of cultural wealth (Jayakumar et al., 2013). Accordingly, the framework expands traditional forms of capital to include six additional forms of cultural capital: social, aspirational, linguistic, familial, navigation, and resistance (Yosso, 2005).

Yosso's (2005) model was useful in helping us understand the lived experiences of high-achieving Black women in STEM and better understand the cultural capital they enacted to help them enter, navigate, and persist in chilly learning environments. We also used this framework as a lens to disrupt the dominant narrative about Black women in STEM – a narrative typically deficit in scope and filled with racialized, incomplete, and false assumptions about Black women and their intellectual capabilities. In this chapter, we share significant lessons from a study of high-achieving Black women in STEM, highlighting forms of cultural capital used and cultivated to empower and retain themselves and others.

BRIEF DESCRIPTION OF THE STUDY

We derived the lessons discussed later in this chapter from a larger study on the experiences of high-achieving African-American undergraduates in STEM majors at a predominantly white institution. We defined high achieving as students who maintained a 3.0 grade point average consistent with other studies on this population (Fries-Britt, 1997). Due to the high attrition rates and lack of representation of underrepresented people of color, we were interested in learning about the experiences of high-achieving Black students in STEM. Rarely told are stories of success for underrepresented populations in STEM. Such stories have the potential to benefit future students and campus administrators. Using a case study approach, we collected data from ten Black high-achieving students in STEM majors at a predominantly white institution. Six of the ten participants were identified as Black women (the remaining four were identified as Black men). For this chapter, we only include data from the six Black women in the study (see Table 2.1). Data collection included individual interviews and a focus group with participants to capture pre-college and college experiences as STEM majors. In addition, we asked participants to write letters of advice to future students on navigating STEM majors successfully as an additional data

Table 2.1 Self-reported Participant Data

Chosen Pseudonym	Major	Classification	Self-Reported GPA
Michelle	Biological Sciences	Junior	4.0
Tonya	Mechanical Engineering	Senior	3.85
Angel	Chemical Engineering	Junior	3.5
Joy	Biomedical Engineering	Senior	3.7
Candace	Biological Sciences	Senior	4.0
Cara	Chemistry	Senior	3.3

source. Maya Angelou's Book *Letter to My Daughter* (Angelou, 2008) inspired this methodological choice.

LESSONS FOR MENTORING AND RETAINING BLACK WOMEN IN STEM

Several themes emerged from the data analytic process. For this purpose of this chapter, we present the major themes from the study as lessons for mentoring Black women undergraduates, with a particular emphasis on Black women in STEM majors. Grounded in the experiences of high-achieving Black women undergraduates in STEM majors at a predominately white institution, we offer three mentoring lessons. The lessons offer a counternarrative to underrepresentation in STEM and provide context for why mentoring and support communities are essential for Black women in college. The first two lessons provide context that speaks to the challenges that high-achieving Black women experience. The third lesson highlights how participants used their cultural capital to cultivate communities of mentoring and support to help them achieve success. We chose the word "lesson" intentionally to highlight what we can learn from Black women in college that has implications for how campuses can better support underrepresented college students and how Black women can support each other. Thus, the lessons have implications for institutional policy and practice. The onus for navigating chilly cultural climates should not fall on the students but should be the institution's responsibility. Further, what institutions learn from the experiences of Black women undergraduates can be instrumental in better supporting Black women in graduate school.

Lesson 1 acknowledges that high-achieving Black women come to college with a wealth of experiences that need to be nurtured and better understood to bolster their success. Lesson 2 highlights the intersectional realities and consequences of the race and gender double-bind. Finally, lesson 3 chronicles how participants navigate toxic cultural environments by creating communities of mentoring and support.

LESSON 1: WHAT BLACK EXCELLENCE LOOKS LIKE

Lesson 1, what Black excellence looks like, foregrounds the need for mentoring and support for high-achieving Black women students in STEM majors. Black excellence represents a counternarrative to deficit perspectives that suggest Black women are not interested or prepared to pursue rigorous areas of study in college (McGee, 2016; McGee & Bentley, 2017). The high-achieving Black women in this study held high aspirations and were well prepared for STEM majors in college. Early enrichment opportunities throughout their K-12 experience helped them cultivate and nurture their interests in STEM. In addition, many of them had relatives and teachers who shaped and influenced their interests in STEM. These high-achieving Black women were also clear about what success looked like for themselves and exemplified Black excellence. Yet, their storied experiences within STEM environments reflect the need for mentoring and support to nurture the Black excellence within them. This kind of support should come from the institutional environment to mitigate barriers that prevent and stand in opposition to Black excellence.

Participants reflected on their hopes and dreams for the future and why they chose STEM majors. Embedded within their aspirations are hints about what motivates them and fuels their success. Specifically, Angel articulated her hopes and dreams, stating, "'But what can I do to improve the medicine industry, or what can I help to make it better? Where can I leave my footprint?' So that was kinda, like, what motivated me." Michelle expressed how her aspirations for a STEM career started as early as her junior year when she transferred to [a math and science-focused high school]. Her aspirations held as she entered college. Michelle stated in her interview, "I am planning on pursuing an MD-PhD program." The aspirations expressed by the Black women participants are related to Yosso's (2005) contention that marginalized students possess aspirational capital, "hope and dreams" that motivates them. What we gleaned from the participants in this study reflects the need for higher education institutions to support and nurture the dreams and aspirations of Black women, particularly as Black women aspire to graduate school.

Many of the Black women participants in the study talked about major influencers or people who positively motivated them to be excellent and pursue their dreams, including parents, siblings, and teachers. Almost all of the Black women in the study shared that their parents encouraged them at an early age to earn good grades, do well in school, and pursue higher education. We focus here on teacher influence data because of the implications for campus environments. Participants talked about teachers who noticed their potential and would nudge them to apply for and pursue opportunities to propel their success. Cara shared, "I had teachers in elementary school and middle school who

25

always gave me a pat on the back and said, 'Good job with things.'" Candace also commented about the positive influence teachers had on her experience. She shared, "my teachers, they were like encouraging and they just made sure that I was challenged also." Angel shared, "My physics teacher, he was really big on seeing me go further. He also saw I was doing well in his class. He was like, 'Hey, you could do this, you can do this, you can go here.'" The importance of having teachers and professors inspire students and show them what's possible cannot be understated. Such individuals fuel aspirational capital by creating a culture of possibility for students to dream regardless of environmental circumstances and structural barriers.

Persevering through challenges, balancing their time, and staying connected to their purpose were all a part of what success looks like for the high-achieving Black women in our study. Further, students need mentoring and support to learn skills and utilize resources to help them navigate college environments. Participants in our study clearly articulated that although pursuing a STEM major is challenging, they had confidence and knew they could do hard things. Many of the Black women in the study talked about some of the challenges they experienced adjusting to differences between high school and college-level courses. For example, Angel revealed her experience preparing for exams: "Engineering exams, you have to start studying like days in advance. Not saying that the tests are just extremely difficult for no reason. It's just; it's a different type of testing." About the test, Angel went on to articulate the critical thinking and problem-solving nature of tests in STEM, which is different from high school tests where you repeat back facts from a textbook. Many participants shared lessons learned from doing hard things and rising to the challenge by advancing their problem-solving skills and applying concepts to different problems. In her letter to a future student, Tonya advised students not to be afraid, stating, "Don't let anything scare you, take advantage of opportunities, study hard, carve out some personal time and you'll thrive ..." Persisting through challenges underscores Yosso's definition of navigational capital – people's skills and abilities to navigate challenging, structurally oppressive environments. Further, Black women need mentoring and support to navigate such environments and how to use their voices to change them.

Again, lesson 1 underscores the need for peer and faculty mentoring for high-achieving Black women undergraduates to help navigate chilly campus climates and challenges institutions to take responsibility for creating equitable and inclusive learning environments. Black women can do hard things. However, they also need mentoring and support because they should not have to, but often do, navigate environments that are not diverse, equitable, or inclusive. As a result, Black women experience realities and consequences tied to their interlocking racial and gender identities.

LESSON 2: REALITIES AND CONSEQUENCES OF THE DOUBLE-BIND

As the Black women in our study matriculated through STEM learning environments, the realities of the double-bind became evident. The women in our study described experiences of being "the only one" who looked like them and the lack of support and mentoring received from the environment. They also described the culture shock they felt, the stereotypes they encountered, and the need to prove themselves. These experiences were exacerbated by not having much in common with peers in their major, not feeling welcomed, and the environment not feeling like a space where they could freely express themselves.

The reality of being the "only one" or one of few in terms of racial and gender identity with their majors reflected a consequence of the double-bind for the Black women participants. Some participants, like Cara and Angel, have always been the only one who looked like them since grade school. Further, participants talked about how it felt being the only Black person or woman in their classes and how it shaped their experience. Candace, for example, shared how she expected to be the only one or one of few in her classes:

> I recognize that I'm an African-American, and I recognize that I'm usually one of the very few African-Americans…if there's not enough people to work with, or you don't actually just click…like a lot of people my freshman year, I took a senior level, advanced anatomy class, it was a 400-level class, so I didn't know anybody in that class.

Angel discussed how stressful it was to think through and figure out what to do in isolating situations – teetering between introducing herself to white peers and asking to be a part of their group or waiting for the professor to assign her to a group because it did not happen naturally. She described her internal fear of introducing herself to her peers and how awkward it felt. Nevertheless, she found the courage to do it but acknowledged it was difficult.

Another variation of the realities and consequences of the double-bind is the culture shock participants experienced entering STEM learning environments. Tonya talked about the differences between her high school culture and undergraduate institution. She said, "there was a whole culture shock and adjustment, so that's one fold of the struggle." Angel was also puzzled because her undergraduate institution was somewhat diverse; yet, people there were not tolerant of diversity. She expressed, "you can expect more ignorance than anything else. Many people at [undergraduate institution] are intolerant or ignorant to diversity." Ravyn talked about culture shock in a slightly different way. She attended high school in a rural part of her state and experienced culture shock when she entered a STEM learning environment. In particular, she noticed the discrepancy in resources and how it impacted her level of preparedness compared to her peers who had access to more resources in high school. Ravyn shared, "I didn't realize I was lacking resources or anything ... I went from being in the top of the class to being close to the bottom."

Living and learning within environments filled with stereotypes is another reality and consequence of the double-bind. Many participants expressed feeling frustrated but not deterred by stereotypes. For example, Tonya came into STEM environments prepared to experience stereotypes and judgments based on what her mom told her about experiencing sexual harassment from her supervisor. Tonya stated, "I'm expecting to encounter a lot of opposition, some prejudice." Participants also expressed frustration about working so hard to get where they were; yet, they heard comments within STEM learning environments about affirmative action and reverse racism. Participants also practiced resistance as a form of cultural capital and in protest against stereotypes and microaggressions. Tonya disclosed:

> You can expect more ignorance than anything else; many people at [institution] may not have interacted with many people of color, especially those from more 'ethnic' backgrounds...It just kind of gives me some more motivation for graduation. 'Hey! Bam! Did it, and I did it better than you.'

Lack of belonging and support is another reality and consequence of the double-bind that manifested through not feeling comfortable or welcomed within the STEM learning environments. Participants expressed lack of belonging and support related to difficulty in finding the resources they needed to succeed. Cara talked about how difficult it was to follow the advice of getting close to your professors. She shared, "I feel like it's kinda hard to do it, and you have to make a special effort to do it..." Angel talked about how difficult it was to find tutors for higher-level gateway courses like calculus and physics.

Another manifestation of lack of belonging and support expressed by participants was having little in common with their peers. Ravyn said she had "no friends in class, and so I sat in the front row, and I just was looking at the teacher." Angel described the same dynamic as intimidating and anxiety-producing. Angel said, "I didn't know how people would respond to me...literally, every class, you're in a group with different people." For Angel, this meant not knowing and not feeling comfortable having little to nothing in common with her peers. Joy discussed the importance of friendships during college, especially within the major. At the same time, she expressed how difficult it was for her to form friendships with her peers in class:

> ...with my peers in my classes, it's just like well, all right, this one class you have together...let's just study for it and then let's be done, which that sounds

bad, but, yeah…But it's just that level of comfortability, that level of similarity that I have with [friends] that I don't have with my peers in my classes.

Most participants formed friendships outside the major but maintained surface-level relationships with their peers in class. The importance of friendships and peer mentoring to a sense of belonging and student success cannot be understated. We revisit this in the next lesson.

In response to chilly STEM learning environments, stereotypes, lack of belonging and support, and being the only one, participants talked about having to prove themselves to navigate the academic environment successfully. Unfortunately, because STEM learning environments are toxic, anti-Black, and filled with stereotypes, Black women spend a lot of time thinking about and performing in ways that refute stereotypes and resist anti-Blackness. The lack of faculty and peer mentoring suggests they must navigate these situations independently. Although Cara and Tonya expressed seeing it as a challenge that pushes them to do better, Joy recognized in her response the time and energy it takes to ensure that stereotypes are "not really being portrayed through our actions." Disproving stereotypes is especially troubling because the stereotyped group feels the need to prove themselves even though the information touted about them is false and inaccurate (Tatum, 2017). Tonya expressed it this way in her letter to a future student, "As a minority and especially in engineering, people expect you to be unsuccessful." Therefore, one of her strongest sources of motivation is "proving them wrong."

LESSON 3: CREATING COMMUNITIES OF MENTORING AND SUPPORT

The previous two lessons set the context for why faculty and peer mentoring are crucial to attracting and retaining Black women in the academy. The Black women participants in this study represent Black excellence. However, the realities and consequences of the double-bind complicated their learning and personal development. To navigate the chilly climate in Engineering, participants intentionally created communities of support for themselves. Cultivating mentoring and support communities included seeking mentors and role models, finding and asking for help, nurturing friendships outside of their major, and involvement in student groups and organizations. Ravyn stated this in her letter to a future student, "I also advise that you surround yourself with positive and motivated individuals that will serve as a support system." Her words speak to the importance of peer support on campus, which is vital to success, especially for Black women. Angel stated in her interview, "[Your] best resources will be your peers." Many participants also spoke of an on-campus mentor, Ms. Apple (pseudonym), a Black woman administrator who ran the summer transition program. Beyond the summer program, she was influential and supportive of their success. These experiences characterize what Yosso (2005) called social capital, *peer support*, and *social contacts*.

Creating communities of mentoring and support meant not being afraid to ask for help, a sentiment articulated by most participants. They recognized that STEM learning environments feel intimidating, but they found ways to push past that to find and create support and retain others. Angel contextualized this best by sharing that it's impossible to know everything alone.

> Honestly, you just gotta talk to the right people. I know I keep – I feel like a broken record, but a lot of the things that I've learned while being here in college have come from mentors. I don't learn anything on my own. There has never been a time where I've been able to sit down with something I don't understand and teach it to myself. I've always had to go and ask somebody else or ask them what they think about certain things. You definitely gain skills and intelligence from somebody else that has had to use skills and intelligence to get through something.

Being bold and asking for help also meant intentionally going to office hours to talk to professors and support staff, although doing so was intimidating. All six participants recalled an experience where they went to office hours to seek information and opportunities to ensure they fully understood a concept discussed in class. For example, Tonya voiced her experience of struggling in her classes, "…if you look at my transcript, it doesn't look like I struggled, but that's because I went to office hours."

Participants also talked about the importance of using campus resources. Candace observed that you may not need every resource available, "but if you know how to use what you do have to your advantage, that's a good thing to help you thrive…." In addition, Tonya named several resources she sought and how each enhanced her college experience. For example, she used the free printing services offered through one of the minority-serving student organizations.

Finally, asking for what you need involves avoiding the tendency to struggle in silence. Participants found the courage to ask and speak up to get what they needed. Ravyn recalled a struggle in class. She eventually found the courage to ask for help.

> I've never been a person to go ask for help, but I was struggling in this one class, and I was like, "I have to go talk to this teacher because I don't know what to do anymore," so I had actually taken the time to actually go and ask questions and show people that I'm trying to learn and I'm not grasping it the way that you want me to grasp it.

This kind of boldness helped navigate group dynamics. In their letters to future students, several participants advised students to be bold and put themselves out there to ask for help or to be a part of a study group. Angel made known the advice that her dad gave her:

> My dad used to tell me 'closed mouths don't get fed.' If you don't ask for help or ask to be a part of a study group how do you expect to get it? Do not let your minority status in your major keep you from being successful.

Putting this into perspective was helpful for Candace, who divulged that she "treated it as strictly business," which helped her deal with the dynamic of having nothing in common with people in her study group. Instead, she advised future students to "seek out other people of color with similar classes" to create a support system.

The importance of having **friendships** in college, particularly for Black women, considering their lack of representation, matters. Joy expressed it this way:

> I think friendships are important for college experience and within the major it's just an added bond, and added struggling together, an added...way to engage with somebody who is going through the same thing that you're going through.

She distinguished the difference between not having anything in common with people in her classes versus having more fluid interactions with her friends outside of her major. Cara appreciated her college friends because they provided advice and shared their experiences. In her words, "...you can learn from their mistakes..." Although many did not have friends in their classes, Ravyn did and expressed the importance of this by sharing, "...we would study together, and that would help me out...having friends in the class really contributed to my positivity."

Participants intentionally cultivated friendships, as classes were not spaces where they all felt comfortable developing close bonds. Most participants attended the summer bridge program before their first year of college, which set the foundation for friendships and cultivating communities of support. Others were more open to putting themselves out there to develop friendships. Candance said how she met many of her friends: "I just went up to them, 'hey, how'd you feel about this test?' and then we'd start talking about it, and the next thing you know, we're good friends...." The conversation from one class carried on to another, and they retained each other as they matriculated through the major.

Three participants talked about how friendships provided much-needed balance, mainly to offset the rigors of classwork or the consequences of having nothing in common with peers and lack of belonging in the classroom. Joy revealed her experience of not feeling comfortable in class, but when she's hanging out with her friends, "it just feels like I'm at home." Tonya affirmed, "I just have to find the balance. So a lot of the people that I'm closer to, my friends, are in [minority engineering program] just because we spend a lot of time together and have that similar background." Finally, Ravyn added an important dimension of balance to friendships relative to mental health. She stated:

> I take some time to have a social life and to have fun, and I think that is very important in college and in life to make sure you have a healthy balance between your schoolwork and your social life.

Further, participants talked about the spillover effect of being in community with friends and studying and supporting each other even if you are not in the same major. Joy put it this way, "...having more friendship and similarity in my outside groups, I find myself studying with them for a different class..."

While navigating their majors, all participants retained each other through **involvement in student groups, organizations,** and programs designed for minoritized student success. For example, many participants mentioned the importance of getting involved in their letters to future students and articulated the benefits of engagement in campus communities. For instance, Joy, in her letter, shared:

> The Minority Engineering Program is designed to help retain and encourage students of color in engineering. The program provides you with a mentor and multiple fun weekend events that help introduce you to other minorities in your major. Talk to your mentor, and talk to your peers. These people will be your support system from your first day of class until you graduate.

The benefits of involvement in campus organizations included mentoring, advice, support, college readiness, leadership development, and the opportunity to find and interact with diverse students. Tonya talked about her experience in the summer bridge program and how it helped acclimate her to college. She shared that it "... was probably the best thing I could have done the summer before my freshman year..." She took one class, and it helped her "...find the balance of fun and studying."

Involvement in student organizations, particularly those created to retain and support minoritized students, offered opportunities for students to develop leadership skills. Over half of the participants expressed having the opportunity to mentor other students. For example, Ravyn entered college looking for opportunities to mentor other students. In her words, "…my goal was to serve as a mentor and a role model for the people back home and to show them what can happen." Involvement in student organizations allowed them to practice leadership by planning events and serving as officers. Involvement also offered volunteer opportunities and increased their effectiveness working with others.

Another benefit of creating mentoring and support communities through involvement in student organizations was the opportunity to interact with diverse students. Given the importance of friendships, participants shared that one of the easiest ways this happened was by putting themselves out there and getting involved. For Ravyn, she was intentional about becoming involved. She shared, "I can get that interaction with other students that are like me." Further, becoming involved and having the opportunity to meet and interact with diverse students helped Ravyn deal with "the shock of it all" – one of the consequences of race and gender realities for participants in this study.

Participants encouraged future students to find their fit because involvement in student organizations yields positive, beneficial experiences. In her letter, Joy mentioned that "there are a plethora of opportunities available to you at [her undergraduate institution], so make sure you maximize on them." Ravyn double-downed on this advice, suggesting that because there are so many ways to get involved, it's important for students to identify activities that relate to their interests and passions. Involvement in student organizations served as a healthy outlet and enhanced her learning experiences and personal development.

Participating in co-curricular activities, engaging in-class topics, lab experiences, internships, and co-ops are how participants described maximizing experiences. Navigating their college experiences through co-curricular experiences highlights their *skills and abilities to navigate social systems,* which Yosso (2005) defined as navigational capital. Many of the participants got an early start on navigating educational spaces through a seven-week summer transition program. They were able to jump start taking classes and build peer mentorship and support. Candace began these experiences in high school through participation in the early college program.

Participants also spoke of their experiences with co-curricular activities. For example, Angel served as vice president for her institution's National Society of Black Engineers (NSBE) chapter. Cara was the vice president of the Multicultural Scientist. Michelle participated in her institution's undergraduate research symposium. Each of these Black women recounted their experience with campus involvement as an enhancement to their academic experience. Given the importance of cultivating communities of mentoring and support, campuses can take responsibility for ensuring that Black women have access and the opportunity to connect with others within the environment in meaningful ways. One practical approach is hiring and retaining equity-minded faculty and staff to mentor and support students and shift campus environments to be more welcoming and inclusive.

HOMEWORK FOR INSTITUTIONAL LEADERS

There are several connections to prior studies and implications for policy and practice when interrogating how high-achieving Black women successfully navigate academic spaces using their cultural capital. First, exploring the experience of high-achieving Black women enrolled in a STEM discipline has implications for policy and practice. In white male-dominated fields, support for marginalized students is critical to success. Second, embedded within the lessons is advice from Black women on retaining themselves and others. Further, this advice extends to what institutions can do to retain and support Black women in science and engineering and on college campuses. Finally, participants' experiences represent opportunities for institutions to create and sustain college environments that better support and retain Black women in higher education. Programming and interventions alone will not resolve the systemic issues that make campus environments challenging to navigate for Black women.

While Black women are achieving and persisting in STEM disciplines by utilizing the cultural wealth they already possess, institutions can do much more to support them. For example, faculty engagement in equity-minded training and workshops could help shift the environment. Further, creating special interest groups (SIGs) for Black women in STEM can be sites for peer mentoring and support. Finally, there is room for more recognition and representation of Black women within STEM disciplines. Representation matters to mentoring and the ability to retain each other.

REFERENCES

Angelou, M. (2008). *Letter to My Daughter*. Random House.

Charleston, L. J., George, P. L., Jackson, J. F., Berhanu, J., & Amechi, M. H. (2014). Navigating underrepresented STEM spaces: Experiences of Black women in US computing science higher education programs who actualize success. *Journal of Diversity in Higher Education, 7*(3), 166.

Commodore, F., Baker, D. J., & Arroyo, A. T. (2018). *Black Women College Students: A Guide to Student Success in Higher Education*. Routledge.

Espinosa, L. (2011). Pipelines and pathways: Women of color in undergraduate STEM majors and the college experiences that contribute to persistence. *Harvard Educational Review, 81*(2), 209–241.

Fassinger, R. E., & Asay, P. A. (2006). Career counseling for women in science, technology, engineering, and mathematics (STEM) fields. In Walsh, W. B., Heppner, M., & Heppner, M. J. (Eds.), *Handbook of career counseling for women* (pp. 427–452). Taylor & Francis.

Fletcher, T., Ross, M., Tolbert, D., Holly, J., Cardella, M., Godwin, A., & DeBoer, J. (2017). Ignored potential: A collaborative roadmap for increasing African

American women in engineering. National society of black engineers, society of women engineers, women in engineering ProActive network.

Freeman, K. (1999). No services needed?: The case for mentoring high-achieving African American students. *Peabody Journal of Education, 74*(2), 15–26.

Fries–Britt, S. (1997). Identifying and supporting gifted African American men. *New Directions for Student Services, 1997*(80), 65–78.

Fries-Britt, S., & Griffin, K. (2007). The Black box: How high-achieving Blacks resist stereotypes about Black Americans. *Journal of College Student Development, 48*(5), 509–524.

Gayles, J. G., & Ampaw, F. (2014). The impact of college experiences on degree completion in STEM fields at four-year institutions: Does gender matter? *The Journal of Higher Education, 85*(4), 439–468.

George-Jackson, C. (2011). STEM switching: Examining departures of undergraduate women in STEM fields. *Journal of Women and Minorities in Science and Engineering, 17*(2), 149–171.

Griffin, K. (2006). Striving for success: A qualitative exploration of competing theories of high-achieving black college students' academic motivation. *Journal of College Student Development, 47*(4), 384–400.

Griffin, K., & Allen, W. (2006). Mo'money, mo'problems? High-achieving Black high school students' experiences with resources, racial climate, and resilience. *The Journal of Negro Education,75(3),* 478–494.

Jayakumar, U., Vue, R., & Allen, W. (2013). Pathways to college for young black scholars: A community cultural wealth perspective. *Harvard Educational Review, 83*(4), 551–579.

Johnson, D. R. (2011). Examining sense of belonging and campus racial diversity experiences among women of color in stem living-learning programs. *Journal of Women and Minorities in Science and Engineering, 17*(3), 209–223.

Kelly, B. T., Gayles, J. G., & Williams, C. D. (2017). Recruitment without retention: A critical case of Black faculty unrest. *The Journal of Negro Education, 86*(3), 305–317.

Matias, J.N., Lewis, N., & Hope, E (2021, September 7). University say they want more diverse faculty. So why is academia still so white? *FiveThirtyEight.* https://fivethirtyeight.com/features/universities-say-they-want-more-diverse-faculties-so-why-is-academia-still-so-white/

McGee, E. O. (2016). Devalued Black and Latino racial identities: A by-product of STEM college culture? *American Educational Research Journal, 53*(6), 1626–1662.

McGee, E. O., & Bentley, L. (2017). The troubled success of Black women in STEM. *Cognition and Instruction, 35*(4), 265–289.

McPherson, E. (2017). Oh you are smart: Young, gifted African American women in STEM majors. *Journal of Women and Minorities in Science and Engineering, 23*(1), 1–14.

Meeuwisse, M., Severiens, S. E., & Born, M. P. (2010). Learning environment, interaction, sense of belonging and study success in ethnically diverse student groups. *Research in Higher Education, 51*(6), 528–545.

Morton, T. R., & Parsons, E. C. (2018). # BlackGirlMagic: The identity conceptualization of Black women in undergraduate STEM education. *Science Education, 102*(6), 1363–1393.

Parson, L. (2016). Are STEM syllabi gendered? A feminist critical discourse analysis. *Qualitative Report, 21*(1), 102–116.

Patton, L. D. (2006). The voice of reason: A qualitative examination of Black student perceptions of Black culture centers. *Journal of College Student Development, 47*(6), 628–646.

Rockinson-Szapkiw, A., & Wendt, J. L. (2020). The benefits and challenges of a blended peer mentoring program for women peer mentors in science, technology, engineering, and mathematics (STEM). *International Journal of Mentoring and Coaching in Education, 10*(1), 1–16.

Seymour, E., & Hewitt, N. M. (1997). *Talking About Leaving* (p. 134). Westview Press.

Seymour, S., & Ray, J. (2015). Grads of historically black colleges have well-being edge. *Gallup.com, 1127.*

Smith, W. A., Allen, W. R., & Danley, L. L. (2007). "Assume the position… you fit the description" psychosocial experiences and racial battle fatigue among African American male college students. *American Behavioral Scientist, 51*(4), 551–578.

Strayhorn, T. L., & Saddler, T. N. (2009). Gender differences in the influence of faculty-student mentoring relationships on satisfaction with college among African Americans. *Journal of African American Studies, 13*(4), 476–493.

Strayhorn, T. L., & Terrell, M. C. (2007). Mentoring and satisfaction with college for black students. *Negro Educational Review, 58(1-2),* 69–83.

Tatum, B. D. (2017). *Why Are All the Black Kids Sitting Together in the Cafeteria?: And Other Conversations about Race.* Hachette UK.

Yosso, T. J. (2005). Whose culture has capital? A critical race theory discussion of community cultural wealth. *Race Ethnicity and Education, 8*(1), 69–91.

Section II

Intersectional Peer Mentoring

Section II of this book examines the intersectional nature of Black women's identities and how these identities shape their navigation into, and through, the academy. Often, the primary identities that are salient for Black women (e.g., race, gender, and sexuality) are deeply embedded in historical and social forms of oppression. While each identity has its own distinct history and social context, when combined they constitute interlocking systems of oppression (Collins, 1990; Crenshaw, 2003) that are reinforced at the organizational as well as the individual level of identity. Black women are challenged to navigate these multiple systems of oppression that often leave them regulated to a marginalized status. The marginalization of Black women in the academy is pervasive, and finding communities of support to help guide their academic journey often remains a challenge through degree completion. The two chapters in this section offer very distinct and important examples of how Black women navigate the academy across and within their intersectional identities.

Setting the stage for this intersectional work is Chapter 3, an insightful examination by Liliana Gordon of the "wayfinding" experiences of Black Queer Femmes who are in the early stages of considering postsecondary institutions and the process of finding campuses that can affirm all aspects of their identity. This chapter draws upon the theoretical evidence of deeply embedded systems of interlocking oppression to lay a foundation and understanding of the layers of invisibility that emerge at every turn for Black Queer Femmes. Gordan takes the reader behind the scenes of what wayfinding looks like for young Black Queer Femmes and how they navigate challenges in society and create important opportunities to enhance their success often within a community of Black Queer Femmes. Utilizing the Black Queer Identity Matrix (BQIM) framework (Howard, 2014), this chapter critically examines the experiences of Black Queer Femmes in a more deeply meaningful way as race, gender, and sexuality are explored simultaneously and deconstructed to convey the experiences of Black

DOI: 10.4324/9781003394648-4

Queer Femmes as they navigate society. Liliana's journey of navigating the early stages of the college choice process included exercising her own sense of agency by reaching out to Dr. Bridget Turner Kelly to learn more from her experience studying Black women. This action opened the space for connection and the building of networks as she navigated her understanding of the doctoral process. As noted by Liliana, the generosity, genuineness, and expertise of Dr. Bridget Turner Kelly were significant in fortifying her success toward building a network. As Dr. Kelly quickly became her mentor, she worked with Lilianna to help her explore and understand what campus commitment to diversity, equity, and inclusion (DEI) should look like as well as key performance measures to help her understand the work of each campus to address DEI issues. We learn from the chapter that campuses approached the discussion of these issues in varying ways. This chapter offers important insights into how Liliana accessed key individuals who added to her exploration and process of college choice. At times, her narrative offers readers a heart-rending view of the within-group violence that can occur for Black Queer Femmes. Even in her most difficult moments, her ability to persevere and to draw upon the collective strength of her community moved her toward success.

In Chapter 4, Stephanie Bent, Kat Stephens-Peace, and Abigail Smith center Caribbeanness as a salient aspect of their identity as they navigate their doctoral journey. They observe, "Caribbeanness is the enactment, essence, and ethos of Caribbean culture, heritage, norms, and behaviors" (Ferrante & Fox, 2016; Glissant, 1997). The authors employ storytelling as a methodology to convey important lessons that they learned on their journey. Through a Caribbean form of discourse of reasoning together, they invite a level of intimacy and authentic communication about their journey as peers creating a community of support that was not available to them in higher education as they *mek yaad* (make home) in the academy. The use of storytelling is a powerful tool in this chapter as it conveys and informs the meaning and essence of Caribbean culture and how it increases the understanding of what the women value and need from each other. Moreover, it highlights the important aspects of their respective heritage to make the academic experience more meaningful as they recalled in their reasoning sessions the richness of their cultural practices and the histories of their Anglophone Caribbean culture (e.g., recognition of Black Power and deep commitment to African roots). These interactions fortified and strengthened their peer connection as they shared their experiences migrating from countries that were majority Black to the United States where direct encounters with racism were common stressors. Remarking on their triple invisibility in the academy as Black, Women, and Foreign, they offer powerful arguments in this chapter on the need in the US educational context to provide support for Afro-Caribbean women and scholars. Learning to navigate in spaces that are racially hostile and not inviting to Black folks was a challenge for the authors as they were impacted by racism as well as the marginalization of foreignness. To resist the invisibility that they encountered, they centered their Caribbean culture in all aspects of their work and expression of self. The authors offer compelling examples of how higher education can better serve and fortify the success of Afro-Caribbean women in graduate programs such as supplemental funding for international research, expanding representation of Blackness in reading to include the work of Afro-Caribbean scholars, helping facilitate space on campus for Afro-Caribbean women to gather as a community of women to discuss their experiences, and building systems of support.

REFERENCES

Collins, P. H. (1990). Black feminist thought in the matrix of domination. In P. H. Collins (Ed.), *Black Feminist Thought: Knowledge, Consciousness, and the Politics of Empowerment* (pp. 221–238). Unwin Hyman.

Crenshaw, K. (1991). Mapping the margins: Intersectionality, identity politics, and violence against women of color. *Stanford Law Review, 43*(6), 1241–1299.

Ferrante, A., & Fox, D. (2016). Introduction: Women and gender: Looking toward "Caribbeanness". *Journal of International Women's Studies, 17*(3), 1–3.

Glissant, É. (1997). *Poetics of Relation.* University of Michigan Press.

Howard, D. S. (2014). *Internet Archive.* Retrieved 2021, from Black Queer Identity Matrix: Towards an Integrated Queer of Color Framework: https://archive.org/details/blackqueeridenti0000howa/page/16/mode/2up

Chapter 3

Omittance ≠ Inclusion

Extending the Narrative of Guided Wayfinding through Higher Education for Young Black Queer Femmes in Secondary Education

Liliana G. Gordon

INTRODUCTION

Black *queer* womanhood is neither understood nor valued (Ashley, 2014; Collins, 1990; Crenshaw, 1989). For Black queer women in secondary and higher education, this creates a dichotomy of identity. Facets of our existences within gender, sexuality, and race paradigms are treated as independently functioning in academia and therefore dissectible (Crenshaw, 1989, p. 13). Interlocking systems of oppression are strengthened by this widespread ignorance of triple jeopardy minority existences. And continual, willful ignorance of these identities contributes to suffocating pressures placed on our psyches as we move through our higher educational goals (Crenshaw, 1989; Howard, 2014).

In addition, because our existences are rarely studied or examined by academics, triple jeopardy minorities cannot trust academia to support us in higher educational wayfinding. Academic institutions cannot grasp what it means to live outside of the constricted bounds of gender and sexuality in our ever surveilled, continuously caricatured Black bodies. Starting from a young age, we are our own problem solvers, teachers, medical practitioners, and advocates. We are often our only resources. We are often our only mentors.

Queer people of color are isolated from mentorship because of exclusive dialogue among people of color and queer communities. The fear of rejection from our religious, familial, and social circles, lack of safety and awareness in our schools, and general apprehension toward romantic expression in public and private spaces is persistent. Black queer women understand that "Don't Ask, Don't Tell" is

DOI: 10.4324/9781003394648-5

disproportionately enforced in our barbershops, classrooms, shopping centers, and churches (Meyer, 2012) and not in white communities. We have seen queer people of color leading global civil rights movements and achieving greater equality for greater numbers, only to be tossed aside and forgotten (Kiesling, 2017). And we are the family, students, and constituents of members of the LGBTQ+, femme, and Black communities who disregard and devalue our very existence.

It is important to have scholarship and studies focusing on queer people of color issues, to understand the plights as well as triumphs of this community, supporting us further in academic circles. Studying the experiences of Black queer young women in higher educational wayfinding also provides clearer insight into how other vulnerable minority populations may maximize opportunities for success inside and outside of academia. Black queer women, like other minorities in such spaces, cannot rely on educational institutions to support them in their academic goals (Pasulka, 2016). Instead, we learn from and seek the experiences of our sisters and foremothers to chart paths in higher educational achievement. Understanding our experiences would not only be resourceful for general strategy in Black femme mentorship but also mentorship in the greater Black community.

But identity scholarship by itself is inadequate. We as Black queer women and triple jeopardy minorities need comprehensive diversity, equity, and inclusion strategies to support us in our higher educational journeys. We need more than your Black Lives Matter statement. We need monetary and instructional support to remove barriers to reaching our educational aspirations. And as Black queer femmes continue to be at the center of marginalization and forefront of social change and intellectualism at your institutions (Green Jr, 2019), you need us to be protected at all levels of academia.

In this chapter, I address and define the Black Queer Identity Matrix (BQIM) framework and why learning and teaching BQIM is an important first step to understanding Black queer femme existences (Howard, 2014). I share what it means for me to be a queer woman of color and how I attempted to understand the experiences of queer people of color in higher education through meeting Black women mentors. And lastly, I reflect on the results of my exploration, and how my own college search process was informed by the mentorship I received along the way.

THE THEORETICAL LENS: UNDERSTANDING THE BQIM

The BQIM is an approach to critically study and decipher the identities existing within gender, sexuality, and race as working in concert with one another in creating interconnecting systems of subordination and/or domination (Howard, 2014). While previous frameworks in sociological scholarship (e.g., Queer [Giffney, 2007] and Critical Race Theories [Ladson-Billings & Tate IV, 1995]; [Bell,

1995]) played pivotal roles in facilitating greater equity in educational and social spaces, they often fall short in accounting for and aiding in the understanding of the experiences of queer of color.

Several frameworks that conjunctly tackle the paradigms of race, gender, and sexuality typically discuss each paradigm separately for critical analysis. Furthermore, such frameworks view the structures of race and gender or sexuality and race as independently functioning rather than intertwined. Consequently, these types of analyses often fail to account for triple jeopardy minority experiences, because they do not directly address the nuances of how these paradigms function together and affect those living in their intersections (Kiesling, 2017). And though some frameworks create wiggle room in exploring interlocking identities by addressing intersectionality in their tenets, scholars of those frameworks usually approach gender, sexuality, and racial studies as separate disciplines, isolating each from the other (Howard, 2014). The BQIM was devised to supplement these traditional identity frameworks by focusing on holistic rather than additive identity, creating more space for triple jeopardy minority study (Howard, 2014).

Additive identity is an approach of study traditionally utilized in social scholarship where each facet of identity is studied largely alone and then amalgamated to understand the total impact of each facet on an individual. However, cumulative identity examines self-identification holistically to recognize how all aspects of identity mold and shift an individual's mobilization through society. An ideal of BQIM is to create a framework to deeply understand how queer of color navigate society (Howard, 2014). Dr. Sheena C. Howard established the BQIM framework with the intention to examine the experiences of Black American lesbian women, including coping behaviors, cultural communication, and gender expression.

Though BQIM itself is a new framework, it is founded on three well-known and long-standing conceptual matrices of Afrocentricity, Standpoint Theory, and the Matrix of Domination (Howard, 2014). These three foundational lenses serve as ways to observe the complexity of the Black identity in depth. Altogether these lenses provide greater context into what it means to be a woman who is Black and queer.

Afrocentricity scholars (Asante, 2009; Reed, 1997; Reviere, 2001; Schiele, 1994) believe African interests and experiences should dominate African political action and researched thought. A core ideal of this framework is that supporting African values means opposing and standing against other forms of oppression that plague the Black community (Asante, 2009). In its entirety, Afrocentricity advocates for the usage of diverse forms of communication to acquire and study data about the diverse, intersectional experiences of African peoples. BQIM draws on the principles of Afrocentricity by providing a vessel to bridge the realities of misogynoir and homophobia in the Black community to African centrality and pride (Howard, 2014).

43

Standpoint Theory promulgates experiential knowledge of minoritized people of various gender and sexuality identities over those of majorities in understanding minoritized people's experiences (Hartsock, 1983). This area of study purports that people who are not in power possess knowledge that is critical and different from those who are. Minoritized people are shaped by materialism, domination, classism, and civil struggle differently than those of a majority culture, without their consent. People with subordinate identities are compelled to navigate a world set by the majority, giving them greater insight into the inhumanity and injustices that trouble our society. To understand social hierarchies and power structures, Standpoint Theorists advocate for the usage of concrete, lived experiences of minorities to inform sociological research, instead of abstract ideas and frameworks (Halpern, 2019). BQIM calls on the principles of Standpoint Theory by positing that adversity is experienced differently for varying gender identities.

Lastly, the Matrix of Domination studies how intersecting systems of oppression are organized and work against and for individuals. As developed by sociologist Patricia Hill Collins, it is the understanding of privileges and disadvantages an individual may have within a society (Collins, 1990; Johnson, 2004). A person can benefit from their privileges of being able-bodied and cis-gendered, while also being discriminated against as a Black woman.

Using the previous frameworks and other theories of identity as a foundation for study, the tenets of BQIM are as follows (Howard, 2014):

1. **Sexual orientation and race exist as social constructs.**

   It is widely though erroneously accepted that people are born with set sexuality and/or exist within a fixed definition of race. BQIM challenges these premises by asserting sexual orientation and race serve as fluid mechanisms to organize communities and form cultural backgrounds, rather than scientific, fixed classifications.

   However, even though sexuality and race are social constructs, sexuality and racialized systems of oppression serve as rigid borders and/or doors to opportunity for Black queer women in higher education. In addition, Black queer women's holding of power is severely limited by these systems of oppression. Social systems conventionally see Blackness, femininity, and queerness as identities lacking power, and Black queer women may internalize a state of vulnerability and powerlessness when navigating these academic spaces.

2. **The experience of struggle is central to the Black queer conceptual framework because of the history of oppression within the Black community.**

   Those subscribing to and existing within the Black queer of color sphere do not enjoy the privileges of those of dominant identities and therefore do not traditionally hold power. Instead, Black queer of color must strategize and struggle through activism, community-centered organizing, and abolition to combat interlocking institutions of subordination (Stanley, 2015). In other words,

> My silences had not protected m. Your silence will not protect you. But for every real word spoken, for every attempt I had ever made to speak those truths for which I am still seeking, I had made contact with other women while we examined the words to fit a world in which we all believed, bridging our differences.
>
> (Lorde, 1984)

3. **Race, gender (as well as gender expression), and sexual orientation are interlocking systems of oppression.**

   Recalling the principles of Afrocentricity and the Matrix of Domination, our dominant and subordinate identities coexist within ourselves, creating an aggregated culturally oppressive impact. There is no single facet of identity that impacts us separately from others. We are advantaged and disadvantaged by our identities simultaneously and see and move through the world based on their relative impact. You cannot be Black on Monday, gay on Tuesday, and a woman on Wednesday. You are holistically, rather than additively, shaped by all three in all forms of your experience.

4. **Different social locations and social knowledge often produce distinct communication patterns.**

   Black queer women have learned for generations how to communicate through secure patterns. Our enslaved foremothers employed coded language to discuss abolition and liberation in their bondage. Terms such as "tracks" and "stations" were spoken so that Black women could share and plan how to reach freedom (Hancock, 2021). In the early 20th century, Black queer women referred to themselves as "dyke" and "butch" so that we could "hide in plain sight" and protect our communities (Wilson, 2009). We continue to do this because we are never free. Unlike other identity groups, triple jeopardy minorities must continuously strategize for survival.

   Overall, the BQIM framework and its tenets are imperative to grasping the complexity and uniqueness of the triple jeopardy minority and Black queer femme experience. However, BQIM also asserts that examining these experiences without listening and critically studying the first-person narratives of those who experience them, potentially opens sociological examination to superficial, over-simplified reflections, reinforcing prejudicial attitudes toward those subjugated identities in the literature. Furthermore, if the Black queer women's experiences are studied without considering the first-hand experiences of Black queer women, an understanding of this minoritized population is lost.

Given the description of the framework and the importance of first-person narratives, I offer my own narrative of how Black queer femininity is presented and explored in secondary education and how Black queer femmes are supported in their journeys to higher education.

THE CONTEXT

During my sophomore year in high school when I was contending with my newly emerging identity as a Black queer disabled young woman, BQIM gave me the tools to explore how I navigated my inner circles as well as those spaces existing outside of me. Before this point, I had not seen my Blackness, gayness, and gender as part of me. Though I had these intersectional identities, I did not feel defined by them. The foremothers in my family and community had fought for my privilege to be an individual. Their generational love and care had supported me to an extent that I never directly experienced academic discrimination until high school. And because of this I did not see myself as defined by my Blackness, my queerness, or my girlhood (Tatum, 2000). I was just Liliana.

My perspective began to shift when I started to plan out my higher educational journey more seriously. Since middle school, I had a very clear goal to attain my doctorate in Sociology. At the time, this meant strategizing my path to successful graduate study by preparing for the undergraduate admissions process. Many of my teachers, family, friends, and mentors warned me and the other, similarly driven, Black students of burning out and becoming too insular to other avenues of vocational success. My white peers were not given this same advice. They were not told they were too ambitious or eager. They were not told to wait.

And as I continued to plan my educational journey by researching colleges, I noticed a similar expectation of white excellence and existence even in diversity admissions for undergraduate programs. From the age of 13, I had attended PWI college tours and information sessions to learn more about campus cultures. Prior to the pandemic, very rarely were Black and Brown identities on campuses discussed beyond the ten-second mention of a Black Student Union. In the spring of 2020, I began to observe more frequent but vaguer discussions around the experiences of queer students and students of color. PWIs typically chose to avoid these issues and/or take the more defensive, offensive messaging tactic of "We are not racist" and "We love gays"; entailing the occasional minority statistic, standard-issued pride flag, two Brown faces on a PowerPoint slide, and (at one institution) one white student touting the inexistence of racism and oppression on their campus.

Though I initially began planning my higher educational journey from my excitement and love of academia, I and several of my other Black queer femme friends understood that planning was a necessity to our long-term success. We could see the uphill battle. We could see the educators at our high school and at PWIs closing the doors to our flourishment, attempting to prevent those like us from accessing higher learning. And we could see how the academic institutions we had dreamt of attending did not want us.

We were all concerned about the lack of demonstrated support universities had for all minoritized student populations. But how could we attend and succeed at these institutions when we existed in several if not all of the minority groups? What would it mean to be a queer, disabled, Black, femme at an R1 institution?

Soon after the pandemic, I decided that I could not rely on the traditional educational pathway through secondary education to prepare me for higher educational success. Instead, I committed myself to informally learn about the Black women's experience on college campuses by attending to Black women's interpretations of this experience. I looked to the Black women around me—those who studied the Black women's experience in colleges and those who thrived in it—to help me along my journey. However, I unconsciously chose to seek out Black women mentors who could speak to intersections of race and gender exclusively. At the time, I could not imagine finding Black queer femme academics because I was told to exist as a Black girl first and a queer person second. As a result, during this journey, I spoke to both Black women who supported my holistic identity and women who loved me until they discovered my queerness.

THE BEGINNING

I began searching for scholars who specialized in the study of Black women in higher education, specifically with a focus on PWI campuses. I eventually found an article from 2018 about an established Black professor at the University of Maryland who studied the stereotypes Black women face on PWI college campuses and how they rise above them (Samoray, 2018). The professor, Dr. Bridget Turner Kelly, worked with other researchers to understand how Black women were shaped by misogynoir in higher education, and how those Black women overcame adversity (Samoray, 2018). I believed she would understand my frustration and slight trepidation about navigating college as a Black young woman. I decided to reach out to her for guidance on my journey,

Subject: Asking for Advice on Navigating College Life as Black Female—High School Student

Good afternoon Dr. Kelly,

I hope you are safe and well during this time.

My name is Liliana Gordon. I am a rising high school junior in MD. I study Engineering at my high school and intend to earn a Ph.D. in Neuroscience.

I read a journal article summarizing your study on expectations and stereotypes black women face on college campuses.

Over quarantine, I have been looking at prospective colleges to go to outside of the DMV. How can I find schools for me that are not only inclusive on paper but also on campus? How have you overcome these challenges? What advice would you give to a person of color, pursuing a doctorate?

Respectfully,
Liliana Gordon

And within exactly six minutes, she replied:

Hello Liliana—Thank you so much for reading a summary of my work. While no school is as inclusive as they should be, I have found most offices of inclusion and diversity to be excellent and would suggest you ask to speak to (zoom appointment) with folx on campus who oversee equity. These titles might be Director of Diversity, Equity, Inclusion or Head of Diversity and Inclusion for the entire campus. Once you connect with staff, ask them if they have students you could speak to who are in Engineering at that institution.

Next, I would think about places you want to live in the U.S. This can be difficult, but sometimes a campus can be inclusive and just be housed in a city that needs a lot of reform. Let me know if you want to talk? I am available for a virtual meeting.
So wonderful to hear from you—Bridget Turner Kelly

I was ecstatic to receive her email. We scheduled a time to virtually meet and discuss her work and my aspirations nine days after our initial correspondence.

When we spoke, she was kind, warm, and interested in my story. She asked me about my interests and reasons for reaching out. I shared my concerns about entering college as a minority and wanted to learn as much about Black women in higher education to prepare myself for success. I desired to find universities that were equitable and would support me in my ambitions to become a social science researcher and learn how I could chart my own path for success to earn my Ph.D.

To help me along my journey, she offered me three, very pivotal steps to take as someone aspiring to earn a Ph.D. and interested in becoming a social science researcher:

1. Direct mentorship for guidance on college searches and interactions between myself and Directors of Inclusion and Diversity at my colleges of interest.
2. The opportunity to connect and receive mentorship with other women of color who graduated from college with a STEM degree and were pursuing their master's in higher education from the University Maryland.
3. The opportunity to write a chapter in her upcoming book, *Black Women Mentoring Each Other for Success in the Ph.D. Journey*, from the perspective of a high school student determined to earn her doctorate, so I may tell my story for other Black queer femmes in secondary education.

THE METHODOLOGY
Step 1—Reaching Out

Over the course of little over a year, with Dr. Kelly's help, I reached out to Directors of Equity and Inclusion (and those of similar positions) at universities. For most schools, finding contacts that could address my concerns was fairly difficult. Many university department websites allegedly dedicated to inclusion and diversity were designed for staff and current student usage. As an outsider, obtaining rudimentary facts about racial breakdowns on retention rates and policy information was extremely challenging. If I was fortunate to find a Director or representative of a department, I sent the following email to them,

Subject Line: *Request for Information from African American HS Junior*
Hello [recipient],
My name is Liliana Gordon. I am a Maryland high school junior and I would like to attend [university]. My CV is attached for your convenience. My mentor Dr. Bridget Kelly, Associate Professor of Student Affairs at the University of Maryland, recommended I reach out to you.
I would greatly appreciate your answers to some of my questions about diversity, equity, and inclusion at [the university]:

1. *Has the university experienced any recent racial conflicts on campus?*
2. *Are cultural exchange programs offered that allow prospective African American students, like me, to connect with current African American students?*
3. *What is [university]'s policy towards organized protesting on campus?*

Finally, I found that Hispanic and African American students have the lowest graduation rates in the undergraduate schools.

4. *To what does the university attribute the disparity in graduation rates between African American/Hispanic students and other students?*
5. *What is [university] doing to address this issue?*
   If you are available, my family and I would be grateful for the opportunity to discuss our questions with you virtually.

Respectfully,
Liliana Gordon

As I was sending emails to Directors in September 2020, I again did not share my queer identity with others. I felt that by labeling myself as a Black queer femme would make me less likely to receive a response from those at the schools, especially considering LGBTQ+ affairs were not the focus of the departments

I found. It is hard enough being a Black woman in academia, but being queer excludes you entirely.

I contacted Harvard University, Carnegie Mellon University, Johns Hopkins University, the University of Pennsylvania, Rensselaer Polytechnic Institute, the Massachusetts Institute of Technology (MIT), Washington University in St. Louis, Stanford University, and California Institute of Technology. The responses I received from universities ranged from September 2020 through March 2021. Of the nine, three did not respond. Of those that responded, four schools replied solely via email, often providing external sites and resources to supplement their answers to my questions. In response to my first question, "Has the university experienced any recent racial conflicts on campus?" one representative cited an incident in 2015 involving the Black Student Union and the university community's attempts to create campus synergy. That representative also shared that while the campus culture lacked racial and gender equity, the university was continuing to work on strategically supporting their diverse student population. Three other universities had similar email responses about their respective schools.

Nonetheless, two schools went through extensive lengths to provide me information. Namely, the University of Pennsylvania and the MIT—whose directors both cishet Black women—were the most helpful in providing clarity on campus safety and inclusion. I am very thankful for their attention and guidance. They helped me extensively in my search as their interactions have implications for how other university personnel might seek to engage with students.

UNIVERSITY OF PENNSYLVANIA (DR. S.)

I reached Dr. S. after my second attempt at contacting the University of Pennsylvania. However, her response to my email was warm and personal. She offered to host a private Zoom call with my mother and I to address my questions about the School of Engineering and Applied Science.

Her answers to our questions were clear and transparent. Dr. S. presented a PowerPoint detailing her journey to pursuing a Ph.D. and the work her office did to support students of color on the University of Pennsylvania campus. My mom and I prompted her on ways the school supported Black women within the student population; how queer students were protected and supported through programs; how safe students of color felt on campus; and how to best prepare for success as a person of color in a competitive school environment. She discussed incidents of racial conflict on campuses and the various ways the administration had and continued to address instances of that nature. She also listed and sent us links to programs designed for the university's students of color (SOCs) before and during enrollment. However, her guidance went beyond answering questions about the school and expanded to how I could, as a Black young woman, prepare for success in a career in the sciences. She gave me advice on how to find mentors, types of Ph.D. programs I should look for, and how to best structure my education around research. However, she was not aware of the support systems available and existences of queer Black students on campus.

Following our meeting, she connected me to a mentee of hers who could speak to the experiences of Black women on campus who were in STEM research. She also invited me to a webinar on Blacks in aviation, a panel for Black professors at the university discussing how to best support Black students on campus going forward, as well as encouraged me to apply to a scholarship for African-Americans in technology. We have continued to stay in contact since our first correspondence in November of 2020, and I am very grateful for all of her guidance and help in my college search.

MIT (DIRECTOR C.)

Director C. was the first representative to respond to my series of emails. She expressed her excitement to meet me and also offered to host a Zoom call to address my mother and I's questions.

Like Dr. S., Director C. was warm and informative. She addressed our concerns about safety for Black women in and around the Boston–Cambridge area and how to best succeed as a student at MIT. She admitted that many students who identified as Black women struggle with imposter syndrome in their freshman year. Her suggestion for combatting these feelings is being grounded in our values, maintaining a growth mindset, and having resiliency. However, she too was unaware of the existences and struggles of queer Black students on campus.

Following the meeting, she connected me to another Director at the university who could answer my more admission-related questions. That Director, as well, was also extremely helpful in aiding me in my search.

Step 2—Building My Network

After connecting with Dr. Kelly's contacts in STEM—two of which are women of color who continue to be close contacts and have helped me review my literature reviews and conference papers, as well as provide guidance on my college search—I began to expand my network. In seeing how kind and warm others could be in helping me along my higher education journey, I have sought out and naturally connected with an assortment of Black women who have guided me along my path. Having Dr. Kelly provide that foundation in Black mentorship made me feel that I had the security to claim and explore my own spaces for reaching out to others. Though, unfortunately, I am unable to list all of my Black women mentors by name, I would like to highlight a few of the Black women who have been invaluable to me along my higher educational journey.

DR. SHAN-ESTELLE BROWN

Dr. Brown is an Assistant Professor of Anthropology at Rollins College and alumni of Yale University (Contributors, n.d.). Her expertise is in understanding the correlation between human organization/interaction and racial inequity in medicine. I was connected to Dr. Brown through her aunt (and my high school counselor) in the winter of 2020 because of my aspirations to earn my Ph.D. in the Social Sciences.

Dr. Brown helped me extensively in preparing for college interviews and providing insight into the Ph.D. journey as a Black woman. From her example, I have continued to learn what strength and brilliance look like. We have stayed in contact, when she was helping me apply to colleges.

MS. DANIELLE (TORI) FINNEY

I met Ms. Finney through my mother. She was a recent graduate from the MIT, and I desired to learn more about her experiences at a PWI as a Black woman. We met over Zoom and have continued correspondence since our first meeting in December 2020. She provided me guidance on college applications, finding my "people" on college campuses, maintaining mental health, and growing into who I am. "Set yourself up to become the person you want to be in college," she told me. "Establish healthy habits while you are in high school, to prepare yourself for success before stepping onto campus."

MS. TAMIKA MAULTSBY, J.D.

I met Ms. Tamika later in the summer of 2021 in my first paid position as a research intern at Friendship Public Charter Schools. In the two months I spent in-person at Friendship Office, she welcomed me into her office every day to talk about my experiences at work, shared her story as a Black woman who studied law, connected me to other Black women who were along their Ph.D. journey, advised me on my educational goals, and provided guidance on maintaining mental health. When I thanked her for all of her kindness and support, she responded, "We Black women gotta look out for each other."

These and several other Black women helped me greatly in my aspiration to earn my Ph.D. They provided me with tools, guidance, and a framework for success in my professional and educational spaces. However, I also experienced great adversity in navigating my experience as Black queer femme.

One of my cishet Black femme mentors initially served as a great support system, friend, and guide for me along my higher educational journey. However, when she later discovered I was queer my senior year, she proceeded to slander, harass, and stalk me at my school. My experiences ranged from her tracking my emotional and academic well-being, to spreading rumors about me among students, administration, and faculty. I was not made aware of her behaviors until I was notified by a community member that she had asked several of my teachers about my mental state.

My experience with her was especially damaging during a time when I experienced assault, harassment, and stalking as a queer person in my larger community. My then transmasculine partner and I were often called derogatory names, followed by cars and bikes on the street, as well as stalked and disproportionately disciplined by adults in our community. At a time when my primary concern should have been transitioning to adulthood and attending college, I feared for my life. Due to these stressors and other underlying medical conditions, I later developed an autonomic disability in February 2022 and spent the remaining of my senior year learning virtually in hospitals and rehabilitation rooms.

As a person seeking to acquire power and clarity in their higher educational journey even as a high schooler, sharing my queer identity made me lose power. Disclosing myself as a member of the LGBTQ+ community presented an opportunity for people—including Black women mentors—to neither value nor protect me.

For me and likely many other Black queer young and mature women who have professional and educational relationships in which they are at a significant power disadvantage, one may have to make a conscious decision to disclose and/or openly live their unseen minoritized experience. The Black femme identity is one that lacks power, while simultaneously enforcing standards of heteronormativity. Therefore, many Black queer women are observed and treated as if they navigate planes of existence as Black and binarily female individuals, rather than as beings existing within spectrums of gender and sexuality. This means that Black queer women are pressed to decide not only how to express their holistic gender and sexuality identities but also if disclosing these facets of their identity is worth losing more clout in their mentor–mentee, power-disadvantaged relationships. And for several Black queer women pursuing doctorates and navigating higher academia (an environment that is notoriously hostile toward Black women), they decide to conceal their queerness and gender identity as I did to preserve the little institutional power they have.

CONCLUSION

Establishing networks of higher educational support in secondary school better prepares all minorities, including Black queer women, for the academic and social rigors of college. Being in predominantly white spaces as a triple jeopardy minority can often be isolating and demoralizing without adequate support. Unlike many of my peers, I was fortunate to be offered the opportunity to speak to successful Black femmes in a variety of fields about undergraduate and graduate studies. I firmly believe their mentorship prepared me for greater vocational success and helped me gain admittance to some of the most prestigious institutions in the country.

However, my experiences also informed me that while opportunities for support were widely available to me as a young Black woman after my search, as a triple jeopardy minority, finding those same communities of support was much more complicated and hidden. The Black, often cishet, women who have mentored me throughout my search provided guidance on maintaining wellness and claiming professional and educational space. They welcomed my femininity and Blackness and taught me that these identities were my strength rather than my shortcomings. They guided me through my college search process so that I could be more confident in my college choices. And they were often the only people who could begin to understand what it was like to navigate a white-centered world in my body.

But in asking the many Black women professionals inside and outside academia, "How do you navigate adversity as a Black woman?" the existence of gender expansiveness and minoritized sexual identities was rarely if ever mentioned in their answers. It is not convention to teach about the existences and experiences of triple jeopardy minorities. And even in unintentionally omitting the existences of triple jeopardy minorities, individuals and institutions promulgate a heteronormative, cis-gendered perspective. It is not enough to discuss Blackness exclusively, and it is not enough to discuss queerness exclusively. Triple and quadruple jeopardy minorities, especially Black queer trans women, are at the intersection of all forms of marginalization in this country. To protect us, you must at least acknowledge we exist alongside you.

HOMEWORK FOR INSTITUTIONS

For institutions to pave higher educational pathways for all, you must make space for triple jeopardy minorities like Black queer femmes. Ensuring the rights and protections of the minority always accounts for the needs of the majority. Black queer women often fall under other identity groups such as low income, first generation, immigrant, undocumented, and disabled. And as an academic institution, it is always your responsibility to ensure that all students have equitable access to your facilities, resources, and learning. Protecting Black queer femmes is not a diversity initiative, it is a bare minimum.

Here are two critical steps that can be taken to meet the needs of all identity groups in higher education:

- Explicitly and clearly communicate the inclusion of minoritized sexuality and gender identities in their spaces.

    While others may argue that it is the Black queer women's responsibility to initiate discussions of queerness, I argue that it is those who are in power who are responsible for doing so. You, and others like you who hold power, must initiate those conversations for those who do not hold power to feel secure. It is necessary to openly discuss queerness issues and experiences and strategically actualize positive outcomes for individuals within those communities.

■ Treat LGBTQ+ identities as a majority rather than a minoritized group.

Even when it is strongly believed that Black women students do not identify with gender and sexuality subordinate identities (and whether the belief was established through personal biases or results from accredited student polls), there should always be an acceptance of the possibility of sexuality and gender minoritized identities existing within educational spaces.

Black queer women and other triple jeopardy minorities do not know we are included if you do not tell us we are included. We cannot afford to assume. We cannot afford to wait. And we do not and should not be our only advocates and experts in the face of adversity. Our existence is a form of resistance and often pushes us to be the activists and warriors in our and other's movements for social justice. Black queer women are already making change on your campuses, inside and outside of the classroom. You need us. So protect us as we fight for all of us.

REFERENCES

Asante, M. K. (2009). *Afrocentricity*. Retrieved September 18, 2021, from Afrocentricity | Dr. Molefe Kete Asante: http://www.asante.net/articles/1/afrocentricity/

Ashley, W. (2014). The angry black woman: The impact of pejorative stereotypes on psychotherapy with black women. *Soc Work Public Health*, 27–34. Retrieved from https://pubmed.ncbi.nlm.nih.gov/24188294/

Bell, D. A. (1995). Who's afraid of critical race theory? *University of Illinois Law Review, 4*, 893–910.

Collins, P. H. (1990a). Black feminist thought in the matrix of domination. In P. H. Collins (Ed.), *Black Feminist Though: Knowledge, Consciousness, and the Politics of Empowerment* (pp. 221–238). Unwin Hyman.

Collins, P. H. (1990b). *Black Feminist Thought: Knowledge, Consciousness, and the Politics of Empowerment*. Unwin Hyman.

Contributors, R. C. (n.d.). *Department of Faculty & Staff*. Retrieved from Faculty & Staff | Department of Anthropology...: https://www.rollins.edu/anthropology/faculty-staff-listing/

Crenshaw, K. (1989). Demarginalizing the intersection of race and sex: A Black feminist critique of anti-discrimination doctrine, feminist theory and anti-racist politics. *University of Chicago Legal Forum, 1989*(1), 139–167.

Giffney, N. (2007). Quare theory. In W. Balzano, A. Mulhall, & M. Sullivan (Eds.), *Irish Postmodernisms and Popular Culture* (pp. 197–209). Palgrave Macmillan. Retrieved from https://link.springer.com/chapter/10.1057/9780230800588_15

Green Jr, D. B. (2019, February 6). *Hearing the Queer Roots of Black Lives Matter*. (N. C. Diversity, Producer). Retrieved January 11, 2023, from Medium: https://medium.com/national-center-for-institutional-diversity/hearing-the-queer-roots-of-black-lives-matter-2e69834a65cd

Halpern, M. (2019, September 30). Feminist standpoint theory and science communication. *Journal of Science Communication, 18*, 1–6. Retrieved September 18, 2021, from Feminist standpoint theory and science communication: https://jcom.sissa.it/sites/default/files/documents/JCOM_1804_2019_C02.pdf

Hancock, A. (2021, February 21). *Coded Resistance: Freedom Fighting and Communication*. Retrieved January 6, 2023, from Electronic Frontier Foundation: https://www.eff.org/deeplinks/2021/02/coded-resistance-freedom-fighting-and-communication

Hartsock, N. C. (1983). The feminist standpoint: Developing the ground for specifically feminist historical materialism. In S. Harding (Ed.), *Discovering Reality: Feminist Perspectives on Epistemology, Metaphysics, Methodology, and Philosophy of Science* (pp. 283–310). Springer. Retrieved from https://link.springer.com/chapter/10.1007/0-306-48017-4_15

Howard, D. S. (2014). *Internet Archive*. Retrieved 2021, from Black Queer Identity Matrix: Towards an Integrated Queer of Color Framework: https://archive.org/details/blackqueeridenti0000howa/page/16/mode/2up

Johnson, A. G. (2004). *Matrix of Domination*. Retrieved from SAGE Reference: https://sk.sagepub.com/reference/socialtheory/n186.xml

Kiesling, E. (2017, November). The missing colors of the rainbow: Black queer resistance. *European Journal of American Studies* (Re-Queering The Nation: America's Queer Crisis). Retrieved from https://journals.openedition.org/ejas/11830

Ladson-Billings, G., & Tate IV, W. F. (1995). Toward a critical race theory of education. *Teachers College Record, 97*, 47–68. Retrieved from https://eric.ed.gov/?id=EJ519126

Lorde, A. (1984). The transformation of silence into language and action. *Sister Outside: Essays and Speeches*, 41. Crossing Press. Retrieved from https://electricliterature.com/wp-content/uploads/2017/12/silenceintoaction.pdf

Meyer, D. (2012, September 24). An intersectional analysis of lesbian, gay, bisexual, and transgender people's evaluations of anti-queer violence. *Gender & Society, 26*(6), 849–873.

Pasulka, N. (2016, March 17). *The 'Criminal' Black Lesbian: Where Does This Damaging Stereotype Come From?* (N. P. Radio, Producer) Retrieved from Code Switch: https://www.npr.org/sections/codeswitch/2016/03/17/456541972/the-criminal-black-lesbian-where-does-this-damaging-stereotype-come-from

Reed, W. E., & Lawson, E. J., & Gibbs, T. (1997). Afrocentrism in the 21st century. *The Western Journal of Black Studies*. Retrieved from ProQuest: https://www.proquest.com/docview/1311806092?pqorigsite=gscholar&fromopenview=true

Reviere, R. (2001, July 1). Towards an afrocentric research method. *Journal of Black Studies, 31*(6), 709–728. Retrieved from https://journals.sagepub.com/doi/10.1177/002193470103100601

Samoray, C. (2018, November 19). *New Study Examines Expectations of Black Women in College.* College Park, Maryland, United States. Retrieved from https://education.umd. edu/news/11-19-18-new-study-examines-expectations-black-women-college

Schiele, J. H. (1994, December 1). Afrocentricity: Implications for higher education. *Journal of Black Studies, 25*(2), 150–169. Retrieved from https://journals.sagepub. com/doi/10.1177/002193479402500202

Stanley, E. A. (2015). *Fugitive Flesh: Gender Self-Determination, Queer Abolition, and Trans Resistance, by Eric A. Stanley.* The Institute for Anarchist Studies. Retrieved January 6, 2023, from https://anarchiststudies.org/fugitive-flesh-gender-self-determination-queer-abolition-and-trans-resistance-by-eric-a-stanley/

Tatum, B. D. (2000). *The Complexity of Identity: "Who Am I?".* Unitarian Universalist College of Social Justice. Retrieved from https://uucsj.org/wp-content/uploads/2016/05/The-Complexity-of-Identity.pdf

Wilson, B. D. (2009, April). *Black Lesbian Gender and Sexual Culture: Celebration and Resistance.* Retrieved from JSTOR: https://www.jstor.org/stable/27784444

Chapter 4

Mek Yaad within Academia

Afro-Caribbean Women Finding Belonging in the Academy

*Stephanie Bent, Kat J. Stephens-Peace
and Abigail Smith*

We liken ourselves to di pimento, thyme, and hol' heap a garlic. The integral combination to spicing up any Caribbean pot. Powerful on their own, but together they make a hearty dish.

We are three Afro-Caribbean women retaining each other through graduate school, supporting each other as we center Caribbeanness in our scholarship and practice. Caribbeanness is the enactment, essence, and ethos of Caribbean culture, heritage, norms, and behaviors (Ferrante & Fox, 2016; Glissant, 1997). Our efforts to retain each other were necessitated by U.S. centric paradigms; this disregard of Caribbean existence reflects the statistical invisibility of Afro-Caribbean students (Fernandez et al., 2016). Although there were over three million non-Hispanic Caribbean people living in the United States in 2019, many U.S. universities do not identify the ethnicity of non-Hispanic Black people (Mwangi & English, 2017; U.S. Census, 2021).

With needs varying across ethnicities, to best support all Black students, university administrators, faculty, and staff must use a diverse set of strategies to avoid marginalizing Black students who do not hold dominant accompanying identities (Mwangi & English, 2017). To share lessons from our experience as Afro-Caribbean women navigating graduate school, we use storytelling as a methodology—providing a non-linear account of the culmination of our stories and centering our experiences as a source of knowledge (Danticat, 2010; McKittrick, 2021; Nakhid-Chatoor et al., 2018). We begin with our individual stories and use academic literature to describe our experiences as Afro-Caribbean women[1] in graduate school. We further describe storytelling as methodology, reasoning[2], and the complications of home for migrants. Then we share our experiences *reasoning* together.

DOI: 10.4324/9781003394648-6

Finally, we provide recommendations to formalize the support we provided one another to retain Afro-Caribbean women through graduate school in the United States.

KAT

My arrival in the United States was made possible by the collective sacrifices of my Guyanese grandmothers and parents. My grandmother migrated years earlier and filed paperwork for my parents, siblings, and I to join her in the United States. In childhood, it was impressed upon me that I owed my people dem to represent, protect, and reify the culture. I remember my American classmates poking fun at the aromatic smell of my *roti and curry* lunches while they had ham and cheese, which was foreign to me. Ironically, in high school, my classmates ditched school to buy Caribbean meals for lunch. As veneration to my late grandmothers and to my lineage, I always *mek yaad*[3] representing my multiethnic Caribbean heritage across the Caribbean Diaspora.

STEPHANIE

Two years before starting college, I arrived in the United States with a love for my Jamaican culture and history. During undergrad, I sought to *mek yaad* in ethnic student organizations. African-American schoolmates disputed my Blackness, while my Caribbean friends questioned my involvement with African-American student groups because "we are not one of them." Proud of my Caribbeanness, along with a friend, I once ran around the residence hall courtyard, draped in Jamaican flags, celebrating Jamaican Olympic gold medalists. In cultural spaces constructed by others as spaces for two different ethnic groups, I was the same person in those affinity spaces bringing knowledge from textbooks highlighting slave rebellions and memories of playfield jokes about Christopher Come-Rub-Us. I understand myself as anti-colonial.

ABIGAIL

During undergrad, my professor asked, "Will you write about the Harlem Renaissance? You're familiar?" I uncomfortably agreed, feeling responsible to *not* do injustice to African-American experiences by refusal. I was the only international and Jamaican Black girl in class. My father suggested, "teach dem bout di Maroons, di Morant Bay rebellion and all di Jamaican connections to di U.S." I spoke with my white professor to propose another topic that did not further marginalize my experience. I attempted to *mek yaad* by always bringing my Caribbeanness into the classroom through research papers and presentations, often seeking supplemental information on my own.

FIWI STORY

Caribbean identity remains most salient throughout our lives. While matriculating through higher education in the United States, our need to *mek yaad* with a community understanding us *and* our intellectual traditions strengthened. Where we did not find groups affirming our experiences, we constructed them, circa 2016. Our trio took formation when Kat invited several Afro-Caribbean graduate women to collaborate on a conference presentation. Kat and Abigail met through a mutual classmate, and Kat and Stephanie met taking an anthropology class on Caribbean culture while master's students. Our quarterly meetings are virtual, we maintain them by a vibrant group chat. There we celebrate accomplishments and share frustrations unique to being Afro-Caribbean women in graduate school. On our doctoral journeys, we find these communities integral in our transitions *to*, and *through* graduate school, *as* Black *and* Caribbean women. Our approaches to scholarly inquiry, the intellectual discourse we present just mek sense to *each oda*. Like the pimento, thyme, and garlic in Caribbean cuisine, our mentorship, fellowship, and friendship remain integral to *mek yaad* in academia.

Plentiful Caribbean experiences preclude us from writing everyone's story (Danticat, 2010). Some Afro-Caribbean women choose assimilation as their path for navigating the challenges of U.S. graduate school (Alfred, 2004), but we choose to understand ourselves through the Caribbean. A regional playground of beach-filled pleasure to many, it exceeds pleasure to us (Sampson, 2018). The Caribbean we know forms rich intellectual thought (Kamugisha, 2019), yaad to Sylvia Wynter, Jamaica Kincaid, Walter Rodney, Frantz Fanon, Paget Henry, Carolyn Cooper, Carol Boyce Davies, Stuart Hall, Richard Allsop, and more. In our reasoning sessions, we extract meaning from our experiences, emotions, histories, and cultural practices to know yaad to be a place of anti-colonial pro-black thought (Nakhid-Chatoor et al., 2019). Sans majority white gaze, majority Black Caribbean countries uniquely provide an inherent gaze toward Black power. An almost cellular recognition and materialization, radical Blackness in Anglophone Caribbean countries ceases to disengage from its African roots to appease whiteness. Insidious colonization ensures some Caribbean institutions lean toward whiteness as *right*, but culturally, historically, and globally, sense-of-self is decidedly Black. From Toussaint's revolution to Nanny of the Maroons, and more, Caribbean people historically and intellectually are rooted in Black resistance against colonial powers. There are Caribbean scholars who theorize/d breaking political ties with colonial powers. Scholarship continually remakes society toward a structure void of the colonial class structure perpetuating inequality, while breaking cultural, ideological, psychological ties with colonial powers through exploring what it means to be Black during neo-colonialism (Fanon, 1961/2004). These intellectual inheritances influence how we identify and navigate the challenges of being Black and Caribbean women in graduate school, which we describe further in the next section.

Afro-Caribbean Women's Triple Invisibility in Graduate School

Our encounter with racism in the United States is a unique stressor. We migrated from majority Black countries to the United States with insufficient socialization to navigate racism in the United States, where Black people are historically excluded from institutional participation (Rahming, 2019). Post-migration, we find the narratives which sustained us in the shadow of Caribbean colonialism failing us in the United States, where educational attainment cannot overcome a class structure built through racialization (Rahming, 2019; Talley-Matthews et al., 2020).

In addition to being racialized, our foreignness is a source of marginalization—adding a third layer of invisibility, Foreignness, Blackness, and Womanhood (Smith, 2015). As immigrants we face unique challenges with xenophobia in our graduate school experiences, in the form of microaggressions toward our foreignness, ranging from common markers like accents or food to complex markers like geographies, histories, and ideologies (Malcolm & Mendoza, 2014). Contrary to our experiences, Afro-Caribbean men reported positive interactions with African-American people, giving them greater belonging among African-American people (Douyon, 2020). We must learn to navigate through our unique experience of triple invisibility.

Caribbeanness as a Response to Triple Invisibility

Centering Caribbeanness is a way for us to resist triple invisibility (Douyon, 2020; Glissant, 1997). We healthily embrace our heritage solely out of sincere pride, using it as a means to resist the centrality of whiteness in the United States (Fournillier, 2010). Incorporating Caribbeanness into scholarship begins with incorporating Caribbean languages and communication styles into academic writing as an aesthetic (Fournillier, 2010). The Caribbean intellectual tradition illuminates the complexity of different histories through which Black people originate worldwide. The visibility of Caribbean people through the Caribbean intellectual tradition adds another layer to the Caribbean aesthetic. In addition to its aesthetic value, Caribbeanness in research is a means to resist colonialism by generating scholarship to address concerns within Caribbean societies and their diasporas (Fournillier, 2010).

Caribbean diaspora mentoring communities can bring a Caribbean aesthetic into the academy. Having encountered isolation in academic spaces,

61

gathering in Caribbean-centric communities counters our invisibility in the academic sphere. These groups are most helpful when we can explore the convergence of Caribbean and academic identities in these communities (Alfred, 2004). Caribbean diaspora mentoring communities honor our collectivist cultures with opportunities for women to learn *with* one another the meaning *of* being an academic in relation to the socio-cultural context (Esnard et al., 2017). These collectivist practices are a means to persist in the academy (Esnard et al., 2017). The practice of using a Caribbean aesthetic serves as resistance against the academy's inculcated individualism (Esnard et al., 2017), and furthers anti-colonialism. These communities provide an additional benefit of mitigating the longing for home by providing a space where professional development centers on using scholarly work to aid our home communities (Esnard et al., 2017). We use our story to showcase how we retain each other through graduate school using Caribbeanness as an aesthetic.

Storytelling through Reasoning

Storytelling through reasoning adds a Caribbean aesthetic to this academic exercise of offering suggestions for supporting Afro-Caribbean women in graduate school (Danticat, 2010; Nakhid-Chatoor et al., 2018). Reasoning, a group activity historically used in Rastafari manifestations, serves as a ritual to uncover wisdom about our existence (Christensen, 2014). In reasoning sessions, we query one another, affirm one another, and offer critique, generating perspectives about biases within structures and discourses in our graduate school experience (Nakhid-Chatoor et al, 2019). We regularly accessed levity through identifying the social processes shaping our experiences, while concurrently generating strategies to subvert harmful social processes (Bamikole, 2017).

We held reasoning sessions while developing this chapter. To adapt reasoning to fit the needs of social science research, we first posed initial questions and then our conversations reverted to the spontaneous nature of reasoning (Nakhid-Chatoor et al, 2019). Our questions were as follows: (1) How have we found mentorship through our group? (2) How has our Caribbeanness facilitated this mentorship? (3) What is it about our experience as Black Caribbean women in the academy that has created a need for this mentorship we provide? (4) What are our immigrant stories? During gatherings, we told stories about our challenges in graduate school (Nakhid-Chatoor et al., 2019). As knowledge, our stories express our meanings of being immigrants, alongside and through stories of fiwi yaad (Danticat, 2010; McKittrick, 2021). Thereby showing the distinctiveness of our experiences to remind the world that Caribbean people tek up space (Danticat, 2010).

Hol 'a reason to Mek Yaad

As Caribbean scholars, we face tensions between the old, the new, and the post-colonial. We are pulled between remembering and forgetting the cultural memory which exists within us (Danticat, 2010). Forgetting can make navigating our new geographies in academia easier, but forgetting also advocates loss of our identity. Remembering is not a glamorous alternative to forgetting, remembering prolongs an unsettled longing for connecting with familiar people and places. Home feels elusive because the tension means home cannot exist in one place. Fully embracing the tension of living between two places leads to new forms of being, recreating home or *yaad* in the diaspora (Danticat, 2010). Reasoning became our site of creation.

Reasoning allows us to *mek yaad* as we see our story within each other's stories, stories of toggling between the old Caribbean and the new American (Nakhid-Chatoor et al., 2019). Collectively, we merge our individual insights to develop practices to subvert a dichotomous construction of our Caribbean lives and our lives in U.S. academia (Esnard et al., 2017; Nakhid-Chatoor et al., 2019). We combine the two through Caribbean postcolonial paradigms to create our Caribbean scholarly practice in the diaspora (Bamikole, 2017). Next, our stories of various interactions with one another illustrate that as we understood our common struggle of blending the old, with the new, *and* the postcolonial, we collectively developed practices of subversion.

Our Reasonings: Mek Yaad in Academia and for wi Sistren

Kat linked Stephanie and Abigail, to construct a panel for the Caribbean Studies Association (CSA) Annual Conference, hosted in Havana, Cuba. Given our shared professional and personal identities, the conference's location, and the theme: *Education, Culture and Emancipatory Thought in the Caribbean,* we submitted a proposal with additional Afro-Caribbean graduate women scholars. Kat was a master's student applying to doctoral programs in higher education, Stephanie was a first-year doctoral student in student affairs, and Abigail, a recent student affairs master's graduate, was a full-time professional with doctoral aspirations. In our initial video call, we felt di group's excitement to present at a conference centered on yaad.

Our proposal, *"Mi Deh Ya Too, Caribbean Students Navigate Bi-Cultural Identity,"* was accepted. Attending the conference allowed us to broaden our supportive academic community and strengthen our yaad within each other through theorizing our positionality while experiencing a conference that was topically and geographically Caribbean. We have bonded over our immigrant stories, higher education journeys, our Caribbean connection, struggles in finding Caribbean

63

mentors, and lack of consistent access to Caribbean journals and scholarship. "Yeah, dat happen to me nuff time." Additionally, this space is liberating, allowing us to feel heard when we realize commonalities in how our racial identities become influenced within the education sphere. "Girl, I know exactly wah yuh ah talk bout." Seeing ourselves in one another, we identified how we have collectively embraced Caribbeanness as a means for navigating the very white spaces we encountered in academia (Esnard et al., 2017; Glissant, 1997). #IslandBrilliance, as Kat introduced to our lexicon (Caribbean Scholar Tings, 2019).

Stephanie used Caribbean postcolonial critiques to disrupt American social justice narratives about allyship, but she needed our reasoning space to discuss the resistance she encountered in the classroom. "Caribbean postcolonialism is rooted in self-definition, rebellion and self-governance. We nah wait pon nuh white ally fi save wi." Simultaneously, Kat brought Edward Glissant's text, *Poetics of Discourses* to her web camera. "It is the Caribbeanness. That is who we are. Wi belong here, tek up space." Stephanie felt understood,

> My critique of whiteness emerges from what I know about Blackness. The Black inna di Jamaican flag is fiwi strength. Can yuh imagine if Caribbean people was ah wait fi ally, wi still would deh unda colonial masta, we fought for ourselves and we govern ourselves.

Marcus Garvey's legacy transcends generations so that we may live and work within the vestiges of Caribbean resistance and self-determination. Our reasoning space allows us to use our historical understanding of Black resistance in the Caribbean to generate paradigms about racism in the United States and globally (Evans-Hall, 2006). We validate our feelings of isolation, stemming from ideological misunderstandings, yet we continue embracing Blackness through our postcolonial Caribbean paradigms, strategizing around *and* through American racism and global neo-colonialism.

Fiwi yaad space has grown to aid in our mentoring and support of each other; Kat and Stephanie recruited Abi as a full-time student affairs professional, interested in theorizing and researching. We both encouraged applications to doctoral programs in the Fall 2021 cycle. Our unwavering support provided Abi with additional confidence in envisioning herself as a researcher. Abi regularly checked in with Kat and Steph, "How mi personal statement sound?" We encouraged her not to lose her voice and ensured it was okay to include Jamaican patwa. We encouraged Abigail to incorporate her Caribbeanness (old and postcolonial), into the U.S. academia (new) (Danticat, 2010; Glissant, 1997).

In anti-colonial fashion via working together (Etienne, 2016), we introduced Abigail to other yaad scholars, which proved helpful in reducing Abi's imposter syndrome. As Abigail received acceptances, Kat and Stephanie held virtual reasoning sessions on navigating offers. Reaching back to the scholars who preceded us, and across to our peers, we have shown no hesitation to impart the importance of our Caribbean heritage on emerging scholars. This Caribbean aesthetic mirrors the behaviors and norms of intergenerational transfer of knowledge among Caribbean women, countering academia's individualism (Etienne, 2016).

Stephanie and Kat supported each other through coursework, before qualifying exams and writing dissertation proposals. Abi would remind us of our #islandbrilliance whenever we forgot. We share articles and books we are using to shape our frameworks and methodological approaches to studying the Caribbean and the Caribbean diaspora. Between reasoning calls, Stephanie or Kat might be on Twitter engaging with the same scholarship before even mentioning it to each other. On our reasoning calls, both Stephanie and Kat arrive with the *same* text or *similar* inquiry at the *same* time, underscoring similar intellectual journeys and trajectories. This affirming space provides us a place to discuss our emerging ideas.

"I love our conversations and how wi build on each other's ideas and ah go back and forth. Wi jus ah develop di idea together. We ah talk to each other, nuh just ah talk bout tings."

"Yuh nuh know what dat is? Dat is 'ow Caribbean people chat",

"Yeah, true ting, reasoning."

Months later, Kat linked an article in the group chat, "*Exploring Liming and Ole Talk as a Culturally Relevant Methodology for Researching with Caribbean People*" (Nakhid-Chatoor et al., 2019), and the appreciation for the article was clear "See it deh, nuh dat wi did ah talk about. Mek mi go find dis because dis mi need fi read." Kat and Stephanie later used this paper in their comprehensive exams. Reasoning, a Caribbean aesthetic, allows us to develop ideas through a non-western form of discourse (Nakhid-Chatoor et al., 2019). Reasoning enables us to push against colonialism. Its anti-colonial strengths are rooted in its stance against *babylon*—what the Rastafari faith names institutional structures, behaviors, thinking that are anti-liberatory in nature—which runs through the academy (Bamikole, 2017; Evans-Hall, 2006).

Despite our support of one another, institutional support remained essential to our integration of the Caribbean aesthetic into our scholarly practice. Abi recalls being nervous to ask her residential life department for funds to attend the CSA conference as most of her other peers were attending traditional student affairs conferences.

ABIGAIL: "How mi ah go mek dis work?"
KAT: "Ask dem fi some money and show dem di connection."

This helped Abigail garner financial support of her transgression of rigid academic boundaries. Still, we have not surmounted all structural difficulties in

65

fully merging Caribbean studies with education scholarship. *After* attending our field's conference, Kat was declined travel funds to Caribbean studies and post-colonial studies conferences, costing her invaluable opportunities with interna-tional senior scholars. There was no rationale shared for this decision, but Kat has received funds from her department before. Stephanie, instead, has cho-sen to use funds from her department to attend Caribbean Studies conferences instead of field-specific conferences, a risk she acknowledges may put her at a disadvantage later in her career, due to loss of networking opportunities within her field.

These challenges continued as in/access to texts. Kat has purchased many costly internationally published texts while Stephanie accessed books and arti-cles through interlibrary loan with a waiting period for access. Their doctoral experiences differed from their shared masters' institution which holds exten-sive collections of books and journals about the Caribbean and its diaspora. Centering our Caribbean identity in scholarship requires that we engage in interdisciplinarity. Folding in scholarship cross-disciplinarily requires funding for academic conferences and access to diverse texts, sans regulation to a sin-gular professional development experience. In/access to texts and conferences is a form of gatekeeping. Our collegiate Caribbean group affirms and refreshes our commitment to our chosen path, but it cannot mitigate structural obsta-cles to our interdisciplinarity. Abi's engagement with scholarship differed as a practitioner-scholar, who, at the time, did not have the demands of rigorous academic writing.

Despite reasonings' limitations, it has allowed us to *mek yaad* in academia (Danticat, 2010). As we feel tensions between the old, new, and postcolonial, through reasoning we describe the nature of our experiences and develop strat-egies of subversion toward integrating our Caribbeanness into our scholarship (Evans-Hall, 2006). This brings cohesion among the old, new, and postcolonial (Danticat, 2010). Our practices allowed us to connect to yaad through each other in academia. In our small network, we collaborated, validated our experi-ences, and shared resources in an accessible way. We frequently introduce each other to new peers in hopes of building a wider consortium of Afro-Caribbean women scholars.

Homework: Supporting Afro-Caribbean Women in Graduate School

We have shared how we supported one another as we integrate our Caribbe-anness (Glissant, 1997) into our scholarship. Our experiences illuminate three strategies for institutions to implement in their support of Afro-Caribbean women in graduate school: diverse representation of Blackness in the curricu-lum, creating communities of support for Afro-Caribbean women, and funding for Caribbean research. These recommendations will aid institutions in creating educational experiences suited for Afro-Caribbean women interested in integrating Caribbean identity into their scholarship.

DIVERSE REPRESENTATIONS OF BLACKNESS IN THE CURRICULUM

Afro-Caribbean women engaging in research about Caribbean people using Caribbean frameworks would be supported by a curriculum that appreciates geographic differences among Black students. In singular understandings of Blackness, the United States' global power elevates American understandings of Blackness as superior to the paradigms immigrants bring from the global south (Mocombe, 2015). The global hierarchy, which is less inclusive of the Global South, has manifested in the curriculum, classroom discussions, syllabus creation, course offerings, library collections and research methodologies (Malcolm & Mendoza, 2014). Black voices within the curriculum and library collections should represent the diversity of the Black population within the United States, including Afro-Caribbean voices (Stewart, 2019). Incorporating Afro-Caribbean voices into the curriculum would enrich the experiences of Afro-Caribbean women by providing us opportunities to discuss our ideas with colleagues within our disciplines. Furthermore, this would enhance the academic experience of all by introducing Caribbean perspectives on decolonizing all aspects of society (Tuitt, 2019). Institutions can further support Afro-Caribbean women with expansion of study abroad opportunities within the Caribbean and forming online graduate course partnerships with the University of the West Indies.

Our isolation stemmed from not having classes in which to discuss Caribbean theories and research. We provided one another mentorship but would have benefited from mentoring from Afro-Caribbean faculty familiar with Caribbean societies and theories. Institutions can better support Afro-Caribbean women in graduate school by institutionalizing mentoring through hiring faculty to teach classes about Caribbean societies and serve on dissertation committees. Caribbeanness' visibility in the academic sphere acknowledges the rich diversity among Black people.

CREATING COMMUNITIES OF SUPPORT FOR AFRO-CARIBBEAN WOMEN

Isolation, alongside invisibility, marginalizes Black students resulting in (un) belonging (Stewart, 2019). To mitigate feelings of isolation, institutions should devise ways for Afro-Caribbean women to meet each other on campus (Esnard et al., 2017). Where percentages of Afro-Caribbean women are low, institutions can partner with peer institutions to coordinate a virtual gathering of

Afro-Caribbean women graduate students. Professional organizations can form networks of Afro-Caribbean women, providing not only a space of support, but these networks can produce collaborative projects in aid of Afro-Caribbean women's home countries (Esnard et al., 2017; Fournillier, 2010). Additionally, providing a space for Afro-Caribbean women graduate students to reason about their experience as Black women can help students leverage the *postcolonial* histories of Caribbean people, creating community knowledge about navigating racism, sexism, and xenophobia in the United States (Nakhid-Chatoor et al., 2019). Furthermore, such spaces can be a place of celebration of Caribbean heritage providing a way to merge the *old*, Caribbean identity, with the *new*, academic identity (Alfred, 2004). Caribbean doctoral students thrive when brought together via professional, academic, and research opportunities (Esnard et al., 2017).

FUNDING FOR CARIBBEAN RESEARCH

Funding for exploring the people, culture, climate, histories, and technologies of the Caribbean is limited (Lewis & Simmons, 2010). Our commitment to bettering yaad brings increased costs of conducting international research (Esnard et al., 2017). Afro-Caribbean women conducting research about Caribbean societies may face increased costs for specialized texts, trips to international academic conferences, or conducting international fieldwork. Pre-research site visits for building relationships with community members are particularly important in the Caribbean context which values face-to-face communication (Joseph, 2015). Institutions can support students with funding, accounting for increased costs associated with incorporating Caribbeanness into academic work.

CONCLUSION

Our story demonstrates that we *mek yaad* in academia through mentoring one another. Our journeys center Caribbeanness in our scholarly identities. Afro-Caribbean women graduate students can use Caribbean cultural practices to support each other academically, socially, and emotionally. Institutions can enrich Afro-Caribbean women's academic experience if ethnicity is visible in faculty and administrators' perceptions of Black students' experiences. Afro-Caribbean doctoral students are best supported when institutions recognize their distinct experiences, support them financially with research funding, and provide professional development from mentors who can develop their scholarship. Caribbeanness should be incorporated into the curriculum, by establishing centers for Afro-Caribbean studies, incorporating Caribbean scholars on syllabi, or programs hiring faculty with research interests in the Anglophone Caribbean. When institutions use a global lens to understand Blackness, Afro-Caribbean students can present their Caribbeanness as a form of Blackness.

NOTES

1. We focus on the experiences of Afro-Caribbean women with ancestry from the Anglophone Caribbean.
2. A Caribbean form of discourse.
3. Literal translation: make home.

REFERENCES

Alfred, M. V. (2004). Making the invisible visible: West Indian immigrant Women and pursuit of a "good education" across the borderlands. In M. V. Alfred & R. Swaminathan (Eds.), *Immigrant Women of the Academy: Negotiating Boundaries, Crossing Borders in Higher Education* (pp. 133–158). Nova Science Publishers.

Bamikole, L. O. (2017). Livity as a dimension of identity in Rastafari thought. *Caribbean Quarterly, 63*(4), 451–466. https://doi.org/10.1080/00086495.2017.1392173

Caribbean Scholar Tings [@CSTDigital]. (2019, November 14)When Caribbean women scholars meet up. The future is ours. #CaribbeanScholarTings #IslandBrilliance [Tweet] https://twitter.com/cst_digital_/status/1195044019685879808?s=21

Christensen, J. (2014). *Rastafari Reasoning and the Rastawoman: Gender Constructions in the Shaping of Rastafari Livity*. Lexington Books.

Danticat, E. (2010). *Create Dangerously: The Immigrant Artist at Work*. Vintage.

Douyon, C. M. (2020). *Black in America but not Black American: A Qualitative Study of the Identity Development of Black Caribbean Immigrants* [Doctoral Dissertation, Boston College]. eScholarship@BC. http://hdl.handle.net/2345/bc-ir:108836

Esnard, T., Descartes, C., Evans, S., & Joseph, K. (2017). Framing our professional identity: Experiences of emerging Caribbean academics. *Social and Economic Studies, 66*(3/4), 123–150.

Etienne, J. (2016). *Learning in Womanist Ways: Narratives of First-Generation African Caribbean Women*. UCL Institute of Education Press.

Evans-Hall, K. A. R. (2006). 'Reasoning' an exploration of pedagogic processes in Jamaican prisons. *International Journal of Learning, 13*(6), 47–53.

Fanon, F. (2004). *The Wretched of the Earth*. (R. Philcox, Trans.). Grove Press. (Original work published 1961).

Ferrante, A., & Fox, D. (2016). Introduction: Women and gender: Looking toward "Caribbeanness". *Journal of International Women's Studies, 17*(3), 1–3.

Fournillier, J. B. (2010). An Afro Caribbean scholar on the higher education plantation/ Plus ca change, plus c'est la meme chose. *Creative Approaches to Research, 3*, 1–13.

Glissant, É. (1997). *Poetics of Relation*. University of Michigan Press.

Joseph, V. (2015). An Ethnography of African diasporic affiliation and disaffiliation in Carriacou: How Anglo-Caribbean preadolescent girls express attachments to Africa. [Doctoral Dissertation, University of Massachusetts Amherst]. Doctoral Dissertations. https://doi.org/10.7275/6962219.0

Kamugisha, A. (2019). *Beyond Coloniality: Citizenship and Freedom in the Caribbean Intellectual Tradition*. Indiana University Press.

Lewis, T., & Simmons, L. (2010). Creating research culture in Caribbean universities. *International Journal of Educational Development, 30*(4), 337–344. https://doi.org/10.1016/j.ijedudev.2009.08.005

Malcolm, Z. T. & Mendoza, P. (2014). Afro-Caribbean international students' ethnic identity development: Fluidity, intersectionality, agency, and performativity. *Journal of College Student Development, 55*(6), 595–614.

McKittrick, K. (2021). *Dear Science and Other Stories*. Duke University Press.

Mocombe, P. (2015). The African-Americanization of the Black diaspora in globalization or the contemporary capitalist world-system. *Journal of Developing Societies, 31*(4), 467–487. https://doi.org/10.1177/0169796x15603226

Mwangi, C. A. G., & English, S. (2017). Being Black (and) immigrant students: When race, ethnicity, and nativity collide. *International Journal of Multicultural Education, 19*(2), 100–130.

Nakhid-Chatoor, M., Nakhid, C., Wilson, S., & Santana, A. F. (2018). Exploring liming and ole talk as a culturally relevant methodology for researching with Caribbean people. *International Journal of Qualitative Methods, 17*(1), 1-10. https://doi.org/10.1177/1609406918813772

Rahming, S. (2019). Social support and stress-related acculturative experiences of an English-speaking Afro-Caribbean female student in United States higher education. *Journal of International Students, 9*(4), 1055–1073. https://doi.org/10.32674/jis.v9i4.343

Sampson, L. (2018). Critical pedagogy through participatory video: Possibilities for post-colonial higher education in the Caribbean. In P. R. Carr, M. Hoechsmann, & G. Thésée (Eds.), *Democracy 2.0* (pp. 127–146). Brill.

Smith, C. R. (2015). Black, female, and foreign: The triple-invisibility of Afro-Caribbean Women in the academy. In M. Y. Zhou (Ed.), *Supporting Multiculturalism and Gender Diversity in University Settings* (pp. 74–100). IGI Global. http://doi.org/10.4018/978-1-4666-8321-1.ch005

Stewart, S. (2019). From slave narratives to "groundings": Moving from the peripheries to the centre of knowledge. In S. Stewart (Ed.), *Decolonizing Qualitative Approaches for and by the Caribbean*. Information Age Publishing Inc.

Talley-Matthews, S., Wiggan, G., & Watson-Vandiver, M. J. (2020). Outsider in the academy: Experiences and perspectives of Caribbean Women attending predominantly white institutions in the southeastern region of the United States. *Race Ethnicity and Education*. Advance online publication. https://doi.org/10.1080/13613324.2020.1718077

Tuitt, F. (2019). Disrupting the colonial gaze. In S. Stewart (Ed.), *Decolonizing Qualitative Approaches for and by the Caribbean* (pp. 205–220). Information Age Publishing Inc.

U.S. Census (2021, June). *National Caribbean-American Heritage Month: June 2021*. U.S. Census. https://www.census.gov/newsroom/stories/caribbean-american-heritage-month.html

Peer Mentoring During a Global Pandemic

The global health crisis of 2019 (COVID-19) had a significant impact on every sector of U.S. society. The effects on postsecondary education were considerable as every aspect of academic traditions was eroded to accommodate the pressing need for the safety and well-being of students, faculty, and staff. The fundamental changes in access to, and delivery of, education severely limited student's ability to successfully navigate their academic experience. The harsh reality of abruptly moving back home, online learning, canceled classes, and graduation were blows set against the mounting loss of life sweeping the nation. The November 27, 2020, issue of the *Chronicle of Higher Education* showcased the many ways that the pandemic was stressing academic life from faculty and student burnout, reckless return policies, and students dropping out of higher education altogether. This coupled with the intensifying racial unrest sweeping across the globe significantly impacted the mental well-being of Black students enrolled in higher education. The chapters in this section represent unique opportunities to understand the behind-the-scene support strategies employed by Black women doctoral students and their peer mentorship networks during this unprecedented time.

Patrice Greene, Ashley Ogwo, and Antoinette Newsome investigate in Chapter 5 what it means to be in a "sisterhood" community of Black women doctoral students invested in each other's success at a predominantly white institution (PWI). Employing Black feminist thought (BFT) and scholarly personal narrative (SPN), the authors examine key elements of their sisterhood and share important attributes of what makes their sisterhood uniquely viable. Setting the context for the importance of the community of Black women, they open the chapter with a personal quote that expresses what compels them to be supportive of each other. Their own words reflect a deep love and desire for success for all Black women, "I believe in Black women. I love Black women. I am a Black woman. I want to see the success of myself and other Black women. It's similar to holding up a mirror to yourself." In this mirror of success, the authors write about the importance

DOI: 10.4324/9781003394648-7

of intentionality in finding and building a community. Key findings of this work emphasize the importance of (1) encouragement through validation, (2) intentional accountability, and (3) authenticity in vulnerability. Each of these elements became important as they found themselves navigating the challenges of COVID and anti-Black racial crisis. They were deliberate in their efforts to communicate with each other to affirm and encourage their skills and abilities to be successful in their doctoral journey. As Patrice stated, "we are intentional about how we talk to one another, what we talk about, and building one another up." As they created these spaces of collaboration and support, they were more successful in navigating the academy and supporting each other's journey. The authors offer several key insights and homework for leaders in academic and student affairs such as expanded mental health services and the creation of affinity groups.

In Chapter 6, Terri McMillian's (1992) bestselling novel *Waiting to Exhale* served as a fitting metaphor for authors Ashley L. Gray, Candace N. Hall, Krystal E. Andrews, and Brianna C.J. Clark to unpack their efforts to find support and to exhale in the academy as they navigated their doctoral program and careers during COVID-19 and the racial unrest touching all parts of the globe. The authors employ critical storytelling as a way to center their experiences while utilizing tenets of Black feminist realism (BFR) and BFT to examine the intersections of race, gender, and class. Both BFR and BFT deepened their ability to explore their experiences in ways that were real for Black women. *Waiting to Exhale* chronicled the life of four Black women in different states of navigating relationships with men, career, and finding love. The deep bond between the women and the strategies they shared for dealing with life's challenges transferred nicely to examining the experiences of the authors in the academy. Like the characters in the book, the authors were at different stages of their doctoral program and professional career. Instead of looking for romantic love, the authors substituted finding the "love for the academy." As they noted:

> For the sake of this chapter we likened their struggles of self-definition and finding love but in higher education. The nature of Black women finding a home in higher education and often reporting the lack of reciprocity in that relationship is familiar to us.

Their compelling narratives convey important lessons in how they were able to catch their breath at critical times along the way. They very artfully bring understanding to the complex interactions that Black women have in the academy with each other, white women, and Black men that give them pause and require them to catch their breath. Their powerful narratives result in a six-part model that Black women can replicate as they continue to support each other to include more self-care and to be retained in the academy.

Chapter 7 focuses on the critical period of writing the dissertation. This often solo and challenging part of the doctoral process can be enormously demanding under the best of circumstances. It was made exceedingly more difficult for Black women who found themselves at this stage during the height of COVID-19 and the intense racial unrest. The authors of this chapter A.C. Johnson, Erica T. Campbell, and Kiara S. Summerville found themselves in this position. Capitalizing on their shared experience as students in the same doctoral program, they became each other's lifeline fortified by a strong connection and friendship over the years. Recapping the intense period of the pandemic and how it was shaping every aspect of daily life in the United States and around the world, the authors reflect on their high levels of anxiety during this time noting, "Some days, we were barely able to function due to the fear, tension, and anger coursing through each of us." Using collaborative autoethnography (CAE) as the research method and a theoretical framework of Black feminist epistemology, the authors center their voices and experiences fully drawing on Collins (1986) notions of outsider within to effectively understand and convey their individual and collective thoughts on how their friendship mattered during the final stages of the doctoral process. The findings of their collective experience illustrate that while they all wanted to complete the dissertation, it was also important for each to decide when and if they would pause, adjust their timeline for completion, and simply extend grace to each other during this period. They found that their friendship was indispensable during this time and helped them to maintain important connections as well as a critical source of motivation to continue moving forward, especially when "all hell broke loose" with COVID. The authors concede that it was friendship and peer mentorship that were crucial for their success and well-being. They close by offering important observations for what academic departments at HWIs can do to provide more support and resources that address Black women's unique experiences.

REFERENCES

Chronicle of Higher Education, November 27, 2020.

Collins, P.H. (1986). Learning from the outsider within: The sociological significance of Black feminist thought. *Social Problems, 33*(6), s14–s32.

Chapter 5

Strategies for Providing Grace and Space on the Journey of Multidimensional Sisterhood in the Academy

Patrice Greene, Ashley Ogwo and Antoinette Newsome

INTRODUCTION

On day one of her PhD program, Antoinette walked into the classroom searching for other Black women, saying, "they don't know it yet, but they are going to be my friends." As Black women navigating college, we learned the importance of finding one another and developing relationships beyond the classroom. These relationships exemplify peer mentorship needed in academic and social spaces. What compels us as Black women to support one another? Exploring this question in community, our responses are found in the following self-quotes:

> I believe in Black women. I love Black women. I am a Black woman. I want to see the success of myself and other Black women. It's similar to holding up a mirror to yourself.
>
> I couldn't imagine...doing this by myself...your success is connected to mine and vice versa.
>
> We're not just retaining each other within this program...this is just one area of our lives...This reciprocal relationship...is genuine...[and] necessary.

As Black women, we have unique experiences navigating challenges, particularly during COVID-19, the national racial crisis, and our doctoral programs. Given these circumstances, the need for mentorship and support for Black women doctoral students (BWDS) is dire; however, BWDS still drop out due to familial responsibilities, workload, stress, need for community, and financial instability (Williams-Robinson, 2019). These reasons, coupled with COVID-19 and the U.S. anti-Black racial crisis, have exacerbated the need for sustained community and mentorship between Black women in doctoral programs.

DOI: 10.4324/9781003394648-8

In recognizing the role of peer mentoring and support in navigating our doctoral journeys, we – three Black women at a predominantly white institution (PWI) in the Mid-Atlantic – believe it is necessary to unpack how sisterhood has been vital for us before and during the shifting racial and public health climates in society. Thus, the purpose of this chapter is (1) to offer personal narratives in showing grace to one another as we co-create spaces with Black women within the academy and (2) to provide strategies for how Black women academics can retain each other in physical and virtual spaces. This chapter explores the zfollowing research questions:

(1) How do BWDS at a Research I institution define their sisterhood and process of retaining one another?
(2) What meaning do we ascribe to the creation of our sisterhood within our doctoral program?
(3) How has adaptation during COVID-19 and the anti-Black racial crisis impacted how we retain one another?

We reflect on how our pre-doctoral and doctoral experiences have broadened our understanding of the term "sister," shaping our intentionality in seeking and building community in the doctoral process. We first provide a literature review on the experiences of Black women graduate students (BWGS). Next, we describe our conceptual framework, Black feminist thought (BFT), to chronicle our experiences at the intersection of race and gender. We then outline our methodological approach, scholarly personal narrative (SPN), to unfold the realities of navigating Black womanhood and provide strategies as new academics retaining each other throughout the doctoral process. Special emphasis is placed on how our sisterhood was impacted by COVID-19 and the U.S. anti-Black racial crisis. We conclude with our findings and homework for academic and student affairs practitioners and faculty interested in retaining BWGS.

LITERATURE REVIEW

In 2017–2018, Black women earned 7.2% of all graduate degrees, making them the most highly educated minoritized group in U.S. graduate education (National Center for Education Statistics, 2020a, 2020b). Additionally, Black women receive 64.3% of doctoral degrees awarded to Black students (*The Journal of Blacks in Higher Education*, 2020). This success, however, is costly to the overall well-being and retention of BWDS (Williams-Robinson, 2019). Literature on BWGS noted it is commonplace for this population to report experiencing microaggressions, feelings of impostor syndrome, isolation, and a pronounced lack of mentoring and access to resources (Apugo, 2017; Beasley, 2016; Lewis et al., 2013). To combat these negative experiences, literature suggests that BWGS seek community and mentorship from others with similar racial, cultural, and gender identities (Coleman-Hunter, 2014; Fries-Britt & Kelly, 2005; Grant & Simmons, 2008; Zachary, 2012). Many BWGS view individuals with similar racial and cultural identities as critical contributors to their success in graduate programs (Zachary, 2012). Success for BWGS is often found in communities where they can unpack their experiences, identities, and values (Sulé, 2014).

These networks also provide space for participants to encounter validation and reciprocal authenticity – feelings not often fostered in classrooms at PWIs (Lewis et al., 2013). These support networks emphasize intentionality, agency, and collaboration while also building professional, academic, and personal relationships in formal and informal settings (Apugo, 2017; Borum & Walker, 2012; Domingue, 2015). These networks are critical in providing BWGS opportunities for dialogue and connection while cultivating skills to navigate stereotyping and persist through adversity (Domingue, 2015; Lewis et al., 2013). At PWIs, Black-women-centered networks that incorporate peer mentorship allow for BWGS to show vulnerability, transparency, and resist assimilation (Beasley, 2016; Domingue, 2015; Minnett et al., 2019). For BWDS specifically, peer mentorship provides space to serve as mentees and mentors to one another, allowing them to recognize their strengths and the importance of adaptability to meet fluctuating doctoral program demands (Minnett et al., 2019).

While existing literature on BWGS discusses the significance of building community with other Black women, there is a need for scholarship that addresses the significance of seeking sisterhood during unprecedented times. At the time of this writing, the U.S. is currently in uncharted territory as its constituents simultaneously navigate a global pandemic and an increasingly charged racial crisis, both disproportionately affecting Black people (Millett et al., 2020). In addition to existing challenges for BWDS, they now face new obstacles such as shifting to virtual educational and social spaces. Given the extenuating circumstances impacting society, it is important for BWGS to make sisterly connections and for literature to capture these current challenges. To fill this literature gap, we focus our sisterhood and experiences as BWDS against the backdrop of the COVID-19 pandemic and U.S. sociopolitical climate.

The combination of COVID-19 and Black Lives Matter protests centered on discussions of anti-Blackness in academia and society. Simultaneously, students had to adjust to asynchronous learning and virtual means of building community with one another (Anand & Hsu, 2020). The realities of COVID-19, anti-Blackness, and police brutality weighed heavily on Black students as they were disproportionately affected by job loss and deaths (Anand & Hsu, 2020). Furthermore, faculty may have an inadequate comprehension of how race and systemic oppression impact students completing a graduate degree (Walsh et al., 2021). To understand Black women's compounding needs during difficult times, we explore our topic through BFT.

CONCEPTUAL FRAMEWORK

Black feminism focuses on the interlocking oppressions facing Black women at the core of their racialized, gendered, classed, and othered experiences (Collins, 1989). BFT allows Black women to ascribe meaning to their own realities (Collins, 1989). BFT's focus on interlocking identities is essential, as Black women have experiences and worldviews that are valid and in need of exploration through Black women's epistemologies (Collins, 1989). BFT is explored through storytelling, narratives, and dialogues among Black women, capturing the strength and scarring of being a Black woman in a racist, patriarchal society (Lorde, 1984). BFT combats the systematically oppressive notion that Black women are not intellectual beings, affirming Black women as experts about their experiences (Collins, 2000). Through an interrogative lens of the legacies of institutional racism and oppression, BFT centers the strength of Black women instead of their deficits (Apugo, 2017; Beasley, 2016; Collins, 1989).

BFT conceptualizes how Black women create community while resisting and challenging institutional oppressions and stereotypes placed upon them (Collins, 2000). BFT consists of four emergent themes: concrete experience as a criterion of meaning, use of dialogue in assessing knowledge claims, ethic of caring, and the ethic of personal accountability (Collins, 1989). As researcher-participants, we utilize BFT coupled with SPN to describe our experiences as BWDS mentoring one another.

METHODOLOGY

Using SPN, we recount our sisterhood. SPN "honors the experiential and intellectual resources of marginalized individuals" (Nash & Viray, 2013, p. 3). SPN validates disenfranchised students' perspectives by using their voices to analyze and construct their worldviews, cultures, and experiences (Nash & Viray, 2013). As Black women whose intersectional identities place them on the margins of scholarly discourse, SPN allows us to center ourselves in academic writing. Because SPN affirms the "validity [and]...necessity" of incorporating ourselves into "dominant scholarly discourse" (Nash & Viray, 2013, p. 4), we use it to write our sisterhood and doctoral experiences into literary existence.

Positionality

We offer positionality statements to establish trustworthiness and to legitimize our lived experiences (Collins, 1989; Merriam, 1995). The study design is described after the statements.

Patrice Greene: My epistemological viewpoints are shaped by the Black women in my life. My first teachers were Black women in my family: my mother and grandmother. I interrogate my reflexivity and how I can support other Black women in my academic, friend, and mentorship communities. As a Black woman, my race and gender are central to my identity with my research pursuits connecting to a transformative view of centering social justice, social action, and equity for Black women in education.

Ashley Ogwo: I am a Black, Nigerian Igbo-American, Christian woman. As a Black woman, I find the most support among other Black women. Black women are central to my retention and success in education. I engage in reflexivity, understanding the importance of highlighting the impact my identities and experiences have on my approach to research. As a critical researcher, I enter the academy to challenge monolithic views of Blackness and celebrate Blackness in all its brilliance, vibrancy, and multiplicity.

Antoinette Newsome: As one of 11 children, growing up as a Black mixed-race woman was centered in my Black Southern community. Community and support from other Black women are central to my being. Without connection to Black women, it would be difficult to navigate life's challenges, especially the doctoral journey. I practice reflexivity by critically reflecting on my experiences. My research uses a constructivist epistemology, elevating marginalized voices by allowing both "researcher" and "researched" to co-create meaning.

Study Design and Data Sources

In developing our study design in Spring 2020, we identified aspects of our academic and personal experiences that best detailed our sisterhood. We discussed our individual journeys leading to our doctoral experiences (e.g., our master's experiences) and agreed that such aspects provided necessary context for understanding how we were navigating sisterhood in our doctoral programs. We deemed it necessary to examine our doctoral experiences prior to and during COVID-19, given the spatial and mental shifts made during the first year of our doctorate. After identifying our pre-doctoral and doctoral experiences – both prior to and during COVID – as foci for our study, we conducted a themed focus group centered on each area of our journey. We then created a bank of guiding questions centered on our three journey areas and used these guiding questions to facilitate discussion. Next, in Fall 2020, we conducted literature reviews and engaged in discussions to create and solidify our focus group questions. We began focus group data collection in Spring 2021.

Alternating the role of facilitator, we collected data through three 60-to-90-minute focus groups highlighting our narratives and discussing how we developed, defined, and exhibited sisterhood in three life stages: (1) Pre-Doctoral, (2) Doctoral, and (3) Racial Crisis/COVID-19.

Data sources included three video-and-audio-recorded focus groups conducted during Spring 2021 and reflective memos written post-focus groups.

79

Data Analysis

Data were collected virtually on Zoom and transcribed using Otter.ai. We conducted member checking by assessing and correcting each transcript. Next, we analyzed data through multiple readings, initial coding, and focused coding (Charmaz, 2006; Corbin & Strauss, 2008; Jones et al., 2014). The analysis process occurred during Spring 2021 and involved a combination of deductive and inductive coding, using BFT themes and data-emergent themes.

We reviewed data individually and collectively, sharing initial data analyses outcomes. We then finalized codes and analyzed them together. Moving from individual to group analysis and discussion, we collectively reflected on emerging patterns. We engaged in memoing, noting, and actively reflecting on the data (Birks et al., 2008). We addressed our positionalities as researchers to illustrate how and why the data may be interpreted and presented as it is (Merriam, 1995). The combination of reflective memos, individual and group reflections, peer debriefing, member checking, and addressing positionalities ensured trustworthiness throughout the writing process (Birks et al., 2008; Merriam, 1995). In reviewing our transcripts and reflective memos, we shifted our initial coding – largely based on relevant quotes – to common themes we expressed in our verbal and written reflections. For example, the theme of authenticity arose from our common use of the word in our dialogue and our post-focus group reflective memos.

FINDINGS

A consistent finding was the necessity of sisterhood throughout our education in providing space to thrive. We found that sisterhood provided various supports within our pre-doctoral and doctoral journeys. Accordingly, we offer three themes that encompass our multidimensional sisterhood: (1) Encouragement through Validation, (2) Intentional Accountability, and (3) Authenticity in Vulnerability.

ENCOURAGEMENT THROUGH VALIDATION

Detailing our individual and collective experiences, we expressed how encouragement through validation was pivotal in our sisterhood. It was important to be intentional in encouraging each other verbally. Ashley experienced an interaction with a professor that helped solidify the importance of this. She recalled a previous Black woman professor telling her "you have a way with words that people need to hear; it would be…a disservice to yourself and to them, to deprive them…and… yourself of being able to speak power to what you believe." The professorial validation Ashley received was affirming because of the rarity of Black women faculty at PWIs. As in Ashley's case, encouragement at critical junctures in Black women's academic journeys can provide the push they need to advance while also inspiring them to create similar validating encounters for other Black women. Such experiences have motivated us to consciously validate others' voices within sisterly spaces.

We are deliberate in our encouragement and support. Patrice stated, "we are intentional about how we talk to one another, what we talk about, and building one another up." Creating a collaborative environment that promotes affirmation helps to sustain one another. Patrice articulated, being "in the trenches with one another" and encouraging each other through difficulties of being BWDS provided reasons to strategically encourage and validate each other. These validating spaces allowed us to flourish inside and outside of the academy. Antoinette shared that as a full-time professional, she relied on our sisterly encouragement to take time away from work for school and self-care. Patrice and Ashley often reaffirmed Antoinette, expressing that we deserve rest. Practicing encouragement and validation with one another is just one way intentionality has been critical in our retention process.

Intentional Accountability

Through dialogue, we defined sisterhood, agreeing that it requires giving time and energy to ensure we have space to navigate life. Patrice shared, "I think [sisterhood] encompasses action and showing up in good and bad times." She defined sisters as those who call her out or in when needed while giving "a different and... better perspective on how to view things." We reflected on how such accountability is valuable within our sisterhood. For example, Ashley discussed how comforting it is knowing that she can call us for any reason and rely on us to hold her responsible. Whether sharing inspirational devotionals linked to personal topics we had recently discussed (e.g., finances, joy, peace), venting, or requesting accountability partners to work with, Ashley utilized our sisterhood to nourish personal, academic, and professional aspects of herself.

During COVID-19, we practiced intentional accountability by conducting frequent self-care check-ins virtually via Zoom or FaceTime. We asked one another how we were making time for our own radical self-care and pushed each other to prioritize our well-being, sharing self-care strategies we were implementing, including taking daily walks, curating and sharing playlists of uplifting songs, and incorporating morning meditations. Antoinette stated, "when thinking about retaining each other in the midst of crises, it's not just through conversations, but intentionally saying '...*how* did you take care of yourself?'" Similar to Walsh et al. (2021), we found that checking in during COVID-19 was important in maintaining communal connection as Black graduate students.

We also held weekly working sessions designed to make progress on school- or job-related items. For example, when Ashley had assistantship or personal deadlines and needed accountability to ensure she made progress toward her goals, she would reach out through the group chat. This resulted in Antoinette and Patrice scheduling various Zoom working sessions for the group. Along with working sessions, we also practiced offering grace to ourselves and to one another. When we did not reach our self-determined goals, we encouraged each other to be kind and understanding to ourselves. We were intentional about ensuring our striving never eclipsed our acts of radical self-care. We celebrated progress but also held each other accountable for our personal well-being by interrogating one another about how we were making time for ourselves.

As illustrated above, our sisterly accountability went beyond academic responsibilities, which was necessary, especially during a global pandemic. The pandemic generated what Antoinette deemed a "swift shift" to a virtual environment. Within the first few months of quarantine, we each relocated to a different state to be with family. In this shift, we missed out on building rapport in-person during our first year in the program. One of the sisterly challenges we faced was finding ways to sustain the community virtually. This called for new strategies of working and checking in while still practicing grace with one another. Exemplifying the need for new methods of maintaining accountability, Antoinette opined that, with the virtual environment, "we're having to think of different methods, like the Pomodoro method, where we 'work for 40 minutes, then chitchat for 10 minutes.' Sometimes it's an hour. We go with what we need at the moment..."

In practicing accountability, we recognized when our working strategies or methods felt stagnant and adapted our working styles as needed. We displayed a consistent willingness to try new styles like shorter, more frequent working sessions to find what worked best for us. Patrice also acknowledged the adaptability we practiced during widespread social unrest, calling it "a testament to how serious we are about maintaining our sisterhood by still getting together virtually and frequently for accountability measures or just to sit and talk." By implementing the techniques above, we developed adaptive working styles; helped each other stay on track with personal, educational, and professional goals; and strategically collaborated to reach benchmarks for larger doctoral goals.

The virtual environment posed challenges to meeting, but our willingness to try new ways of maintaining community reflected reciprocal care, accountability, intentionality, and support regardless of setting. As Ashley stated, "...while the environment in which we've had to work has shifted, the nature of our sisterhood has not." She described the responsiveness we displayed in our sisterhood, noting shifts we made "to give ourselves and each other those small pockets of peace... that we needed," as well as our recognition of "one another's need to shift or step back…" Finding these small pockets of peace involved taking work breaks, carving out intentional times for rest, setting cutoff times to stop working for the night, and relaxing high expectations or strict timelines where possible. Although challenging, the virtual environment also provided benefits the physical setting could not, such as accommodating flexibility in last-minute schedule changes. COVID-19 and the racial crisis increased our intentionality in connecting, while the virtual setting provided us a new communication method despite being in separate states. Overall, while we faced unprecedented circumstances, COVID-19 and the racial crisis provided opportunities for our sisterhood to center authenticity and growth in valuable ways within and beyond academia.

Authenticity in Vulnerability

Our sisterhood emphasized a high level of care and comfort in being our most authentic, vulnerable selves. These were vital aspects of sisterhood, with Ashley describing sisters as "women that I could be my full self around, and not hide… parts of my identity." At the center of authenticity was peer mentorship that fostered affirmation, reciprocity, and peace. We consistently expressed comfort sharing our shortcomings and successes, and wariness regarding the impact of COVID-19 and anti-Blackness, while simultaneously breeding a sisterhood that, as Ashley stated, incorporates the "intimacy of letting folks see you when you're hurt or not alright."

Displaying vulnerability by sharing difficulties has been instrumental in developing sisterhood among ourselves and other Black women in our program. As we collectively stated, we need "people to vent to, be open and honest…to process during racial tension and conflict." Authenticity in vulnerability became key in supporting one another through COVID-19 and U.S. racial injustices as we recognized the salience of our identities as Black women and educators. For example, we discussed unspoken expectations for Black women educators to educate non-Black people on anti-Blackness while balancing their own personal and professional issues resulting from COVID-19 and anti-Blackness. As Black women navigating PWIs during racial and public health crises where Black people were disproportionately affected, we were honest about our self-care, desire to disconnect from spaces that expected too much from us, and concerns about COVID-19's impact on our families. Antoinette had multiple family members who had COVID-19, Patrice was concerned about her parents' older age and presence in a state that undermined COVID-19 guidelines, and Ashley's parents had work responsibilities that made them more susceptible to exposure. As these concerns affected our mental well-being, we prioritized processing together and encouraged individual use of therapy with a licensed counselor via telehealth during the pandemic, with Patrice and Antoinette starting therapy during quarantine.

83

DISCUSSION

Our findings illuminate key points that align with BFT's themes. Through dialogues and reflections, we shared concrete experiences as a criterion of meaning, while using dialogue to assess our knowledge claims (Collins, 1989). Our stories highlighted how other Black women's mentorship and guidance affirmed and validated our identities as BWDS. In Ashley's case, a professor's affirmation of her storytelling ability forged her foundation for how sisterhood should be conceptualized in academia. In describing concrete experiences as a criterion of meaning, Collins (1989) stated "living life as Black women requires wisdom since knowledge about the dynamics of race, gender, and class subordination has been essential to Black women's survival. African-American women give such wisdom high credence in assessing knowledge" (p. 758). Through Ashley's conversation with her professor, her knowledge, essence, and experiences as a Black woman were validated and seen as essential to changing academia.

Antoinette's story of our doctoral retention process during COVID-19 illustrates how our sisterhood and commitment to one another center intentionality and our desire to facilitate our success in transitioning from physical to virtual community. We created authentic spaces centering the ethic of caring, highlighting how "personal expressiveness, emotions, and empathy are central to knowledge-validation" (Collins, 1989, p. 766). Our anecdotes illustrated how sustained dialogue created spaces that centered trust, grace, and rapport in our doctoral process. In defining sisterhood, we emphasized foregrounding transparency and authenticity. Our use of dialogue in assessing and affirming our knowledge and vulnerability underscore "connectedness rather than separation" (Collins, 1989, p. 763).

The ethic of personal accountability captured the importance of community, retention, and sisterhood as we managed our doctoral program, COVID-19, and racial injustice. Collins (1989) described the ethic of personal accountability as "an assessment of an individual's knowledge claims simultaneously to evaluate an individual's character, values, and ethics" (p. 769). Patrice's definition of sisterhood highlighted that being a sister and peer mentor is as much about support as it is about ensuring we, as Black women, are responsible for each other's successes through the doctoral process. There is no sisterhood or growth without accountability. We showed each other grace by acknowledging priorities outside of school and created space to complete personal tasks for work, internships, and more resulting in our bond transcending academics. Additionally, we created a culture of care for each other's family by extending support to process concerns and demonstrated a commitment to mental and physical well-being by promoting therapy and exercise. We created space for vulnerability, authenticity, encouragement, and validation by using various methods of retaining each other in virtual learning environments.

84

Through dialogue and affirmation, we shared how we adequately model community and support, thus providing each other space and grace through a BFT perspective. Furthermore, we must remind Black women to show grace to themselves and others as they discover the multidimensional meaning of sisterhood within the academy. The co-creation of spaces with other Black women on this doctoral journey is rooted in community to help us thrive.

Homework for Institutional Leaders

BWDS encounter racism, sexism, and lack of support as barriers to attending and navigating college, graduating, and receiving a degree (Borum & Walker, 2012; Lewis et al., 2013). Our findings illustrate how sisterhood can help mitigate some of these barriers by providing BWDS with intentional spaces of community, support, and connection. With academic affairs personnel, student affairs personnel, and faculty in mind, we propose homework for institutional leaders based upon our experiences as BWDS navigating academia during COVID-19 and a racial crisis/anti-Blackness.

Mental Health Services

With affirmation, validation, encouragement, and vulnerability as the foundations of sisterhood, campus counseling centers should promote mental health services specifically for BWDS. Therapy was essential in allowing us to process the mental impact of COVID-19 on ourselves and our families. While some of us sought off-campus therapy, we acknowledge that off-campus counseling services are not always accessible or affordable. Therefore, we suggest intentional marketing of on-campus services and resources for BWDS, given stigma associated with seeking these services. Stakeholders providing these services should meet students where they are most comfortable, speaking directly to programs and groups that center BWDS communities (e.g., Black Graduate Student Associations). In the midst of COVID-19, campus counseling centers could also highlight mental health spaces outside of the academy. For example, Therapy for Black Girls (TFBG) focuses on destigmatizing mental health and provides accessible information for Black women dealing with sexism and racism, the impact of COVID-19, and collective grief (TFBG, 2020). TFBG's website displays therapists that center Black women's needs and podcasts that discuss COVID-19 vaccines, positive affirmations, and battling seasonal depression (TFBG, 2020). Although external mental health resources may require a financial investment from BWDS, we believe that these investments may be worthwhile for those BWDS who need additional or more tailored support for maintaining their mental health and well-being that may not be offered on their campuses. Overall, key stakeholders should emphasize that the emotional and mental well-being of BWDS is just as pertinent as their academic achievements.

Affinity Groups

We also recommend that institutions create Black-women-specific affinity groups for BWDS where they can comfortably dialogue with one another. Our experiences demonstrated the benefits of holding space for connecting on both academic and personal (i.e., non-academic, non-professional) levels. These spaces were integral in recognizing our full selves outside of the academic sphere that brought us together. Given the role of dialogue in affirming our identities both inside and outside of academia, we believe institutions should intentionally create such dialogic spaces, as university-sponsored groups could be beneficial in ensuring BWDS have access to university staff and resources. The affinity groups can take the form of monthly meetings where BWDS discuss pertinent topics such as balancing commitments. These groups could create opportunities for BWDS to hear about other Black women's experiences and connect with older BWDS. Like our sisterhood model, these groups could also establish accountability partners, which would allow BWDS to work toward self-defined monthly goals, such as practicing self-care. Accountability partners would allow BWDS to connect and check in outside of group meetings to increase communal connections. Academic and student affairs professionals can collaborate to ensure BWDS affinity groups are supported at their institutions. These groups should foster a welcoming and intersectional environment to ensure that non-binary, queer, and Black women with other minoritized identities can feel supported in these spaces.

CONCLUSION

Our story is a reminder that Black women are powerful, valuable, and necessary. As Patrice stated, sisterhood is "beautiful, it's challenging. There's highs, there's lows, it's frustrating. It's all of that." We share love and appreciation for the spaces we create and sustain as we advance in our doctoral journeys. We communicate our sisterhood, community, and dialogues to reimagine the academy by centering Black women's experiences. Our narratives accentuate what "sisterhood…feels and looks like and we are challenging [ourselves] to recreate that space not just for [us] but for other Black women." These stories serve as encouragement for other scholars to create spaces where Black women can collaborate and support one another. As next-generation researchers, we have the power to shift how knowledge creation is validated and by whom. We must push the envelope by being daring, courageous, and brave enough to continue setting the standards for others by going beyond systemic limitations placed on Black women. That is our power and our way of effecting change. With more to share about our multidimensional sisterhood, our hope is, as Ashley stated, "many Black women [will] benefit from hearing our stories. Because our stories together are love, trial, joy, and so beautifully us."

REFERENCES

Anand, D., & Hsu, L. (2020). COVID-19 and Black lives matter: Examining anti-Asian racism and anti-Blackness in US education. *International Journal of Multidisciplinary Perspectives in Higher Education, 5*(1), 190–199.

Apugo, D. (2017). We all we got: Considering peer relationships as multi-purpose sustainability outlets among millennial Black women graduate students attending majority white urban universities. *Urban Review, 49*(1), 347–367.

Beasley, M. (2016). *The Adjustment of First Year African American Women to Predominantly White Institutions: Implications for Best Practices* [Doctoral dissertation, University of San Francisco]. https://repository.usfca.edu/cgi/viewcontent.cgi?article=1308&context=diss

Birks, M., Chapman, Y., & Francis, K. (2008). Memoing in qualitative research: Probing data and processes. *Journal of Research in Nursing, 13*(1), 68–75.

Borum, V., & Walker, E. (2012). What makes the difference? Black women's undergraduate and graduate experience in mathematics. *The Journal of Negro Education, 81*(4), 366–378.

Charmaz, K. (2006). *Constructing Grounded Theory: A Practical Guide through Qualitative Analysis.* Sage.

Coleman-Hunter, S. (2014). Portraits of four African-American women who earned doctoral degrees from a predominately white institution. *College of Education Theses and Dissertations, 58.* https://via.library.depaul.edu/soe_etd/58

Collins, P. H. (1989). The social construction of Black feminist thought. *Signs, 14*(4), 745–773.

Collins, P. H. (2000). *Black Feminist Thought: Knowledge, Consciousness, and the Politics of Empowerment* (2nd ed.). Routledge.

Corbin, J., & Strauss, A. (2008). *Basics of Qualitative Research: Techniques and Procedures for Developing Grounded Theory* (3rd ed.). Sage.

Domingue, A. (2015). Our leaders are just we ourself: Black women college student leaders' experiences with oppression and sources of nourishment on a predominantly white college campus. *Equity & Excellence in Education, 48*(3), 454–472.

Fries-Britt, S., & Kelly, B. T. (2005). Retaining each other: Narrative of two African American women in the academy. *The Urban Review, 37*(3), 221–242.

Grant, C., & Simmons, J. (2008). Narrative on experiences of African-American women in the academy: Conceptualizing effective mentoring relationships of doctoral students and faculty. *International Journal of Qualitative Studies in Education, 21*(5), 501–517.

Jones, S., Torres, V., & Arminio, J. (2014). *Negotiating the Complexities of Qualitative Research in Higher Education: Fundamental Elements and Issues* (2nd ed.). Routledge.

Lewis, J., Mendenhall, R., Harwood, S., & Hunt, M. (2013). Coping with gendered racial microaggressions among Black women college students. *Journal of African American Studies, 17*(1), 51–73.

87

Lorde, A. (1984). *Sister Outsider: Essays and Speeches.* Crossing Press.

Merriam, S. (1995). What can you tell me from an n of 1?: Issues of validity and reliability in qualitative research. *PAACE Journal of Lifelong Learning, 4,* 51–60.

Millet, G., Jones, A., Benkeser, D., Baral, S., Mercer, L., Beyrer, C., Honermann, B., Lankiewicz, E., Mena, L., Crowley, J., Sherwood, J., & Sullivan, P. (2020). Assessing differential impacts of COVID-19 on Black communities. *Ann Epidemiol, 47,* 37–44.

Minnett, J., Gallaway, J., & Owens, D. (2019). Help a sista out: Black women doctoral students' use of peer mentorship as an act of resistance. *Mid-Western Educational Researcher, 31*(2), 210–238.

Nash, R. & Viray, S. (2013). The who, what, and why of scholarly personal narrative writing. *Counterpoints, 446,* 1–9.

National Center for Education Statistics (2020a). Doctor's degrees conferred by postsecondary institutions, by race/ethnicity and sex of student: Selected years, 1976–77 through 2017–18. https://nces.ed.gov/programs/digest/d19/tables/dt19_324.20.asp

National Center for Education Statistics (2020b). Master's degrees conferred by postsecondary institutions, by race/ethnicity and sex of student: Selected years, 1976–77 through 2017–18. https://nces.ed.gov/programs/digest/d19/tables/dt19_323.20.asp

Sulé, V. (2014). Enact, discard, and transform: A critical race feminist perspective on professional socialization among tenured Black female faculty. *International Journal of Qualitative Studies in Education, 27*(4), 432–453.

The Journal of Blacks in Higher Education (2020). *African Americans Making Slow But Steady Progress in Doctoral Degree Awards.* https://www.jbhe.com/2020/12/african-americans-making-slow-but-steady-progress-in-doctoral-degree-awards/

Therapy for Black Girls (2020). To be seen, to be heard, and to be understood. *Therapy for Black Girls.* https://therapyforblackgirls.com/about/

Walsh, B., Woodliff, T., Lucero, J., Harvey, S., Burnham, M., Bowser, T., Aguirre, A., & Zeh, D. (2021). Historically underrepresented graduate students' experiences during the COVID-19 pandemic. *Family Relations.* https://doi.org/10.1111/fare.12574

Williams-Robinson, C. (2019). *Navigating a Doctoral Program While the Ship Is Sinking: A Black Woman's Journey* [Doctoral dissertation, California State University, Long Beach].

Zachary, L. (2012). *The Mentor's Guide: Facilitating Effective Learning Relationships* (2nd ed.). Jossey-Bass.

Chapter 6

Finding Spaces to Breathe in the Academy

How Black Women Build Sustaining Communities to Fortify Success

Ashley L. Gray, Candace N. Hall,
Krystal E. Andrews and Brianna C.J. Clark

INTRODUCTION

> Racist, sexist socialization had conditioned us to devalue our femaleness and to regard race as the only relevant label of identification. In other words, we were asked to deny a part of ourselves—and we did. We clung to the hope that liberation from racial oppression would be all that was necessary for us to be free. We were a new generation of black women who had been taught to submit, to accept sexual inferiority, and to be silent.
>
> (hooks, 2014, pp. 1–2)

hooks' (1981; 2014) statement not only reflects the marginalization of Black women in society but is also representative of our presence within the academy. For decades, there have been clear and distinct inequities against women within higher education, ranging from lack of access to sexism. However, the subject of racial and gender inequities in the context of postsecondary education traditionally only considers Black men and White women as the universal standard of research (Hull et al., 1982). As a result, Black women and our multiple identities are silenced.

In this chapter, we explored our experiences as four Black women doctoral students and professionals in the academy at the intersections of race, gender, and class through friendship and sisterhood. Centering the tenets of Black Feminist

DOI: 10.4324/9781003394648-9

Realism (BFR; Green et al., 2016), we examined our challenging experiences and support strategies. Terry McMillan's (1992) iconic book-turned film, *Waiting to Exhale,* captured the love and losses of four complex Black women and created a blueprint to share our own need to exhale in the academy. The women in Morrison's novel were our age navigating what often felt like impossible circumstances in finding love of self and romantic partners. For the sake of this chapter, we likened their struggles of self-definition and finding love but in higher education. The nature of Black women finding a home in higher education and often reporting the lack of reciprocity in that relationship is familiar to us. Much like the women in this novel, we have leaned on each other through crises, victories, and to find our breath. Additionally, the novel is centered around the reunion of these four women who were seeking refuge. Much of our reunion used conferences as free-breathing spaces to recharge and renew our mission(s). In many cases, conferences were the only travel many of us could afford, making it essential to gain scholarly information and recharge. We have engaged in shared economics and space since 2018 to ensure our sister-scholars have conference access.

This story of our sisterhood proves that sisterhood in scholarship among Black women benefits all of higher education. Additionally, we negotiate our postures while faced with the academy's extreme duality of glory and labor. At the beginning of 2020, we were unexpectedly suffocated yet again by a global crisis that no one could prepare us for; the COVID-19 pandemic. This pandemic disproportionately impacted the Black community, including Black women doctoral students who were denied the opportunity to commence our journey within the academy as graduates. With the full awareness that we, as Black women, graduate with our families, friends, and communities, we created a national virtual ceremony for Black doctoral students and their families. This ceremony, affectionately named Sankofa, created an opportunity for us to work together closely, celebrate achievement, and recognize the cohorts of Black doctoral graduates impacted. Simply put, we stood in a gap (yet again) that higher education did not have the imagination or intention to fill. This chapter explored the experiences of the sister-scholars through a literature scan, robust conceptual framework, methodology, personal vignettes, and included a model of homecoming for Black women.

Literature Review

The number of Black women earning doctoral degrees increased 73% within the last ten years (National Center for Education Statistics, 2011; 2019). As scholarship examining the experiences of Black women doctoral students continues to emerge (Apugo, 2017; Johnson & Scott, 2020; Patterson-Stevens et al., 2017; Shavers & Moore III, 2014), we offered a brief literature review to situate our personal experiences within the current research.

Black Women Doctoral Students

While doctoral study has inherent challenges such as critical examination of issues and theory, navigating socialization experiences, and executing scholarly research, Black women doctoral students across institutional types experience marginalization, institution-sanctioned violence, and silencing (Gildersleeve et al., 2011; Patterson-Stephens et al., 2017; Patton & Njoku, 2019). Moreover, Black women doctoral students experience challenging environments in their academic programs (Howard-Baptiste & Harris, 2014; Shavers & Moore III, 2014), and as a consequence, Black women create their own support networks to persist through the doctoral process.

Support Networks

While doctoral study has inherent challenges such as critical examination of issues and theory, navigating socialization experiences, and executing scholarly research, Black women doctoral students across institutional types experience marginalization, institution-sanctioned violence, and silencing (Gildersleeve et al., 2011; Patterson-Stephens et al., 2017; Patton & Njoku, 2019). For example, Johnson and Scott (2020) drew attention to the doctoral socialization experiences of Black women and found they often had to seek support externally, particularly post coursework. As a result of limited faculty–student interaction beyond coursework, Black women doctoral students must often create support networks to meet their own needs. These support networks, also referred to as fictive kin (Brooks & Allen, 2016; Cook & Williams, 2015), may include peers, faculty and staff members, romantic partners, and community members. These networks function as sources of empowerment, motivation, support, and accountability (Alexander & Bodenhorn, 2015; Apugo, 2017; Cook & Williams, 2015).

Peer Mentorship

Several studies highlight the significant role of support networks in the academic performance and self-efficacy of Black women doctoral students, while serving as sites of resistance (Dortch, 2016; Fountaine, 2012; Jones et al., 2015; Minnett et al., 2019). For example, Minnett et al.'s (2019) collective Black feminist autoethnographic study presents a peer mentoring framework that fosters a site of resistance from academic spaces that are unwelcoming of Black women's intellectual contributions and presence. The authors of this study identified as Black women doctoral students and desired to examine their cultivation and application of peer mentorship as a form of resistance in their navigation of the academy. Their peer mentoring framework features three central tenets: (a) radical coping, (b) communal sista scholarship, and (c) the cultivation of authentic self that ground the model in peer support. Findings from this study illustrate that bonds between Black women doctoral students can span beyond the academy and that peer mentorship "serves as an opportunity for us [Black women doctoral students] to define our inherent forms or resistance for ourselves" (Collins, 1986; Minnett et al., 2019, p. 226).

As an example of mentoring and socialization support at a broader level, Jones et al. (2015) provided examples by highlighting the Sister of The Ω–Academy's Signature (SOTA) Research Bootcamp ® as a space for engagement with Black women senior scholars to gain mentoring networks and socialization experiences that promote a deeper sense of research knowledge and connection to peers. Black women and the need to use networking models, peer mentorship, and collective scholarship led to the creation of the Sankofa Commencement Recognition Ceremony. This ceremony, created by the authors, provided space for Black doctoral graduates to be recognized in the presence of their full communities when universities were not holding in-person ceremonies or restricting the ceremonies because of COVID-19. To summarize, the presented literature situates the focus of our chapter on our individual experiences as doctoral students and how our friendship provides a site for collective support, scholarship, recognition, and resistance.

Theoretical Framework

As we situated the literature on Black women doctoral students' experiences with mentorship and peer support with our own lived experiences, we utilized a theoretical framework of BFR to examine our unique individual experiences with peer mentorship and support through our sisterhood. Cultivated from the foundational underpinnings of racial realism (Bell, 1992) and Black Feminist Thought (BFT; Collins, 2000), BFR (Green et al., 2016) was the theoretical approach employed by the authors for this chapter. BFR strives to convey the complete or real experience of Black women in the academy without the reproduction of the white gaze and can be situated as an addition to the BFT lineage. As a promising practice, we must (un)learn individual and systematic behaviors that cause harm to Black women as a collective in the academy. As such, BFR leverages an intersectional lens to address the whole experience of Black women that contextualizes the real outcomes of Black women's salient identities without having to choose between race, gender, or class. Three central tenets ground this framework:

(1) survival and sustainability of the eurocentric interests at the individual and institutional level will continue to dominate and replicate due to its critical mass; (2) a segregated knowledge not subjugated amongst stakeholders of the academy persists; all actors within the structure occupy the same space yet the production of knowledge has limits; and (3) there is no "exodus." The academy as

an institution was not designed with the knowledge production of Black women scholarship in mind. It replicates the demands of mainstream society as it was designed to do (Green et al., 2016, p. 296).

BFR provides a contextual lens through which we understand our individual and collective experiences. Drawing on these tenets, we created a list of questions such as *were there times that we felt the air being sucked out of us in higher education* and *how do our future career goals fit within the current academy*, that framed our critical storytelling session. Further, each author's vignette presents our experiences as scholars, faculty, and administrators and how we are influenced by the role of white supremacist patriarchy in our institutional spaces, and how we leverage our sisterhood as a conduit for rest, encouragement, and mentorship. These testimonials capture a snippet of critical instances of air deprivation.

Methodology

We employed critical storytelling (Barone, 1992; Lewis & Hildebrandt, 2019) as a framework to co-construct space to center our experiences in the academy. Because we have been silenced by white supremacist patriarchy in the academy, we disrupted the researcher–participant binary to tell our stories (San Pedro & Kinloch, 2017). We conducted one critical storytelling session that included guiding questions influenced by the BFR theoretical framework. Our storytelling session lasted 120 minutes via Zoom. The recording was transcribed and analyzed for thematic analysis. Additionally, we utilized reflective field notes from our biweekly check-in calls to continually make meaning of the interconnectedness and impact our interactions across higher education (Merriam & Tisdell, 2016). Using the novel characters from Waiting to Exhale, each author provided a vignette of her experiences in the academy of creating a soft-landing space for one another to exhale.

VIGNETTES—NARRATIVES OF BLACK WOMEN IN THE ACADEMY

Savannah—HBCU Graduate

How I Got Over

My academic journey was really hard, and I'm not sure I would've made it without my sister-scholars. Bernie and I grew up in the same city and attended the same college, Robin was introduced through our doctoral program, and Gloria was introduced through a mutual friend. It's no surprise that when we connected, we hit it off as a unit of budding researchers, administrators, and Black women. The sister-scholars are my sounding board, accountability partners, and constant encouragement throughout a journey that was anything but easy. One way they help me is encouragement that I am a scholar who is deserving of healthy work environments and success. This might mean saying my name in rooms I'm not always in or citing my research. In fact, the romanticized idea that some things should be easy left me feeling like perhaps I missed my ride on the easy train. While it didn't start or end with my tenure in a doctoral program or in my role as a researcher of women, the hurt has concentrated in these spaces. My expectation that Black and women's spaces were to affirm Black women left me in respiratory distress in both. The sister-scholars create space for me to share my despair while reminding me that hope always abounds. We typically have life updates about partnership, family, work, and more before jumping into any business. This has helped us to engage in our personal and professional lives meaningfully.

Co-opting

Over the years, I used the concept of intersectionality to describe many of the experiences of study participants, family, friends, aunties, and more. However, the more I found myself in "women's" spaces, the more I understood that white women seldom self-select to explore their racial identity and its implications. And even more so, white women were not interested in discussing mine. Many of the women refusing to examine their whiteness used the language of inter-sectionality when describing their womaness. This framework, established to give voice to the erasure of Black women in legal and racial discourse, was now being used to silence that very group. I've survived the violence of white women not exploring their own privilege, and it emphasizes what momma described as "waiting on the other shoe to fall." It's been my experience that at any moment a white woman can go from disrupter to instigator through the mobilization of tears. The tears tug at the pride of patriarchal white supremacy and give per-mission in some cases to incite violence. And I have one too many wounds from this example. Until white women see themselves in the capacity to induce gen-dered racial violence against Black women, this cycle will remain. It is my un-fortunate shared trauma that makes reflecting on this with my sister-scholars so necessary. We coach, mentor, and counsel one another in ways that only we can understand because we know what it's like to live and exist as outsiders-within a sometimes-ugly academy. Even the heaviness of statements like "Now you know how these folks are" made me feel like I wasn't alone. How freeing it is to be understood even without words and don't we all deserve that?

Tell Me Who I Have To Be To Get Some Reciprocity

I've been socialized to expect that racism will rear its ugly head in white space; however, sexism in Black space hurts differently. There's something to be said about expecting one trauma, while the other trauma cuts like the first time, every time. I had a utopian assumption of a world with egalitarian Black spaces—a reality far from my own personal experience of my childhood in the Baptist church and even my doctoral experience at an HBCU. My whole life, I saw Black women serve tirelessly in Black spaces and seldom be represented in leadership positions. For some, it was mere coincidence that four Black women college presidents were dismissed from their HBCUs in a two-month time span, notwithstanding that all women of color account for 5% of all college presidents (Gagliardi et al., 2016). Black women presidents I've studied mentioned ways they did the job before getting it and in many cases cleaning up their predecessor's mistakes. It reminds us that while men are hired for their potential, Black women are hired based on work they have already done—often in service to others. Why should that be our higher education story? Do Black women have to learn resilience through trauma? While I don't have the answers, I hope the narrative on Black women and strength unroots itself from trauma.

Bernadine—The Professor

As a mother, wife, full-time employee, and doctoral student, I struggled being all things to all people at all times. Yet, as a Black woman, it was all I saw growing up. Many days, I felt like I was drowning and could not catch my breath. Being in community with other Black women encouraged me to persist. Most often, attending academic conferences afforded me the opportunity to exhale. Not only did it provide space to be renewed and energized professionally but also personally. The conference space functions as a respirator to my soul, giving me everything I need to exhale. No pressure to be all things to everyone all the time. Though only a few days, those moments of exhaling with my girlfriends carry me through tough times that always seem to lie ahead for Black women. The sighs of relief made all of the preparation—the hair combing, meal prepping, scheduling—worth it. In the between times, virtual hangouts sustained me until the next time. Yet sometimes, it isn't enough.

As a doctoral student, I had few spaces to exhale in the academy. Now as an assistant professor, I aspire to create the spaces I needed as a student for Black women to breathe. I want to help my Black women students navigate the academy and thrive holistically because we retain each other. Thinking back to my first day as a faculty member, I frantically walked through the hallway to my classroom. I received a text message from my best friend that read, "Good luck with class tonight. Remember to take up space and don't shrink. Love you." Those would be the words I needed to hear to confidently command the room that night. When I saw two Black women students in my class, my fears began to dissipate. I remember the huge smiles on their faces and them whispering to each other, "OMG, I have never had a professor that looked like me here!" In subsequent conversations, I realized I had become a possibility model for them. They shared what it meant for me to be their professor; for me to wear my hair in its natural state and shirts with affirmations such as "Bet on Black Women" and "Black Girl Magic."

Need to Breathe

In my first year as a faculty member, there were many reasons to quit—unmet expectations, pandemic parenting, and unrelenting workload to name a few. Navigating the remote learning schedules of three children under ten years old while doing my best to support my students also struggling left me tired and weary most days. Much of my energy was expended supporting so many people that I often did not make time to catch my own breath. The absence of in-person conferences due to the pandemic canceled my annual trip to exhale with my girls, and I felt as if I was on life support. But in the moments I felt like giving up, the notion of retaining each other came more alive not only through my girls but also with my students. My Black women graduate students have been quick to look out for me and check on me. They challenge me to practice what I preach and prioritize my well-being in a myriad of ways. From scheduling self-care hours under the guise of meetings on my calendar to handwritten notes and the occasional text message, my students challenge me to find my joy. My graduate students and my girls remind me we retain each other through mentorship. Faculty-student and peer mentor relationships are important as we navigate white spaces. So, as I think of the Black women who came before me, who provided me space to breathe, I want to be that soft landing for Black women standing alongside me and coming after me to exhale, to breathe.

Gloria—4th-Year Doctoral Student

Reflecting on my own experiences, I've had several times where I've felt like I was gasping for air. When I am in community with my girlfriends during conference season, it always feels like refilling my oxygen tank, a respite free of pretense and pressure. The space we share is full of laughter, affirming words, and warm hugs as we attend sessions while going on adventures to find the cutest shops and restaurants. The experience is rejuvenating, affirming, and healing because when I return to campus, I have to put my armor back on to navigate living in a rural college town at a university where I have to be hyper-aware while wearing multiple masks such as the non-intimidating Black woman or the always cheerful and open to take on new labor. For me, community with my girlfriends in-person or digitally is vital to my persistence as a doctoral student.

All Skinfolks Ain't Kinfolks

During my doctoral journey, I encountered all of the traditional socialization experiences; however, one experience I never expected was to be harmed in the classroom by a Black male faculty member. As a Black woman in the zacademy, I desire support of Black faculty because I want to see them thrive. As such, I found myself gasping for air after this peculiar encounter. One day in a research methods course, we read a text that was an example for a particular methods approach and discussed racial equity in education. The class discussions around the book were productive until the decision was made to discuss race in education. The professor allowed the teaching assistant to give a lecture on how the text connected to popular culture. However, the class discussion included anti-Black rhetoric along with stereotyping that made the classroom environment feel uncomfortable. To address my concerns, I met with my professor during his office hours to discuss what happened and my feelings about the lecture. I expressed my disappointment and let it be known that the labor of teaching race is not the responsibility of Black students in the course to hold. He told me his plans of addressing the situation with the whole class the following week. However, there was never an attempt made to address the elephant that remained in the room. During this difficult time, I found myself constantly negotiating between advocating for a better experience, addressing the missteps of the situation, and/or just going with the flow. It felt like I was in a perpetual state of sacrifice and survival. What this situation revealed most to me is that I must manage my expectations of how I think Black faculty choose to show up in the classroom and who I don't want to be as a faculty member. As a means of support, my sister-scholars provided emotional support through various phone calls that gave me space to vent and to plan for how I would respond to my professor and finish the course. I know definitively that without their support, my navigation of this situation would not be successful.

Guiding Light

Talking through my emotions with my girlfriends as I navigated this experience and other personal experiences provided me with invaluable support and encouragement. Even as we navigated the COVID-19 pandemic and persistent racial injustice, my sisterhood community has strengthened through digital platforms when it was not safe to be in-person. Through this journey of doctoral study, my relationships with Black women have become the balm for my weariness. Our sisterhood provides space for both scholarship and public engagement through our establishment of the Sankofa virtual commencement recognition ceremony for Black doctoral graduates and our collaboration on book chapters and conference presentations as a means to engage and create scholarship that matters to us and is reflective of our experiences. My engagement in this space has been a vital lifeline for my persistence through this doctoral journey.

97

Robin—Doctoral Candidate

I have been gasping for air for what seems like every single day throughout my personal, professional, and academic life. Over the years, as a student and administrator within higher education, there has been this unspoken hustle I felt the need to embrace. As a Black woman in this space, I always felt the need to be *on* while subconsciously ignoring my pain and suffocation. For so long, it was ingrained in me that I had to *perform* in some capacity to be embraced and valued truly. In possessing this thought process, it has taken me years to genuinely discover the tangible beauty of my Black womanhood and the joys of being in community with other Black women within and outside of the academy, who only want the best for me. The deep-rooted internal work began as I started my doctoral program, and at the time, I honestly thought I was only going to be stretched academically. However, I quickly realized that *my* work had to start from within before I could accomplish what I had labored so hard for. By allowing vulnerability and interrogating racial and gendered roles that I shad grown accustomed to by simply spending time with other Black women on the same journey as me, I was able to restore the woman I always knew I was called to be.

Struck Down, But Not Destroyed

This journey has challenged me in many ways, from working multiple jobs to fund my education and survive in one of the most expensive cities in the country to unexpectedly losing loved ones who will not get to see me graduate. Although I have begun the dissertation process, some days feel like I do not have the fortitude to finish for those very reasons. During my doctoral experience as a Black woman, I have been disappointed and hurt, which developed this mundane cycle of focusing on what I lacked instead of all that I have gained along the way. It is easy to feel like you are navigating an experience alone with nowhere or anyone to turn to. *OH*, but Black women, the Black women who have found their way to occupy my heart and feed my spirit in ways I did not know I needed through intentional sisterhood and mentorship, have been there for every trial but also every victory.

Growing Pains

I started this Ph.D. exploit in my mid-twenties and was unaware that my entire life would experience a shift. Simply put, it was tough. Heck, it still is. However, I slowly realized that I was not alone and that I have a community cheering me on that also has no problem with challenging me and "snatching my edges." The biggest challenge I faced was feeling inadequate—**like an imposter.** My sisters constantly challenged me to see my worth and, more importantly, believe that

I belonged. Sometimes this would come in the form of a hug and happy hour, and other times, it would be a true come-to-Jesus moment that would often involve tough conversations that I did not always want to have but in retrospect needed. By being mentored and challenged in love by my village; my sister-friends who are brilliant Black women, I have been empowered to learn myself, as a doctoral student, educator, and, most importantly, as a Black woman with purpose. As I exhale, I take comfort in knowing my purpose is a form of resistance on this lasting and ever-evolving journey.

Homecoming

Alas, higher education is a microcosm of society at large, and as a Black woman, finding your breath is not only essential but radical. Coming together to share our stories and to make meaning of our experiences served as necessary research, mentorship, and space for healing. Themes of self-advocacy, belonging, and setting healthy boundaries emerged as we shared. Self-advocacy came in the form of defining ourselves for ourselves. Not allowing the narratives of patriarchal white supremacy to tell us who or how we are to be. Belonging emerged as a radical reminder for us to make space for ourselves and other Black women and people. This theme was particularly present in our creation of the Sankofa ceremony. Essentially, there was a need, and we as Black women rose to meet it, thus creating a unique for-us-by-us (FUBU) experience. Lastly, the theme of setting boundaries remains a prevalent survival technique as we navigate the evolving landscape of higher education. While the themes may indicate deficits, we are more committed to creating space for Black women to exhale in higher education. As our theoretical framework, BFR, illustrates, our nuanced experiences as Black women within the academy are often bounded by the concept of "survival" and white supremacist ideals. By intentionally choosing to come together with our distinctive memoirs and leveraging our sisterhood as a form of mentorship and support, we found space to reflect, breathe, and just be. Our stories resulted in the production of a six-part model that Black women doctoral students can replicate as conduit for self-care and retention.

1. Connection. Making meaningful connections with other Black women who are not in the same roles, institutions, academic programs, or research interests is important for creating a diversity of thought and scholarship. We did this by meeting up with other scholars in networking receptions, attending their conference sessions, and inviting them to be speakers in the Sankofa Recognition Ceremony. We also all sought out mentors in a few capacities including subject matter expertise in our interest areas, support, and personal value alignment.

2. Scholarship. Upon creating a group, it's essential for Black women scholars to engage in research together, thus creating writing groups wherein publications and presentations become the expected outcome. We knew early on that we wanted to establish ourselves as critical researchers and began to meet about common interests. We also keep each other informed of conference, writing, and employment opportunities.

3. Refresh. Using conferences as spaces for intellectual capacity building and spaces of personal refresh was essential to us maintaining throughout our various doctoral programs and career milestones. To do this, we shared rooms when our institutions didn't cover costs, spread coverage across sections capturing notes for each other, and introduced each other to faculty mentors to build networks at conferences.

4. Recognition. The Sankofa Black Doctoral recognition ceremony was created to fill a need but also to celebrate our own achievements when we were robbed of commencements and other village-wide celebrations due to COVID-19. Since the creation of this ceremony, we have been conscious to celebrate accomplishments beyond educational goals including holidays, new jobs, submitting first faculty role applications and more. Recognition is essential and the glue to making this model work. We learned to celebrate each other in a field that often feels thankless. In order to do this, we relied upon our national networks of graduates, current students, and Black faculty/staff scholars to serve roles such as keynote speaker, name reader, master or ceremony, and much more. This nation-wide engagement not only served Black student graduates but seeks to add to the service component of faculty dossiers. Additionally, this virtual ceremony created access to celebrate graduates that some families and communities otherwise may not have access to because of a tanking economy. Simply put, when we retain and support each other, the entire academy and community wins. As we enter into our third year of planning and brand building and as the pandemic evolves, we intend to continue celebrating the hard work and achievement of Black scholarship including a faculty spotlight. The pandemic was a catalyst but certainly not the only reason to sustain this FUBU ceremony.

5. Check-in. Beyond our capacities as scholars, our sisterhood requires regular check-ins mostly taking place via Zoom during the height of the COVID-19 pandemic. Other check-ins include texting, group facetime calls, and social media messages. We've realized through our collective experience, the power of a "hey sis, you good?" message.

6. Homework—not for us but assigned by us to the academy. We found affinity spaces to be critical in affirming us as Black women in the academy with the longing to exhale. Yet this labor should not rest solely on the

shoulders of Black women. Although as Black women, we are socialized to do what needs to be done, institutions' homework is to recognize the important work we are doing to recruit, retain, and support one another in the academy. The academy directly benefits from this work, and it is time this work is recognized beyond a pat on the back. One way we propose this work be rewarded is through the tenure and promotion process. Studies have shown Black women as disproportionately burdened by service, yet it does not factor in tenure and promotion decisions as much as research and teaching (Chang et al., 2013). This work matters, and it should count. Institutions should explore and strategize how they can create welcoming environments to support Black women throughout their doctoral education. This includes, but is not limited to, intentional funding opportunities, professional development, and early faculty training programs. Critical practice must include mixed-methods climate assessments and exit interviews to fully explore the lived experiences of Black women scholars. Further, we challenge departments and faculty to think critically and intentionally about how they retain and support Black women doctoral students. For recruitment without a plan for retention is destined to fail.

7. Consider the following critical questions/actions steps to better engage, recruit, and retain Black women:

   a. Ask Black women what we need without assumptions based on what other women report as needs.
   b. It's incumbent upon higher education to continue to ask, "How can we center the needs of Black women not in proximity to whiteness as a standard?"
   c. We ask that allies of Black women continue to engage in reflexivity and self-examination.

We look forward to the day when our shared experience of higher education can widely feature elements of belonging and inclusion—a place where Black women can freely affirm our own breath. Until that day comes, we'll be using our co-constructed model to be in community with Black women scholars (formal and informal). It is in that community that we find affirmation in being our authentic selves.

Statement on choosing NOT to capitalize "white": We the authors of this chapter chose to keep the "w" in white lower case: (1) to disassociate ourselves from the historical capitalization of "white" by white supremacists, (2) as an intentional disruption of solely centering whiteness in scholarship, and (3) to recognize that racial oppression doesn't impact the aforementioned racial group.

REFERENCES

Alexander, Q. R., & Bodenhorn, N. (2015). My rock: Black women attending graduate school at a southern predominantly white university. *Journal of College Counseling, 18*(3), 259–274.

Apugo, D. L. (2017). "We all we got": Considering peer relationships as multi-purpose sustainability outlets among millennial Black women graduate students attending majority white urban universities. *Urban Review, 49*(2), 347–367.

Barone, T. E. (1992). Beyond theory and method: A case of critical storytelling. *Theory Into Practice, 31*(2), 142–146. https://doi.org/10.1080/00405849209543535

Bell, D. (1992). Racial realism. Connecticut Law Review, *24*(2), 363-380.

Brooks, J. E., & Allen, K. R. (2016). The influence of fictive kin relationships and religiosity on the academic persistence of African American college students attending an hbcu. *Journal of Family Issues, 37*(6), 814–832.

Chang, A., Welton, A. D., Martinez, M. A., & Cortez, L. (2013). Becoming academicians: An ethnographic analysis of the figured worlds of racially under-represented female faculty. *Negro Educational Review, 64*(1–4), 97–118.

Collins, P. H. (1986). Learning from the outsider within: The sociological significance of Black feminist thought. *Social Problems, 33*(6), 14–32.

Cook, D. A., & Williams, T. (2015). Expanding intersectionality: Fictive kinship networks as supports for the educational aspirations of Black women. *The Western Journal of Black Studies, 39*(2), 157–166.

Dortch, D. (2016). The strength from within: A phenomenological study examining the academic self-efficacy of African American women in doctoral studies. *Journal of Negro Education, 85*(3), 350–364.

Fountaine, T. P. (2012). The impact of faculty—student interaction on black doctoral students attending historically black institutions. Journal of Negro Education, *81*(2), 136–147.

Gagliardi, J. S., Espinosa, L. L., Turk, J. M., & Taylor, M. (2017). *American College President Study 2016.* American Council on Education. https://www.aceacps.org

Gildersleeve, R. E., Croom, N. N., & Vasquez, P. L. (2011). "Am I going crazy?!": A critical race analysis of doctoral education. *Equity and Excellence in Education, 44*(1), 93–114.

Green, D., Pulley, T., Jackson, M., Martin, L. L., & Fasching-Varner, K. J. (2018). Mapping the margins and searching for higher ground: examining the marginalisation of Black female graduate students at pwis. *Gender and Education, 30*(3), 295–309. https://doi.org/10.1080/09540253.2016.1225009

hooks, b. (1981). *Ain't I a Woman: Black Women and Feminism.* South End Press.

hooks, b. (2014). *Ain't I a Woman: Black Women and Feminism* (2nd ed.). Routledge.

Howard-Baptiste, S. & Harris, J. C. (2014) Teaching then and now: Black female scholars and the mission to move beyond borders. *The Negro Educational Review, 65*(1–4), 5–22.

Hull, G. T., Hull, A. G., Bell-Scott, P., & Smith, B. (Eds.). (1982). *All the Women Are White, All the Blacks Are Men, But Some of Us Are Brave: Black Women's Studies*. Feminist Press.

Johnson, J. M., & Scott, S. (2020). Nuanced navigation: Narratives of the experiences of Black 'All but Dissertation' (ABD) women in the academy. *International Journal of Qualitative Studies in Education*. https://doi.org/10.1080/09518398.2020.1852485

Jones, T. B., Osborne-Lampkin, L., Patterson, S., & Davis, D. J. (2015). Creating a "safe and supportive environment:" Mentoring and professional development for recent Black women doctoral graduates. *International Journal of Doctoral Studies, 10*, 483–499.

Lewis, P. J., & Hildebrandt, K. (2019). Storytelling as qualitative research. In P. Atkinson, S. Delamont, A. Cernat, J. W. Sakshaug, & R. A. Williams (Eds.), *SAGE Research Methods Foundations*. https://www.doi.org/10.4135/9781526421036754858

McMillan, T. (1992). *Waiting to exhale*. Viking.

Merriam, S. B., & Tisdell, E. J. (2016). *Qualitative Research: A Guide to Design and Implementation* (4th ed.). Jossey-Bass.

Minnett, J., James-Galloway, A., & Owens, D. (2019). Help a sista out: Black women doctoral students' use of peer mentorship as an act of resistance. *Mid-Western Educational Researcher, 31*(2), 210–238.

National Center for Education Statistics. (2011). *Digest of Education Statistics: Doctor's Degrees Conferred by Degree-Granting Institutions, by Sex, Race/Ethnicity, and Field of Study: 2009–10*. https://nces.ed.gov/programs/digest/d11/tables/dt11_307.asp

National Center for Education Statistics. (2019). *Digest of Education Statistics: Doctor's Degrees Conferred to Females by Postsecondary Institutions, by Race/Ethnicity and Field of Study: 2016–17 and 2017–18*. https://nces.ed.gov/programs/digest/d19/tables/dt19_324.35.asp?current=yes

Patterson-Stephens, S. M., Lane, T. B., & Vital, L. M. (2017). Black doctoral women: Exploring barriers and facilitators of success in graduate education. *Higher Education Politics & Economics, 3*(1), 157–180.

Patton, L. D., & Njoku, N. R. (2019). Theorizing Black women's experiences with institution-sanctioned violence: A #Blacklivesmatter imperative toward Black liberation on campus. *International Journal of Qualitative Studies in Education, 32*(9), 1162–1182.

San Pedro, T., & Kinloch, V. (2017). Toward projects in humanization: Research on co-creating and sustaining dialogic relationships. *American Educational Research Journal, 54*(1), 373–394.

Shavers, M. C., & Moore III, J. L. (2014). Black female voices: Self-presentation strategies in doctoral programs at predominately white institutions. *Journal of College Student Development, 55*(4), 391–407. https://doi.org/10.1353/csd.2014.0040

Chapter 7

"If it mattered to them, it mattered to me"

How Friendship Shaped Three Black Women's Doctoral Experience during a Pandemic and Racial Injustice

A.C. Johnson, Erica T. Campbell and Kiara S. Summerville

As we, Black women doctoral students, were in the writing phase of our dissertations, we found ourselves in the middle of a global pandemic due to COVID-19 and racial unrest. The writing stage was already difficult, but because of the pandemic, we were no longer allowed on campus and had to stay at home. Writing a dissertation is an isolating experience, but the fear of the pandemic intensified our anxiety. Moreover, during the time when we were asked to stay home, the three of us, along with others in the Black community, witnessed how our lives continued to be disregarded and did not matter. Almost daily, we received the news that another one of our Black brothers and sisters was murdered, arrested, or brutally beaten. Some days, we were barely able to function due to the fear, tension, and anger coursing through each of us. We knew that we had to lean on one another in order to get through this incredibly difficult time and to finish writing our dissertations. Each day presented a new hurt and a new fear because as Black women, we were facing unique challenges that only we understood.

LITERATURE REVIEW

Although Black women's enrollment in higher education continues to grow, they face challenges that affect their experiences. They endure discrimination while

DOI: 10.4324/9781003394648-10

attending HWIs due to their race, gender, and other identities. Black women graduate students experience issues including battling stereotypes, microaggressions (Apugo, 2017), and not having diverse faculty mentors (Patton & Harper, 2003). These challenges are intensified due to isolation (Dortch, 2016), especially during the writing phase (Wilson & Cutri, 2019), coping with psychological stressors (Shavers & Moore, 2014a; Shavers & Moore, 2014b), and feelings of imposter syndrome (Gardner & Holley, 2011). Feeling imposter syndrome is harmful at any stage of the doctoral journey; however, it is especially damaging during the writing stage due to the ways that doctoral students are continuing to find their scholarly voices while writing and managing their studies independently.

To fight these challenges, Black women graduate students often turn to peer relationships to cope (Apugo, 2019; Dortch, 2016; Johnson, 2021). These peer relationships are even more vital when Black women find peers who are at the same stage as them in their doctoral journeys, particularly the dissertation-writing stage. Peer relationships provide a safe space to "ease tensions" within harsh environments (Apugo, 2019). For these women, due to "a lack of faculty of color and sufficient role models, the support of peers become an essential element in doctoral student persistence and success" (Dortch, 2016, p. 355). Peer relationships are multilayered and contribute to Black women's achievement.

Along with peer relationships, Black women graduate students have created ways of coping with "racial and gendered oppression" as well (Patterson-Stephens & Vital, 2017, p. 2). Black women protect themselves and their well-being through coping mechanisms that involve cultivating various "selves" by compartmentalizing their academic self, private self, and other parts of themself and roles (Shavers & Moore, 2014a). These coping mechanisms help Black women connect with one another by discussing and authenticating their experiences and by challenging racism to persist (Apugo, 2019). Coping mechanisms assist Black women in their doctoral journeys to persevere and to serve as positive ways to combat racism and sexism; however, these tools are also detrimental to their health (Shavers & Moore, 2014b). On one hand, the coping mechanisms help Black women successfully achieve their academic goals. On the other hand, this "duality" (hooks, 1981; Shavers & Moore, 2014a; 2014b) causes health issues due to compartmentalization, dualism, and not being able to be their authentic selves in historically white spaces.

Additionally, self-efficacy plays a role in the persistence of Black women doctoral students. Dortch (2016) discussed ways that Black women doctoral students' success derives from elements of Bandura's (1997) self-efficacy theory: how they "perceive setbacks," observe others' experiences, receive feedback, and deal with stress. Responses to their doctoral journey help shape and influence Black women doctoral students' resilience. Even though literature points to issues that Black women graduate students endure at HWIs, there is a growing amount of research that highlights the ways that these women continue to persist (Brown, 2019; Cropps, 2020; Dortch, 2016; Howell, 2014; Johnson, 2021;

Patterson-Stephens & Vital, 2017; Patton, 2009). Additionally, the global pandemic and social injustices occurring in the United States caused more stress for doctoral students (Brochu et al., 2021). Along with the uncertainties of the pandemic and the murders of Ahmaud Arbery, George Floyd, Breonna Taylor, Nina Pop, Tony Dade, and many others, writing a dissertation during this time created feelings of anger and frustration.

Through developing and nurturing one another in peer relationships, creating coping mechanisms, and believing in their own capabilities, Black women doctoral students continue to persevere. Even though they do persist, institutions need to create better resources and support systems for Black women. Black women doctoral students should not have to carry the responsibility of their success and retainment in these programs. In the following sections, we include a brief overview of Black feminist epistemology and an explanation of how we employed collaborative autoethnography (CAE). Then, we discuss the findings and provide implications for practice.

CONCEPTUAL FRAMEWORK

We turn to Black women's ways of knowing, or Black feminist epistemology, to frame this research study. Black feminist epistemology includes the voices of Black women researchers and scholars who have created lines of inquiry that center the unique experiences of Black women (Collins, 1990; hooks, 1981; King, 1988). Black women often have shared experiences at the intersections of race and gender, but they also express their Black womanhood in different ways based on various life experiences and identities (Collins, 1986). Seminal work on Black feminist epistemology considers how Black women see the world from the outside-in and the inside-out or as an "outsider-within" (Collins, 1986, p. S14). With Collins' (1986) theoretical position in mind, we understand our situatedness in academia as a privilege, though our livelihood is not yet fully recognized in academia. Additionally, we honor each of our individual and shared experiences as Black women who entered our program at different seasons of life, yet with the same goal to earn a doctoral degree and amplify Black women's voices. We were fortunate to not only develop a friendship, but we also found ourselves at the writing stage of our journeys at the same time.

METHODOLOGICAL APPROACH

We used CAE as the research method to understand our individual and collective thoughts on how our friendship mattered during the final stages of our doctoral studies. Autoethnography is a methodological approach that uses the researcher's personal experience as the primary data (Chang, 2016). Autoethnography is "highly personal" and "highly social," in that it involves the researcher(s) examining their interactions with others in specific contexts and how their lived experiences have been shaped by social forces (Chang, 2016).

As a methodological variation of autoethnography, CAE involves two or more researchers telling their personal stories and personal experiences (Chang, 2016). CAE was a productive methodological approach to situate our experiences as doctoral candidates who were navigating through the final stages of dissertation writing within a particular socio-cultural-political context [e.g., writing a dissertation during what was (un)known about COVID-19, "outsider-within" (Collins, 1986) status in the academy, and social unrest and injustice in relation to Black lives mattering in the United States].

The idea for this book chapter came through casual conversation with each other. Once we found a scholarly platform on which to tell our stories, we considered what CAE would look like for us. Given that we were almost-exclusively glued to our computers to be in community with each other during the time, we used digital platforms, such as Zoom and virtual writing spaces, for data collection. Together on Zoom, we identified a topic and decided to digitally journal our thoughts on general feelings about writing a dissertation during a global pandemic, the social unrest happening in light of the murder of George Floyd, and how our friendship with each other mattered in the midst of it all.

In a shared document, we each typed about how our friendship mattered to us during doctoral studies and, specifically, how we *kept* each other during the dissertation-writing process. We held two individual journaling sessions before we scheduled a time to have inter-dialogue between each other, written and verbal, about our collective thoughts toward our friendship in the current socio-cultural-political context of what was happening in our world. In the inter-dialogue, we read each other's individual narratives and used Black feminist epistemology as the lens through which we created patterns from those thoughts. Specifically, we considered individual and shared experiences within our narratives, in addition to how our race and gender shaped how we navigated the nationwide crisis happening around us as we wrote our dissertations. With the created patterns in mind, we identified themes and pulled quotes from the individual narratives to write the Findings section of this book chapter. We met over Zoom numerous times, too many to count, to brainstorm the structure of the study, write our narratives, discuss our narratives, and write this book chapter. Overall, the process of the CAE, from conceptualization of the study to completing our first draft of this book chapter, took us 13 months.

Our use of CAE was an act of resisting notions of isolation within the doctoral experience. Together, we completed the entirety of the research study and this book chapter in a digital space. We conceptualized this book chapter, documented our individual thoughts, discussed our collective thoughts, wrote this book chapter, and made edits to the book chapter while also being on a video platform with each other. During our individual journaling or editing time, we muted our voices and our videos, all the while still being available to each other for feedback and writing breaks, which typically happened every 25 minutes. For us, completing this book chapter together mirrored what was core to our friendship – knowing that we were in it together. Writing and editing together also held us accountable for doing the work. Using CAE as a method was a way to preserve our individuality through telling our personal stories, and its use also "create[d] a unique synergy and harmony" (Chang et al., 2012, p. 24) of our shared experience as researchers and Black women doctoral candidates.

BLACK WOMEN DISSERTATING IN 2020

We met as doctoral students in the same academic program. Through shared enrollment experiences in courses, we forged our relationship. Over time, we built a friendship that extended beyond our coursework. We initially bonded over being one of a few Black women doctoral students in our program, and we had similar research interests which were broadly situated on the experiences of Black women in academia. Though we shared being Black women doctoral students, we entered our doctoral program during different seasons in our lives. Although we were individuals with different life experiences, we found that our friendship was a necessity in the year 2020.

At the beginning of 2020, the three of us were in the "all but dissertation [ABD]" stage and preparing for the final leg of our doctoral journey. The COVID-19 pandemic swept into our lives and shaped how we conducted our research studies and defended our work. Notable milestones in doctoral studies sometimes felt all but celebratory because of the added stress of maintaining our own health and being careful toward the health of our loved ones. On top of adjusting to new ways of life due to the COVID-19 pandemic, in May 2020, we watched the murder of George Floyd take place and witnessed the demonstrations that happened afterward to defend and *plead* the preciousness of Black lives. As scholars and as people, the three of us needed each other more than we could have imagined. In the following section, we discuss how our friendship helped us to survive and maintain our academic progress.

WHERE WERE WE IN THIS PROCESS?

In order to provide context regarding each of the authors, we share our identities and other pertinent information to provide a glimpse of who we were when we wrote this chapter. Shaped by our various identities and life experiences before and during our doctoral journeys, we felt it is necessary to include this information.

A.C. Johnson

During the doctoral journey, I was a first-generation college graduate; mother of a college-aged child, who was living at home due to the pandemic; and caregiver of my mother. I was also a full-time doctoral student and worked for the university as a graduate research assistant. My family played a huge part in my perseverance, and my daughter was my biggest cheerleader. When we started writing this book chapter, I was in the middle of data collection and writing up my findings. Because my dissertation was about first-generation African-American women doctoral students, I felt guilty because I asked Black women to tell their stories while the world was on fire. Black people were feeling an array of emotions, but these women were so gracious to sit with me and talk about their experiences. Many of them were working from home because of COVID-19. Along with that, we were seeing the murders of so many of our Black sisters and brothers. It was a difficult time, and I felt like my stress of being a doctoral student was insignificant compared to what was happening.

Erica Campbell

My dissertation-writing process was characterized by being a cisgender, heterosexual Black woman who was a full-time Ph.D. student and Graduate Research Assistant. The pandemic's beginning made me glaringly aware of the lack of proximity to family as my parents were in the Midwest, and my siblings lived in other states and countries. Also, sandwiched between a recent knee injury, several family deaths, a Co-President role of a Black Graduate organization, church involvement, and dating, the pandemic brought many challenges, grief, and change to the forefront amid writing my dissertation proposal.

Kiara Summerville

When I started writing this book chapter, I worked full time as an administrator. I completed data collection and was writing my final chapters of my dissertation. I had expectations of when I wanted to finish, and COVID interfered with that. I tried to keep that deadline for sentimental reasons. I worked from home during this time, and I wrote every time I was not working. Work was demanding, but I balanced those obligations along with my personal ones (e.g., staying in touch with friends and family, activities outside of work, dating, etc.).

FINDINGS

There were three themes that we found important to highlight about being in community with each other as friends during the dissertation-writing process. In the following section, we discuss the challenges we faced while writing a dissertation, such as working through high expectations we set for ourselves. Then, we discuss how our friendship brought us joy and helped us navigate through the final stages of our doctoral journey. Finally, we discuss what it meant to write a dissertation studying Black women at the genesis of a global pandemic and in the face of racial injustice.

Dissertating through Personal Challenges

Each of us was concerned about completing the dissertation process given the national context, changes impacting higher education, and our personal struggles. The challenges included maintaining high expectations of ourselves amid a global pandemic, anxiety about how the COVID-19 pandemic would shape our completion of doctoral work, physical and mental exhaustion, and dealing with our emotions about the racial injustice that was happening in the United States. We all had the drive to finish our dissertations, but in different ways, we decided to pause, evaluate our timelines, and extend grace to ourselves and each other.

Kiara wrote about her self-made expectations to complete her dissertation, and how the stress of completing it began to take a toll on her physically:

> You could not tell me that I was not going to finish in the summer! I told A.C. and Erica my plan... they supported me and cheered for me. None of us really knew if we were "doing it right," and by it, I mean dissertating. Moving as I often do, which is expeditiously, I turned in my IRB, completed edits quickly, got approval, started and completed interviews for my dissertation study, and self-transcribed all ten of them in a month's time. I was in grind mode... I hit a wall, though. My body started talking to me. I had spent the last month isolated in my apartment trying my best to tune-out what was happening around me, put my head down, and finish. The isolation, though different at first, was productive for me in that I could not do much else but work from home with my full-time job and write... The high expectations I had set for myself, though, made me move at a speed so fast that I had not taken the time to listen to my body.

The uncertainty about dissertating in the "right" way was due to confusion about a research method, suggested by a committee member, which had a heavy emphasis on ethnographic interviewing. Kiara had trouble conceptualizing what ethnographic research would look like while physically isolating during a global pandemic. Ultimately, Kiara listened to her body and took a pause, which gave her time and clarity to work with her dissertation committee to consider alternate research methods for her study. A.C. and Erica listened and supported Kiara through her decision to slow down and re-imagine her research study.

As Kiara determined it was best to slow down and rest more, Erica decided that slowing down was also imperative to her process. Her concern was staying on track with her self-imposed deadline. She decided to work at her own pace and reminded herself that if A.C. and Kiara could write through everything happening in the world, so could she:

> Needing a serious break, sitting at home on a nationwide lockdown, and needing to grind on my proposal was not it…but it had to be done… My Sista PhDs were forging forward. I was a little overwhelmed with COVID shutting everything down but to be honest, I needed a break from campus… I realized that I needed to continue my process at my own pace… If they can do it, I can do it.

Erica used that time to rest by not writing for a few weeks, examined what she needed most, and then began the writing process again at a slower pace.

A.C., however, felt helplessness and anger through her process. Her challenge was to learn how to use those feelings and channel that energy into her dissertation:

> To write and talk with other Black women about the effects regarding… the isolation, microaggressions, racism and sexism within these institutions… was very painful… Because I wrote about Black women, I also found myself scared that I would not do their stories justice; however, Erica and Kiara encouraged me to keep going and to not let fear get in the way, so I kept writing through that fear.

The challenges of writing a dissertation in the middle of a global pandemic (i.e., physical exhaustion, writing in isolation, shattered personal deadlines due to changes in research methods), racial injustice, and civic discord (i.e., the murder of George Floyd and protests on police brutality) and trying to do justice to our research participants caused us to re-evaluate our expectations and our timelines. Each of us had different concerns. Kiara previously set a time that she wanted to complete her dissertation, but her body spoke to her, and she decided to change her expectations of herself. Erica's concerns centered around moving at her own pace and using A.C. and Kiara as motivation. Finally, A.C. was afraid that she would not do justice to the stories of other Black women. Even with these challenges, leaning on one another and reassuring each other before and during the global pandemic was vital for each of us to push through the challenges, especially during the writing stage.

Friendship

Even with the aforementioned challenges, our friendship retained us and was made stronger through our common interests, especially in researching and writing about Black women. We motivated one another to keep going. Kiara expressed how the consistency in our friendship helped her feel less isolated and provided her support:

> Though life was changing around me, what did not change was the relationship I built with A.C. and Erica...Prior to the Spring 2020 semester, A.C., Erica, and I spoke almost daily about school, family, dating...Our friendship helped to demystify stories of isolation during doctoral work. Because our friendship and support for one another extended beyond the classroom, it was natural to continue to lean on each other when the COVID-19 pandemic started to re-shape those things that we spoke about almost daily- school, family, dating...but, especially school.

Erica appreciated when we would check in with one another and how we cared about each other's well-being. Our conversations ranged from talking about the circumstances in which we had to write our dissertations and our experiences with romantic relationships:

> The conversations were as simple as "How are you doing this week?" or "How is the dissertation going?" Often, we would take a moment to allow space for venting and celebrating each step of the dissertation process and other areas of our lives. Questions such as "How are you weathering the quarantine period?" or "How's the dating process going?" were often. While being in the same PhD program and supporting each other through the dissertation process is what brought us together, we truly cared about each other's holistic life. In other words, finding a qualified partner was just as important as completing this degree. The historical context and societal tropes of dating as a single Black educated woman was a shared experience that only we could understand. We cared enough about each other to offer support and friendship through the ups and downs of dissertating, while discussing dating and other life challenges. If it mattered to them, it mattered to me.

Having regular check-ins and discussing all aspects of our PhD journey helped each of us persevere through the challenges. A.C. reflected on how she felt motivated by Erica and Kiara:

> I needed a safe space to talk through my frustrations but still push forward with my dissertation. Throughout this time, I leaned on Erica and Kiara... Along with assisting one another through this trying time, they helped me think through my study, and we would write together and motivate one another. If I felt frustrated, which I often did, they would either provide reassurance that we would get through this or validate my feelings. We would check in

with one another to make sure that we were okay mentally, physically, and spiritually. Along with checking in, we also used laughter to counteract the difficult times. We had a group chat and would send texts, memes, gifs, etc. about the job market, being Black in the academy, but most importantly, we sent messages that provided a much-needed laugh. Finding humor during this time was not always easy, but we all love to laugh. Having a sense of humor but also having a shared understanding about our experiences as Black women (e.g., our discourse with one another, not having to explain microaggressions, cultural references, etc.) made us come together even through the challenges.

Throughout our time together, even when discussing challenges, we always found joy through our friendship. We moved between being mentors for one another, being sounding boards for each other's dissertation study, and simply being friends. We supported one another by celebrating one another's accomplishments and by sharing helpful resources, especially resources that were not presented to us in our program (e.g., how to network and find other Black women students; organizations on campus made especially for Black women; tips on how to navigate the job market; etc.). We wanted to be sure we were all mentally, physically, and spiritually healthy; our friendship extended beyond our shared experience as PhD students. It was, and continued to be, our safe space, especially when it felt like the world was falling apart around us.

ALL HELL BROKE LOOSE

As we discussed previously, there were many factors that contributed to our challenges during the dissertation phase. In this section, we turn to how our friendship carried us through the hardships of the social unrest due to the murders of Black people and, again, the global pandemic that caused us to quarantine while writing a dissertation. It felt like all hell broke loose around us, yet we had each other to process what was happening. When our campus operations halted and we were told to go home, we did not understand how this would impact us. Kiara expressed, "At the beginning of shutdown and quarantine-period, life was changing, but in hindsight, I don't think it hit me that we were truly in such a pivotal moment in time."

Erica also felt the impact of the shutdown; however, she explained how the social injustices impacted her as well, particularly being a Black woman:

What does it look like when you have to balance the world on your shoulders and carry the world on your back, as Black women proverbially have been doing since the beginning of time? For me, it has been a journey. A certified triathlon. Taking each step, roadblock, obstacle, experience, as new chartered territory. In particular, the constant stress and challenge to resist controlling images such as the superwoman and mammy. But to do this during a global pandemic...also with a continued (re)surgence of police brutality influencing my Black brothers and sisters, how is one to think through a triathlon while carrying the world on my back?

Moreover, Erica felt that even with these events happening around her, she still had to stay on course. She also spoke about how our friendship provided some stability:

We supported each other despite the lack of support through areas such as socialization to the program, and consistent mentorship and guidance we received from the program. We saw each other as a pillar of strength, even in our weakness of trying to fight to remain strong during the dissertation process. Our dissertations were about Black lives. To continue to write during this season was difficult and draining. However, we did persist. We had to fight for Black lives through achieving the milestone of a Ph.D., through friendship, and checking in with each other weekly for accountability and conducting research that will shift the support and overall livelihood of Black women on college campuses.

In addition to what Erica described as "difficult and draining," A.C. also had strong emotions regarding her dissertation and the Black women who graciously agreed to talk with her. The process of recruiting and interviewing during these tough times heavily weighed on everyone:

To have to recruit other African American women during this time was hard because we were all feeling the pain of yet again, our Black lives not mattering. All the women who participated in my study were stressed and felt the brunt of the social injustices and the effects of the pandemic. We talked about how they were affected, and I checked on them after the interviews.

Having to write about Black women doctoral students during a time when we felt the pain of the murders of Black people in the United States was difficult; however, we understood one another in ways that no one else could.

Along with that pain, A.C. also expressed how she felt about the lack of response at their HWI:

In addition to the encouragement and support we provided one another, we were all outraged by the lack of response that we saw within our department and institution. At times, in the past, we saw statements coming from the department or institution about social injustices and how the institution would support the students; however, we did not receive any reassurance during this time. We wanted to know that we were seen, that people cared about our well-being and mental state. We spoke to one another about the marches and the injustices and how quiet many white peers and "allies" had become.

We vented to one another about our feelings regarding the responses to the murders of our Black brothers and sisters. The silence from our own institution was deafening. These events played a pivotal role in not only how we chose to re-spond to one another through weekly check-ins, sharing dissertation resources, writing sessions, and shared laughter and support but also how we viewed those around us too. Since it was clear that we did not have the support of the institu-tion, our friendship was what carried us through these trying times.

DISCUSSION

In this study, we chose to discuss the challenges of writing a dissertation during the COVID-19 pandemic and social unrest, and we highlighted how our friend-ship mattered to us during this time. Although we had each other, we considered how higher education professionals must improve the ways that they support Black women doctoral students. As we have seen by research, Black women graduate students thrive with peer mentorship (Apugo, 2019; Dortch, 2016; Patton, 2009). In these relationships, they receive the support and resources that they need to better succeed. This point was evident in our study, too.

The three of us expressed that the friendship and peer mentorship we pos-sessed was crucial for our success and well-being. Kiara appreciated the consis-tency of the friendship when it seemed there was a lack of consistency during the writing stage of the dissertation. Erica talked about how we checked in with one another and how we leaned on each other to share resources that were not readily available within our program. A.C. also shared this same gratitude and expressed how she was filled with emotions during this crucial time of the doc-toral journey. The relationship between the three of us demystified the isolation that we find prevalent for Black women graduate students, and this happened due to the friendship and peer mentorship that the literature suggests (Apugo, 2019; Dortch, 2016; Johnson, 2021; Patton, 2009).

In addition, we found that our findings were consistent with the Black women graduate students enduring psychological stressors as well (Shavers & Moore, 2014a; Shavers & Moore, 2014b). These showed up in various ways for each of the women, but all of them expressed that they put unrealistic pressure on them-selves. For Kiara, she wanted to complete her dissertation by a certain deadline but doing so began to cause her health to suffer. Erica also needed to reassess her "self-imposed deadline" and slow down to keep herself healthy. A.C.'s pressure derived from her desire to ensure that she did justice to the Black women's stories in her dissertation. In these ways, the literature about the psychological stressors was nuanced when compared to these Black women graduate students because there was more focus on unrealistic timelines and expectations; however, these women still experienced issues related to the oppression due to their race and gender (Patterson-Stephens & Vital, 2017). In the following section, we offer ways that higher education administrators, academic departments, and Black women doctoral students themselves can support Black women students.

HOMEWORK

Challenges are inevitable during the doctoral journey, but institutions need to improve how they support Black women graduate students by providing more mentoring opportunities through helping bridge the gap between Black women faculty and administrators and Black women graduate students (Patton, 2009). To add to this point, institutions need to hire and retain more Black women faculty and administrators in the first place (Patitu & Hinton, 2003), especially if certain programs yield high numbers of Black women graduate students. In doing so, Black women doctoral students may feel supported in their dissertation-writing process to persist in achieving their doctoral degree.

Academic departments at HWIs should have higher levels of support and resources that address Black women's unique experiences. Too often, Black women's experiences are not represented in curriculum, and Black women graduate students have to find ways to re-shape material to understand dominant theories and concepts through the lens of their own identities (Summerville et al., 2021). Within our study's findings, we found that because we did not see ourselves in the curriculum, we discussed and shared our own resources. We were fortunate that each of us had a desire to write about Black women's experiences at HWIs, so we shared resources such as articles, names of scholars who wrote about the same issues and worked with Black women, and even advice from Black women mentors. Because we shared these, and much more, with one another, it made our writing stronger. We leaned on one another, but not all Black women graduate students will be able to do so. Academic departments need to amplify the work of Black women researchers and scholars through course materials, lectures and seminars, and collaborative research and professional development opportunities.

To our fellow Black women doctoral students, current and future, we encourage you to develop friendships with other Black women graduate students at your institution; however, we recognize the complexity of this advice. The onus should not be yours to carry as institutions need to improve the ways that they connect you with people who look like you (Johnson, 2021). For these reasons, this is why mentorship is vital (Patton & Harper, 2003). We were fortunate to find one another during our coursework to provide peer mentorship, but this is not always possible; therefore, institutions should reach out to Black women students to (1) Ask them what do they need in order to be successful and to feel less isolated, (2) Listen to this feedback! And (3) Connect Black women graduate students with other Black women peer mentors, faculty, and/or staff by holding events especially for them.

CONCLUSION

As Black women doctoral students journeying through the final phases of our program, we felt it is necessary to share how our friendship sustained us through challenging times. In writing this chapter, we felt a sense of responsibility to contemplate our realities, not only as doctoral students but as Black women with nuanced familial relationships and responsibilities, work and employment obligations, health- and wellness-related experiences, all the while taking care of our souls. To us, the writing of this chapter was also a way to extend our hand to other Black women scholars who may or may not feel as if they have community in their doctoral program. We leaned on our friendship as we navigated the dissertation-writing phase, all the while dealing with the harsh realities of the COVID-19 pandemic and the racial injustice that continued to plague the nation to which we call home.

This book chapter is a vulnerable space for us. We know that we have colleagues, former professors, and administrators who may read this chapter and must sit with the aforementioned homework. We hope that our stories inspire action to better support Black women doctoral students, not only at historically white institutions but at all institutional types and all levels of college affiliation (i.e., undergraduate students, graduate students, staff members, faculty, and administrators). As researchers who commit to Black feminist ways of knowing, we use our Black womanhood as an entryway to equitable experiences for all oppressed identities. With that said, we hope that this chapter inspires action to better support doctoral students from any marginalized identity. This chapter, at its core, is an account of how the friendship between the three of us mattered in our doctoral studies and retained us in our graduate program.

When we started our doctoral studies, we did not anticipate that the final leg of our journey would be spent mostly virtual, having to write, study, and check-in with each other on a screen. We did not anticipate virtual final dissertation defenses. We did not anticipate that, due to social distancing guidelines, we would not be hooded by our doctoral advisor at graduation. We did not anticipate that the world as we knew it would change, that we would have to deal with the complexity of doctoral-level work and the uncertainty of what life looked like within and after a global pandemic. We did not anticipate having to question if our lives mattered to those who supported us as scholars and people. Administration eventually released a statement about how we mattered, but this happened only after they were told how Black people felt dismissed and neglected. It may not have been an afterthought, but it felt like it and only reinforced the feelings we already carried.

We also did not anticipate that our friendship would develop in a space that was not historically conditioned for us. We relied on each other to process the challenges of finishing a dissertation in a global pandemic, as well as feeling fatigued from racial injustice. We relied on each other to make it. We created space for us to be ourselves with each other, to retain each other from start to finish.

REFERENCES

Apugo, D. (2019). A hidden culture of coping: Insights on African American women's Existence in predominantly white institutions. *Multicultural Perspectives*, *21*(1), 53–62.

Apugo, D. L. (2017). "We All We Got": Considering peer relationships as multi-purpose sustainability outlets among millennial Black women graduate students attending majority white urban universities. *The Urban Review*, *49*(2), 347–367.

Bandura, A. (1997). *Self-Efficacy: The Exercise of Control*. Freeman.

Brochu, K. J., Bryant, T. R., Jensen, A. J., Desjardins, D. R., Robinson, R. M., & Bent, L. G. (2021). Redefining Roles: Female scholars' reflections and recommendations for coping during the COVID-19 Pandemic. *Impacting Education: Journal on Transforming Professional Practice*, *6*(2), 54–60.

Brown, L. (2019). "*I've been conditioned to navigate": First-Generation Black Doctoral Women and Their Persistence at a Predominantly White Institution* (Doctoral dissertation, University of Georgia).

Chang, H. (2016). Individual and collaborative autoethnography as method: A social scientist's perspective. In Jones, S.H., Adams, T.E., & Ellis, C. (Eds.), *Handbook of autoethnography* (pp. 107–122). Routledge.

Chang, H., Ngunjiri, F., & Hernandez, K. (2012). *Collaborative Autoethnography*. Left Coast Press.

Collins, P. H. (1990). *Black Feminist Thought: Knowledge, Consciousness, and the Politics of Empowerment* (1st ed.). Routledge.

Collins, P. H. (1986). Learning from the outsider within: The sociological significance of black feminist thought. *Social Problems, 33*(6), s14–s32.

Cropps, T. A. (2020). *Disappointed but not Surprised: A Critical Narrative Inquiry of Black Women's Doctoral Experiences in Agricultural and Life Science Disciplines* (Doctoral dissertation, Purdue University Graduate School).

Dortch, D. (2016). The strength from within: A phenomenological study examining the academic self-efficacy of African American women in doctoral studies. *The Journal of Negro Education*, *85*(3), 350–364.

Gardner, S. K., & Holley, K. A. (2011). "Those invisible barriers are real": The progression of first-generation students through doctoral education. *Equity & Excellence in Education*, *44*(1), 77–92.

hooks, b. (1981). *Aint I a Woman: Black Women and Feminism*. South End Press.

Howell, C. D. (2014). *Black Women Doctoral Students' Perceptions of Barriers and Facilitators of Persistence and Degree Completion in a Predominately White University* (Doctoral dissertation, The University of North Carolina at Charlotte).

Johnson, A. C. (2021). *"I deserve to be here more than anybody else": First-generation African American women doctoral students' experiences at Southern HWIs* (Doctoral dissertation, University of Alabama).

King, D. K. (1988). Multiple jeopardy, multiple consciousness: The context of a black feminist ideology. *Signs*, *14*(1), 42–72.

Patitu, C. L., & Hinton, K. G. (2003). The experiences of African American women faculty and administrators in higher education: Has anything changed?. *NewDirections for Student Services*, *2003*(104), 79–93.

Patterson-Stephens, S. M., & Vital, L. M. (2017). Black doctoral women: Exploring barriers and facilitators of success in graduate education. *Academic Perspectives in Higher Education*, *3*(1), 5.

Patton, L. D. (2009). My sister's keeper: A qualitative examination of significant mentoring relationships among African American women in graduate and professional schools. *Journal of Higher Education*, *80*(5), 510–537.

Patton, L. D., & Harper, S. R. (2003). Mentoring relationships among African American women in graduate and professional schools. *New Directions for Student Services*, *2003*(104), 67–78.

Shavers, M. C., & Moore III, J. L. (2014a). Black female voices: Self-presentation strategies in doctoral programs at predominately white institutions. *Journal of College Student Development*, *55*(4), 391–407.

Shavers, M. C., & Moore III, J. L. (2014b). The double-edged sword: Coping and resiliency strategies of African American women enrolled in doctoral programs at predominately white institutions. *Frontiers: A Journal of Women Studies*, *35*(3), 15–38.

Summerville, K. S., Campbell, E. T., Flantroy, K., Prowell, A. N., & Shelton, S. A. (2021). Finding ourselves as Black women in Eurocentric theory: Collaborative biography on learning and reshaping qualitative inquiry. *Qualitative Research Journal*, *21*(4), 456–468.

Wilson, S., & Cutri, J. (2019). Negating isolation and imposter syndrome through writing as product and as process: The impact of collegiate writing networks during a doctoral programme. In *Wellbeing in Doctoral Education* (pp. 59–76). Springer.

Section IV

Centering Healing in Peer Mentoring

The final section of this book examines the importance of healing to fortify Black women in peer mentoring relationships. The three chapters in this section illuminate the ways that Black women enhance their lives with deep reflective practices of spiritual uplift and communal collaboration and sharing. These chapters remind us that a foundation of well-being for Black women is a conscious decision and an act of resistance. It must be built intentionally by and for Black women. Navigating the academy for Black women is by its nature a decentering of joy and peace. Peer networks hold an important space for trust, healing, and bringing the fullness of Black womeness into the healing process. In this section, we learn that Black women's centered networks, and by extension Black women's lives, contain a tremendous amount of joy, intellectual power, strategic thinking, love, peace, spirit, and dignity. We endeavor to be fully present in each other's company. However, when we fall short, it is usually because *Black Life Making* in the United States, especially the academy, has required too much of our reserves, tenacity, and grace. This is when peer mentor networks are at their best – the knowing without saying, the being – without asking – the restoration of strength and peace. These chapters provide a glimpse of how the barriers, opportunities, and competing demands that Black women doctoral students balance in the academy are addressed in more deeply meaningful ways.

The opening dialogue in Chapter 8 conveys the apprehensions that many have for how Black women show up and occupy space in the academy. The *murmurings* in the hallways and office spaces on campus about Black women who are always talking about race, not afraid to push back and ask questions in the classroom, will be familiar to many. Chapter authors Alexis Morgan Young, Mary Johnson (MJ), Courtney A. Douglass, and Blake O'Neal Turner offer a critical look at how their peer network generated such *murmurings* as the sisterhood they created became a conscious act to use their peer network and power to become an embodiment of ethic of care, love, and mentoring to survive the threats of the academy. Their work is centered around several key questions (1) in what ways is attending to the specificity of Blackness as a sister cohort a political act, particularly at an HWI? (2) How is sisterhood enacted, inside and outside the academy, as a means of retaining each other? And (3) what kinds of academic and intellectual support did we develop through mentoring each other? Employing Black feminist thought (BFT) and Black critical theory (BlackCrit), they offer examples of the ways that they pushed back and asserted themselves in a context meant to "shrink" them. Using Sista Circle Methodology (SCM), they created a safe space to review and make meaning of their experiences as they gleaned insights from shared class notes, academic planning sessions, text messages, and other sources of data exchanged between them. A poetic and penetrating rhythm runs through this chapter as the authors draw upon the insights and lessons from community elders, artisans, and way makers to offer direction and light for wholeness and healing. Writing about the mind and active remembering, they note:

> In our sister-cohort, the heart is a pathway to the mind. Our intentional kinship provides space to remember ourselves as multidimensional beings reclaiming our gifts and relationship with the world. Alexis Pauline Gumbs--visionary poet and Black feminist scholar--reminds us there is comfort in knowing we are all in the process of remembering ancestral wisdom. Individually and collectively, we find ourselves constantly answering the question, how can embodying our sister cohort be an invitation into a deeper experience of our whole selves?

Young et al. center and protect themselves against a system that erodes the well-being of Black women by an introspective process of reflection. This work invites the reader to do the same in deeply meaningful ways that lead to a fullness of being as Black women in the academy.

Niah S. Grimes, Roshaunda L. Breeden, Jenay F. E. Willis, and Konadu Y. Gyamfi set forth in Chapter 9 a critical examination of living the "theory of mentoring and retention" desiring instead to center the importance of the spirit in their success. The chapter starts with a discussion of the irony of the juxtaposition of dealing with the rising deaths in society from COVID-19 and racial unrest all while needing to write this very chapter on how they are retaining each other. They observe:

> We have been writing about how we retain one another while in the thick of trying to retain each other. Our doctoral journeys have been riddled with daily grief and shock due to the multiple pandemics impacting our nation. We are experiencing what it means to live 'theoretical ideas of mentoring and retention' at the margins of doctoral education.

The "theoretical ideas of mentoring and retention" held little power for the authors to convey and capture the important lessons of their experience. Grimes et al. instead turn to Endarkened Feminist Epistemology (Dillard, 2006) as an epistemological lens that held integrity for them and resonated with their spirit and intellect. Rooted in history, memory, and healing, Endarkened Feminist Epistemology allowed the authors to ground their chapter in, "... spirit-led values rooted in community, honesty, love, and responsibility to ourselves, nature, and God." Utilizing the methodology of narrative inquiry, they were able to center their voices and stories to make meaning from their experiences and the extended community to offer recommendations to the academy. Throughout this chapter, there is a critical analysis of the features of the academy that stand in the way of Black women showing up as their full selves. By pushing back on the language and processes in the academy, they were able to position themselves in their fullness. Offering a compelling set of examples, they creatively capture the challenges and recommendations in a re-imagined conversation that is rooted in their own experiences and narratives. This artistic rendering adds power and impact that is distinctly unique.

Similarly, in the closing chapter, Sharon Fries-Britt and Bridget Turner Kelly come full circle in their efforts to center the importance of mentoring for Black women doctoral students in ways that affirm and value their well-being in the academy. While they acknowledge the importance of peers as an important network circle, the chapter title *There Is Only So Much That Peers Can Do* leads them into a discussion of the importance of having multiple levels of mentorship. They offer key observations about the underlying ways in which they too had to reframe, re-imagine, and re-assert themselves within the academy to find success. The chapter starts with a recap of the importance of building a multidirectional approach to mentoring followed by an examination of two key themes: (1) access to Black women faculty mentors and (2) increasing support for Black women doctoral students. Across these themes, they draw upon the lessons throughout this book offering examples of how these were affirmed across various chapters. Fries-Britt and Kelly also provide examples from their own institutional context of how they have employed some of the strategies in this book. Writing about their campus, they observe:

> The University of Maryland, College Park (UMD)...serves as a unique case to highlight because of the structural racial and gendered diversity within the faculty and students, but also the current climate of intentional efforts to work on issues of systemic oppression and racism.

REFERENCE

Dillard, C. B. (2006). *On Spiritual Strivings: Transforming an African American Woman's Academic Life*. State University of New York Press.

Chapter 8

Cultivating a Conscious Cohort

Sisterhood as a Site of Institutional Change

Alexis Morgan Young, Mary Johnson (MJ),
Courtney A. Douglass and Blake O'Neal Turner

INTRODUCTION

They called us difficult. We do not have full clarification of the origins of this comment, just murmurings in shared office spaces, hallways, and a "friend" who will not reveal their source. "*They* said y'all are always taking up class time talking about Blackness", "*They* said y'all challenge professors", and a knowing "Yeah, we've heard about your cohort" – are some of the phrases we have heard from student peers and faculty attempting to make sense of the ways we navigate the academy. We, a sister-cohort of four Black cis-gendered Black women, are knowledge makers and world shakers both within and outside the confines of the academy – that is not up for debate. Where there is room for conversation, however, is what this means for how we are perceived and the subsequent treatment, both positive and negative, we receive as a result. As such, we have intentionally created an ecosystem to sustain us and provide mentorship as we navigate the epistemic violence of higher education.

In this chapter, we use an iterative storytelling process, guided by a framework uncovered from data collected in sista circles (Johnson, 2015), to discuss how our sisterhood contributes to social change. We elucidate how our sister-cohort is a living being requiring a politics of care, love, and mentoring to survive. This chapter asks, (1) In what ways is attending to the specificity of Blackness as a sister-cohort a political act, particularly at an HWI? (2) How is sisterhood enacted, inside and outside the academy, as a means of retaining each other? and (3) What kinds of academic and intellectual support did we develop through mentoring

DOI: 10.4324/9781003394648-12

each other? We analyze how the deployment of explicit and collective strategies used to navigate our doctoral program makes our existence as a sister-cohort a political act. In this context, a political act refers to an action, intentional or not, resulting in social change (Hanchard, 2010; Pitsoe & Mahlangu, 2014). We illuminate the ways that "sisterhood is still powerful" (hooks, 2000, p. 13) as we boldly assert the "unapologetic acknowledgment of our right to be in these spaces" (Cook & Williams, 2015, p. 165).

METHODOLOGY

In order to gather the experiences we used to tell the story of building, sustaining, and enacting our cohort as a political act, we employed Sista Circle Methodology (SCM) (Johnson, 2015). SCM is both a qualitative research methodology and a system of support that specifically attends to the lived experiences and social relationships of Black women and femmes. Wilson (2018) underscored the relationship between SCM and Black feminist thought (BFT) and argued that SCM "provide[s] a safe space for Black women's consciousness to be nurtured and fosters a collective self-defined standpoint" (Collins, 2002, p. 36). In our sista circles, we made sense of our collective recallings, shared class notes, academic planning session notes, agendas, and transcripts from text message threads as our data sources. We used an iterative storytelling process guided by themes uncovered during sista circles (Johnson, 2015), in which each person added to the story to make a living narrative about the ways in which our sisterhood functions as a political act. While the academy places value on the author's position in a citation, we want to be very clear that this work is a collective endeavor where each of our voices begins where the other ends. This work, like our sister-cohort, is an amalgamation of our individual voices.

CONCEPTUAL APPROACH
Black Feminism and Black Critical Theory

We lean on the theoretical offerings of BFT (Collins, 2002) and Black critical theory (BlackCrit) (Dumas & ross, 2016) to illustrate the ways that our sister-cohort has audaciously stepped out of the margins and asserted ourselves into contexts meant to shrink us. Taken together, they provide a critical analysis of the peculiar nature of being Black women doctoral students at an HWI. While both theories address concerns of Black folks facing the dominance of white supremacist systems, they depart from each other in their principal framings. BFT contends with the nature, and collective knowledge, of Black women and femmes living under racism, patriarchy, and misogynoir. BlackCrit provides a lens to analyze the specificity of anti-Blackness along with the disgust and disdain for the Black (Dumas & ross, 2016). These lenses ground our assumptions that

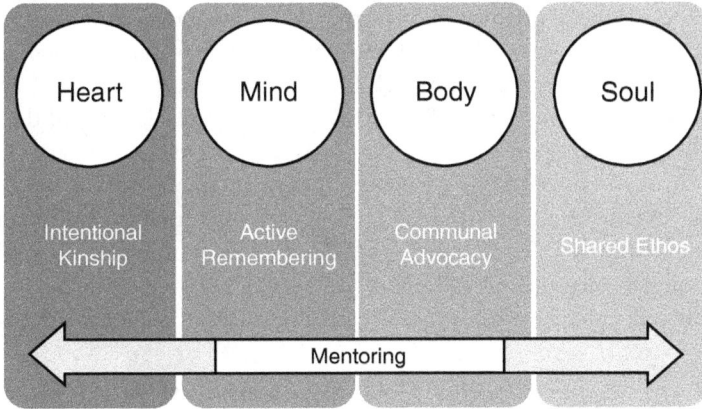

Figure 8.1 Cultivating a conscious cohort

we will continue to experience gendered, anti-Black violence in and outside the confines of institutions. In tandem, these frameworks help us to elucidate the phenomenon of being Black women in a doctoral program studying Blackness with a love-centered orientation and how the fictive kinship (Cook & Williams, 2015) of our sister-cohort sustains these endeavors (Figure 8.1).

CONCEPTUAL FRAMEWORK: CULTIVATING A CONSCIOUS COHORT

Our sister-cohort is a noun; a living, evolving being that requires nurturing, care, and resources to see it, and each other, as a whole. Conceived with intentionality and born out of the womb of resistance, this living manifestation of our commitment to warding one another must have its basic needs met to continue sustaining its purpose. To exist, we must tend to all of its components: its heart must be loved, its mind must be stimulated, its body must be nourished, and its soul must be affirmed. The absence of one of its vital organs, or its essence, would result in a failure to thrive – thus, ceasing the collective force that maintains our ability to exist amid our political struggles. Next, we describe how each of these pieces works in tandem to cultivate the conscious cohort that is our sisterhood.

THEMES/LITERATURE REVIEW

The Heart (Intentional Kinship): Sisterhood Is Still Maternal

The heart is the aspect of our sisterhood that envelopes our praxis of loving, caring, mentoring, nurturing, and healing. To attempt survival in a space where we do not belong, are not truly welcomed, and are subjected to violence, we

127

must be consistently filled with and covered by the maternal affection given to us by Black women faculty, women scholars of color, and by one another. The power and strength of a mother's love are sustaining, fortifying, and life-giving, even in places of pain, suffering, and death. As Black women, this motherwork is personal, political, and our resistance to anti-Blackness (Collins, 1994). Through our care, we recognize that our maternal orientation "is the antithesis [of anti-Blackness] because of its inherent function in proliferating and preserving Black life" (Smith, 2016, p. 32). By reflecting upon our sisterhood (and its implicit mentorship) through a lens of stages of pregnancy and birth, we illuminate and capture essential features of the stages of our evolving bond and maternal heart.

Intentional kinship is the act of choosing a familial bond whether or not blood ties exist. This choice of creating a family is heart led and is also reflective of maternal care. Much like a mother, or othermother (Edwards, 2000), who makes intentional choices for herself and her children, our cohort has developed through intentional decisions. Our sisterhood was formed naturally (but on purpose) through various stages of our journey, mirroring those found in pregnancy and birth. Although all mothering is not aspirational to all women and femmes, this metaphor is especially salient to our particular collective due to Alexis' positionality as a mother to two daughters and the commitment Courtney shows to mothers and Black families as a doula.

In the stage of *Preconception* (Klaus et al., 1993), we did not recognize ourselves as a sister-cohort. Though we made intentional choices to talk to each other, find each other in a room of strangers, or sit together in class, we were not yet bonded by our collective experiences or our desire to be "rah rah". Though it's difficult to identify a specific date of *Conception* (Klaus et al., 1993), there were moments and incidents of pain that were the catalysts for being more intentional in our time together. Reckoning with intellectual brutality, we began sharing our struggles, our lives outside of grad school, our scholarship, and what we needed beyond making it through our most violent course.

As our sister-cohort reached the stage of *Gestation* (Klaus et al., 1993), we found ways to ensure our circle remained healthy and viable. We engaged in individual and collective acts of nurture, care, vulnerability, learning, and growing into ourselves and each other. These acts looked like buying MJ houseplants when she was having a tough time, watching a movie together at Blake's house, being mindful of Alexis' commitments to her family, and taking turns offering to drive Courtney across campus to her car after an exhausting class. We also became more comfortable asking deeper questions, sharpening each other's thinking, and internally recognizing ourselves as a unit even as we spent more time nurturing our individual relationships. We became more honest with ourselves and one another about why we were in the academy and if we would remain despite the violence. During this stage, any time we spent on campus was with at least one member of our collective. As we were growing our relationship, we were protective of the space, time, and access that we allowed other people to have. These small acts of nurturing our friendships became the foundation for birthing our sisterhood.

The *Birth* (Klaus et al., 1993) phase was where we recognized that being a unit was no longer just something we saw within our group. In our gestation phase, we had, in fact, begun "showing" as a unit to others. This realization led to birth in the sense that we were now both privately and publicly a sister-cohort. Our critical vocabularies, actions, decisions, and scholarship took on a collective language and process. Much like physical birth, our journey to that moment was wrought with aspects of pain, joy, and even healing. Like women in labor, we relied on our intuition and trusted our "body" to do exactly what was needed at the moment, whether in class, with a professor, or when centering Blackness in white spaces. We learned that we could carry both isolation and community in juxtaposition because we had a space to call our own.

We are currently in the *Mothering* (Klaus et al., 1993) stage of our sister-cohort. Similar to the work of birth and postpartum doulas who bear witness, hold space, and emotionally support women by mothering the mother (Klaus et al., 1993), our sister-cohort engages in acts of caretaking and mentoring by mothering ourselves, each other, our work, and others. At this stage, we no longer have all our classes together, we hardly see each other in person (in large part due to a global pandemic), and we have various responsibilities and relationships that require more of our attention, but our bond is unyielding. Through our instincts, we know when something is not right, when someone is not saying their whole truth, when sticking to an agenda is not what is needed, or when someone is trying to push through something that has nothing to do with academics. Through our intentionality, we carefully prioritize our time together, doing work just as much as we do mothering. We take hikes, celebrate birthdays, practice wine down Wednesdays, and connect over trash tv with the same energy we give writing feedback, go to each other's presentations, check on Alexis' girls, and support each other's scholarship privately and publicly. Like entry into motherhood, this protective, resourceful, resilient, truth-telling, loving sisterhood has given us space to see the world with new perspectives.

The Mind (Active Remembering): Sisterhood Is Still Calling You In

In our sister-cohort, the heart is a pathway to the mind. Our intentional kinship provides space to remember ourselves as multidimensional beings reclaiming our gifts and relationship with the world. Alexis Pauline Gumbs – visionary poet and Black feminist scholar – reminds us there is comfort in knowing we are all in the process of remembering ancestral wisdom. Individually and collectively, we

129

find ourselves constantly answering the question, "how can embodying our sister cohort be an invitation into a deeper experience of our whole selves?" In the *Finding Our Way* podcast hosted by Prentis Hemphill (2020), Gumbs expressed that it is important to listen to the wisdom of what was, what is, and what is possible for freedom. As a sister-cohort, we have used this time post coursework to be still and witness the wisdom of our ancestral lineage, loved ones, friends, and our own essence. We find wisdom, and channel our remembering, in spiritual altars, Zoom heart-check-ins, old journals, books, family getaways, or total isolation immersed in Earth. Like many in the world, we are unsure what is next on our (professional, political, spiritual) journey. Still, it is affirming to know that as a sister-cohort, we can trust each other to be compasses, illuminating a path toward being more free. Gumbs (2021) shared, "…it feels really powerful to be trusted as a compass… I am hoping to be this landing place of ancestral light so it can guide us". When you see Alexis know she embodies ancestral light. When you catch glimpses of Blake, watch how she sparkles. When Courtney walks in the room know that the floor is glowing. When MJ is present, her essence is radiant. As Black women, remembering ourselves as trustworthy co-creators of this world is an invitation to be limitless and courageous researchers, mothers, relationships builders, and sisters.

To be clear, freedom starts in the mind first. We have spent the last four years unlearning and remembering our relationship with Blackness. Now is the time to nourish our minds and fill them with the love and compassion we deserve. Yet, Toni Morrison unveiled in *Beloved,* "freeing yourself is one thing; claiming ownership of that freed self was another" (p. 95). As we continue through our doctoral program, we are learning new ways to claim ownership of our freed selves. Although this requires deep introspection, we still lean on our sisters during this process. During our sista circles, we reflected on our personal statements and how our research has transformed socially and politically. For example, Blake's research has transformed from how mathematics education is an instantiation of a white institutional space (Martin, 2013) to how mathematics education researchers can support and create Black liberatory mathematics. The catalyst for this shift was her evoking the wisdom of other Black critical mathematics scholars and Black mathematicians through time and space. Together, our scholarship is a direct response to remembering how our ancestors, loved ones, and all Black life could and should live freely. Furthermore, MJ ensured that we held semesterly wrap-ups for our sister-cohort. She spent time reflecting on where we had been and where we wanted to go next. During the year three sista wrap-up, we documented the wisdom we learned through an audio recording to share with our past, present, and future selves as well as other graduate students in our program.

We acknowledge that individually, and collectively, we came into this kinship as fragmented beings remembering ourselves whole. Now we look toward ways to not defend the intentionality of our connection but instead be active with the wisdom we have available. We each are Black storytellers who provide an important perspective on what it means to be multidimensional beings that support each other's intellectual and educational pursuits. That is how we move toward communal advocacy.

THE BODY (COMMUNAL ADVOCACY): SISTERHOOD IS STILL SACRED

The ecosystem of our sister-cohort is organized, sustained, and emboldened by our love for each other and the dreams we have about liberation. Our sister-cohort allows us to be fully human in a world that denies our humanity. In our sister-cohort, we find a space to hope, laugh, love, and experience joy. In our sister-cohort, we learn to strategize against a common enemy, find ways to engage in creative insubordination, and plan for a life on the other side of anti-Blackness. Because of our sister-cohort, we can lay down our "academic masks" (Shavers & Moore, 2014) and engage in the "real work" of dismantling the world. In our sister-cohort, we allow ourselves to be vulnerable and transparent so that we can find ways to protect each other based on our needs as individuals and as a collective. In sum, our sister-cohort is the place where "all that truly matter[s] in life [takes] place – the warmth and comfort of shelter, the feeding of our bodies, the nurturing of our souls. There we learned dignity, integrity of being; there we learned to have faith" (hooks, 1990, p. 41). Our sister-cohort is a hallowed site of refuge.

Our sister-cohort is a sacred space where we mentor each other to be the best versions of ourselves. We regularly send each other job postings, fellowship announcements, and journal calls. We actively support each other by providing feedback on ideas, writing, or research projects, even when we apply for the same opportunities. We celebrate each other's successes, and we push each other to step out of our individual comfort zones academically, professionally, and personally. The deep, fierce love we feel for our sister-cohort allows us to simultaneously experience physical and spiritual connections to one another that transcend beyond the confines of the academy. Each of us profoundly loves Black folks, and it is this quest to not only advocate for ourselves, but for the communities we love, that binds the body of our collective. As Black women, we have been validated and loved in our sister-cohort, which has helped us step into our power. Being in a sister-cohort has been a constant reminder of the magic that Black women possess and that our purpose transcends our individual-level actions.

Our sister-cohort functions as a particular kind of homeplace (hooks, 2000) where we make plans for navigating academia and our relationships with each other. We did not form, and we do not maintain our sister-cohort haphazardly;

instead, we developed the mind of our cohort by establishing rules of engage-ment. For example, we do not disagree with each other publicly and show up as a collective front. Instead, we reserve tough conversations for private. However, in public, we maintain the body of this supportive ecosystem by advocating for the needs of the cohort. This looks like amplifying the scholarship of one another, sharing resources, and positioning each other as the experts in our respective scholarship.

The body of our ecosystem protects us in tangible and psychic ways. In our work describing how our cohort supports each other in the academy as a direct response to anti-Blackness, we detail how, "in our Black bodies, we deliberately move as a unit. We sit together. We run together. We decide together. We ad-vance together. We invoke one another when one or more of us is not present" (Turner et al., forthcoming). We intentionally position ourselves as a unit, both when we are together and when one or more of us is absent. As a consequence, when you see one of us, you see all of us. We are keenly aware that each of us represents our sister-cohort. Each of us has been in classes, meetings, or conver-sations where someone has made references to our cohort: "How is *your* cohort doing?", "This reminds me of the point that *your* cohort brought up in our last class", and "Is *your* cohort going to participate?" Early in our program, we pre-pared for this in study sessions by curating a list of talking points for our cohort. As we progressed, our increasing grasp of theory helped to facilitate our abilities to affirm, amplify, and/or defend an absent sister. In many ways, each of us be-ing one part of a body, signals to others that we are a force. Our sister-cohort, a homeplace which in itself is a site of mentorship (Calafell, 2007), helps us to understand "intellectually and intuitively the meaning of homeplace as a site of resistance" (hooks, 1990, p. 45). Recognizing our power as a site of resistance emboldens us to demand that others see us the way that we see ourselves – as fugitives, as difficult women, as human, as a sister-cohort.

THE SOUL (SHARED ETHOS): SISTERHOOD IS STILL POLITICAL

In our sister-cohort, we practice mentorship by encouraging, challenging, and supporting each other to be critical scholars that unabashedly center Blackness. An unwavering commitment and love for Black folks is at the crux of our polit-ical and social engagement with the academy. Our soul is the immortal piece of our sister-cohort that binds us. We are keenly aware that to be in community with each other, the spirit of loving Black people must be fed first. One of the most contentious parts of doing this work is that we do it in an institution depen-dent on our subjugation (Dancy & Edwards, 2020). We are acutely aware that while Black folks are being murdered by arms of the state, we are simultaneously worried about the sentence structure. Thus, it is paramount that we make our commitments to the work and to our sisterhood abundantly clear. We walk into class not only as a daily routine but also as a political act. We dare to be bold in our quest for Black liberation and disruption of whiteness in spaces we occupy – spaces that were not made for us. Our shared ethos has influenced the way we have engaged with the academy. For instance, when we discovered that a class that looked good on paper did not meet our needs in practice, we collectively dropped it. This action prompted the instructor to contact us, provide us with research aligned to our research agendas, and follow up with us a year later to ask us to take a different course under her tutelage. We declined. We did not make any special announcements, cause a disruption, or debate the content of the class – we left quietly. However, our departure certainly made noise.

We made an ontological and epistemological stance concerning the ways that we individually and collectively navigate the academy and make conscious decisions concerning refusal *in* and refusal *of* oppressive systems and meritocracy (Martin, 2019). These stances are sometimes in direct contention with the institutional norms to which we are expected to assimilate. To be clear, moving with a collective stance comes with internal challenges. Although we are one body in the sense of our sister-cohort, we are four separate individuals with varying commitments inside and outside of academic spaces. The soul of our unit has been challenged when putting theory into practice. One striking example of this was a missed opportunity for collective refusal that we have been grappling with since our first semester. In a space that was particularly anti-Black, as exemplified by the instructors disregarding theories centering Blackness as "non-rigorous" and allowing racially violent sentiments to be expressed in class, we had the chance to make a collective statement. However, at the time we were not all principled enough, or brave enough, in our politics to potentially lose the sponsorship of the people in power in that space – power we all know now means nothing in the fight for Black liberation. Power we have since rebelled against in such a way that that particular space has been radically transformed by a change of the instructional team, an overhauling of the curriculum, and the inclusion of books and articles that we suggested.

Wanton anti-Blackness is validated by white institutional norms in the academy and society writ large. As such, there is no defined place for an uncompromising love of Black children and adults. There is no systemic place for an academic devotion to our people, yet we are still here, studying, theorizing with our communities, and still seeking refuge in theory. Still here taking up space and altering the rules of engagement where we see fit. Together, we are still here, studying with and for Black people in an institution that contributes to our ontological and social death. There is no grammar for Blackness in the academy; however, Collins (2002) prepared us for this when she offered the sentiment that "loving Black people ... in a society that is so dependent on hating Blackness constitutes a highly rebellious act" (p. 250).

IMPLICATIONS

We took it upon ourselves to establish fugitive educational spaces (ross, 2020) where we learned to edify and challenge one another absent of the white gaze. There should be mechanisms in place for more easily fostering spaces to help Black women transition into and through the academy. We were fortunate to come in as a group of four; however, we know that there are times where Black women enter the academy without a "built in" support system. As such, it is imperative that institutions do a more robust job of facilitating and bolstering cohorts for Black women. It is not enough to admit Black women into the academy, the culture of these institutions has to directly respond to the phenomenon of being a Black woman academic. As such, we recommend these specific ways that institutions can aid in developing conscious cohorts among Black women and specific strategies graduates can deploy to cultivate a cohort independently if no support is offered.

We recognize that some institutions do not currently have established programming to recruit, retain, and matriculate Black women graduate students. However, higher education institutions could and should work with Black women graduate students to develop programming that centers their needs. Institutions of higher education are white institutional spaces and as such are often committed to maintaining white supremacist ideologies and policies dependent on anti-Blackness (Dancy & Edwards, 2020). Thus, in the absence of institutional support, Black women graduate students can develop the body on their own, as our cohort did. This programming can look like a listserv exclusively for Black women at a particular institution, affinity groups, and paid-mentorship structures. For our sister-cohort, these supports in practice looked like a Black woman graduate student providing us mentoring. Our cohort also engaged in sharing fellowship or journal calls, providing support for each other even when we were applying for the same opportunities. We made deliberate efforts to co-author together. These spaces, both physical and intellectual, must be structured in ways that encourage advocacy and decenter the temptations caused by the myth of meritocracy.

However, in the absence of formal support from institutions, cohorts of Black women can still join together to form and maintain a shared ethos which can be accomplished through mentorship. Our program is led by a brilliant Black woman that has provided boundless support. It is not uncommon for her to take us in a room, close the door, and let us just be and learn together. The institution has limited investment in creating this type of intentional kinship among Black women. While programs can be intentional about ensuring cohort models are utilized for admittance, they cannot foster deeper relationships needed to sustain Black women through the process. As such, it would bode Black women well to intentionally seek these sisterhoods and maternal relationships within the academy, even if they are across departments or institutions. The hallmark of our political identity was developed through peer mentorship. MJ entered the program with a strong theoretical grounding and poured into us as some of us were still developing our own. We were intentional about learning nuances of theories provided to us and then decided what felt most salient to us individuals. Although some of the tenets of the theories we engage with are in tension with each other, the urgency of improving conditions for Black people is a shared commitment through the work and authors we cite. For other groups of Black women, the shared spirit of the collective may be grounded in another topic or concern; however, mutual respect and love across the work is essential for developing a soul that is the life force of the collective body. It is in this pursuit of thinking together, separately, that "we have the good fortune to know every day our lives that sisterhood is concretely possible, that sisterhood is still powerful" (hooks, 2000, p. 18).

HOMEWORK

To develop the heart, it is imperative that institutions of higher education foster a welcoming, nurturing, and respectful environment for Black women students and faculty. It is imperative that institutions recognize the labor of Black women faculty who support Black women graduate students. Our faculty were our guides into birthing our sisterhood. They were our doulas who mentored us, allowed us to mentor each other, and taught us to mentor other Black women entering the academy. Institutions of higher education need to regularly audit the amounts of unpaid labor provided by Black women and other women of color who take up the task of aiding in retaining and sustaining graduate students of color and provide compensation for that work.

To develop the mind, it is vital that institutions of higher education provide space for group inquiry beyond the classroom. Black women faculty deserve compensation for developing Black educational fugitive spaces (ross, 2020). Additionally, higher education institutions need to elicit the expertise of Black women graduate students and faculty to share how they engage in creative insubordination. As a reminder, this work should be compensated. Just as we reflected on the ways that our scholarship and praxis centered Black life and Black freedom, stakeholders in institutions of higher education need to continuously ask themselves, "How are you being held responsible for your work and its functions towards Black life and Black freedom?"

To develop the body, institutions of higher education have to create, sustain, and develop formal institutional support systems. For our cohort, admittance to the Ronald E. McNair Graduate Fellowship (McNair) Program before we formally committed to our program was an invisible thread that joined us together. By chance, we were all McNair Fellows. Through McNair, we were provided space to engage with other Black women academics. Our presence as a cohort shifted the programming that McNair offered to provide support for us. For example, one of the participants in Bacon's (2014) *Sisters in the Dissertation House* was invited to a McNair programming event to provide us with practical tools to navigate the dissertation process as Black women. The McNair program centered our specific needs as Black women and provided targeted programming to address them. The McNair program went beyond recruitment and found ways to retain us. McNair opened the door and then made sure that the space was welcoming and deserving of our presence.

To develop the soul, institutions of higher education must provide Black women graduate students space and opportunities to build a collective identity absent of the white gaze (Morrison, 1993), which will bode well in establishing the foundation for cohorts to develop the souls of their collectives. We assert that HWIs, as white institutional spaces, exist to reproduce and maintain societal norms that harm Black women. As such, they cannot be responsible for developing a shared ethos that solely benefits Black women – however, they undoubtedly have an obligation to provide structures and support that allow groups of Black women to create and sustain their collective identity. In practice, this can look like sponsoring affinity groups, planning and implementing targeting programming for Black women graduate students, and working to mitigate the "Black tax" (Givens, 2016). Despite tuition remission, we undoubtedly are paying for the spaces, physically and ontologically, that we occupy.

CONCLUSION

Together, the heart, mind, and body cultivate the collective spirit and politics that manifest the soul of our sister-cohort and allow us to demand transformational changes across space and time. Our ecosystem moved the starting line for folks that want to engage with us. We are very clear in our scholarship, in our conversations, in our movements, in who we are, in our sister-cohort, that Black lives matter. We love Blackness loudly, deeply, and fiercely. Our existence as a sister-cohort means that we no longer engage in conversations that require us to justify the humanity of Black adults and children as a principle. Institutions of higher education – including faculty, staff, and administrators – must also make this same commitment to Black graduate students. There has to be an explicit commitment to and love of Black graduate students that is evidenced in praxis, policies, funding, programming, and curriculum. Drawing on the work of Woodson (2020), we hold as truth that "Black humanity is an ontological reality. We are already enough. With no further recognition, we are already enough. With no new legislation, we are already enough. We. Are. Already. Enough. Already" (p. 19).

REFERENCES

Bacon, J. N. (2014). *Sisters in the Dissertation House: A Dissertation Narrative*. New Forums Press.

Calafell, B. M. (2007). Mentoring and love: An open letter. *Cultural Studies ↔ Critical Methodologies, 7*(4), 425–441. https://doi.org/10.1177/1532708607305123

Collins, P. H. (1994). Shifting the center: Race, class, and feminist theorizing about motherhood. In E. Nakano Glenn, G. Chang, L. Rennie Forcey (Eds.), *Mothering: Ideology, Experience, and Agency* (pp. 45–65). Routledge.

Collins, P. H. (2002). *Black Feminist Thought: Knowledge, Consciousness, and the Politics of Empowerment*. Routledge.

Cook, D. A., & Williams, T. J. (2015). Expanding intersectionality: Fictive kinship networks as supports for the educational aspirations of Black women. *The Western Journal of Black Studies, 39*(2), 157.

Dancy, T. E., & Edwards, K. T. (2020). On labor and property: Historically white colleges, Black bodies, and constructions of (anti)humanity. In C. A. Grant, M. J. Dumas, & A. N. Woodson, (Eds.), *The Future Is Black: Afropressimism, Fugitivity and Radical Hope in Education* (pp. 31–46). Routledge.

Dumas, M. J., & ross, k. m. (2016). "Be real black for me": Imagining BlackCrit in education. *Urban Education, 51*(4), 415–442. https://doi.org/10.1177/0042085916628611

Edwards, A. E. (2000). Community mothering: The relationship between mothering and the community work of Black women. *Journal of the Motherhood Initiative for Research and Community Involvement, 2*(2), 87-100.

Givens, J. R. (2016). The invisible tax: Exploring Black student engagement at historically white institutions. *Berkeley Review of Education, 6*(1), 55–78.

Hanchard, M. (2010). Contours of Black political thought: An introduction and perspective. *Political Theory, 38*(4), 510–536. https://doi.org/10.1177/0090591710366379

Hemphill, P. (Host). (2020, October 19). *Remembering with Alexis Pauline Gumbs*. (No. 20) [Audio podcast episode]. In *Finding Our Way*. https://www.findingourwaypodcast.com/individual-episodes/s1e7

hooks, b. (1990). *Yearning: Race, Gender, and Cultural Politics*. South End Press.

hooks, b. (1993). *Sisters of the Yam: Black Women and Self-Recovery*. South End Press.

hooks, b. (2000). *Feminism Is for Everybody: Passionate Politics*. Pluto Press.

Johnson, L. S. (2015). *Using Sista Circles to Examine the Professional Experience of Contemporary Black Women Teachers in Schools: A Collective Story about School Culture and Support* [Unpublished doctoral dissertation]. University of Georgia.

Klaus, M. H., Kennell, J. H., & Klaus, P. H. (1993). *Mothering the Mother: How a Doula Can Help You Have a Shorter, Easier, and Healthier Birth*. Addison-Wesley.

Martin, D. B. (2019). Equity, inclusion, and antiblackness in mathematics education. *Race Ethnicity and Education, 22*(4), 459-478.

137

Martin, D. B. (2013). Race, racial projects, and mathematics education. *Journal for Research in Mathematics Education, 44*(1), 316–333.

Morrison, T. (1993). *Playing in the Dark: Whiteness and the Literary Imagination.* Vintage Books.

Pitsoe, V. J., & Mahlangu, V. P. (2014). Teaching values in education as a political act for social change. *Journal of Social Sciences, 40*(1), 141–149. https://doi.org/10.5951/jresematheduc.44.1.0316

ross, k. m. (2020). On Black education: Anti-blackness, refusal, and resistance. In C. A. Grant, M. J. Dumas, & A. N. Woodson, (Eds.), *The Future Is Black: Afropressimism, Fugitivity and Radical Hope in Education* (pp. 7–15). Routledge.

Shavers, M. C., & Moore III, J. L. (2014). Black female voices: Self-presentation strategies in doctoral programs at predominately White institutions. *Journal of College Student Development, 55*(4), 391–407.

Smith, C. A. (2016). Facing the dragon: Black mothering, sequelae, and gendered necropolitics in the Americas. *Transforming Anthropology, 24*(1), 31–48.

Wilson, J. A. (2018). *"Ain't I a Woman?": Black Women Negotiate and Resist Systemic Oppression in Undergraduate Engineering and Mathematics Disciplines.* [Unpublished doctoral dissertation]. University of South Florida.

Woodson, A. N. (2020). Afropessimism for us in education. In C. A. Grant, M. J. Dumas, & A. N. Woodson, (Eds.), *The Future Is Black: Afropressimism, Fugitivity and Radical Hope in Education* (pp. 16–21). Routledge.

Chapter 9

"Retention Ain't Enough"

The Spiritually Guided and Intersectional Narratives of Four Black Women Doctoral Students

Niah S. Grimes, Roshaunda L. Breeden,
Jenay F. E. Willis and Konadu Y. Gyamfi

INTRODUCTION

We ain't got white people money class privilege problems, we got different "prolems."

We got our momma's power off, and she needs money to cover the bills "prolems."

We got reparenting ourselves in the midst of trauma "prolems."

We got drive-by shootings and family members being incarcerated for being Black "prolems."

We got they think we money bags now because we are doctors, but the gag is there is no sustainable money "prolems."

We got I'm carrying a village on my back, if we don't make it our families don't eat "prolems."

We got seeing ourselves lynched and our elders killed by a virus to hear don't forget that deadline on Monday problems.

We got different kind of problems, poem by Niah Grimes.

We have been writing about how we retain one another while in the thick of trying to retain each other. Our doctoral journeys have been riddled with daily grief and shock due to the multiple pandemics impacting our nation. We are experiencing what it means to live "theoretical ideas of mentoring and retention" at the margins of doctoral education. Mentorship and retention take on new meanings entirely for us after experiencing a global pandemic, government-supported political coup, and national trial for the wrongful murder

DOI: 10.4324/9781003394648-13

of our brother George Floyd. Every day we awake to traverse through doctoral education not built for scholars that look, act, think, or write like us. Our worth, intellect, and belonging are constantly challenged, while simultaneously we are being championed for our successes and privilege as Ph.D. students. Despite campuses and doctoral programs' access and creation of knowledge that outlines the hardships doctoral students in the margins face, institutions of higher education continuously perpetuate systems of oppression, assuring the *spirit murdering* of Black Indigenous scholars of color (Love, 2016). Lack of access to resources, structures of oppression, daily microaggressions, and societal trauma plague Black students while we are simultaneously being placed in competition with each other to win awards, and secure valuable lines on our curriculum vitas, simply to sustain our basic needs and hopefully silence questions of our worth. For this chapter, we were tasked with answering the question, how do we retain each other through insurmountable odds?

As Black women scholars living theory, we ground our chapter in spirit-led values rooted in community, honesty, love, and responsibility to ourselves, nature, and God. Acting in alignment with those values is what has retained us in higher education. Our goal is to share our journey and pass along the knowledge we have acquired to retain ourselves. We hope it will allow others to build communities of freedom and to utilize this chapter as an expression of spirit and an embodiment of our critical framework. In this chapter, we first discuss the critical framework that shaped our work, we discuss the methods used to collect our narrative data, outline our positionality, and then we present our findings through a re-imagined conversation and brief implications institutional agents can consider right away.

After a celebratory dance once our chapter was accepted, because celebrating is a foundational piece of our retention work, we reconvened to discuss next steps and immediately began to trouble the language "mentoring." The language "mentoring" did not fit our experience of retaining each other. The language mentoring evokes a hierarchy or vision of our elders. Although mentoring has been a piece of what has sustained us throughout this process, without communities of freedom and joy, where we can actualize our authentic selves and release socializations of harm, we would have little to sustain us from the multiple lashes we endure each day fighting for a degree that takes more from us than is given to support us. We are championed for gaining grants, fellowships, and publications in top-tier journals. Our institutions maintain their power off of the sweat and blood of our work and the work of our ancestors continuously (Boss et al., 2021; Nzinga, 2020; Roland et al., 2021). Our advisors barely have time to advise us because they are being beaten down by the neoliberal wheel of global capitalism that higher education is complicit in. Mentoring is not as widely valued in most processes for tenure for our faculty. That leaves our most direct mentors in duress, while the wounded support each other, making what little we can muster work.

This chapter focuses on our distinct narratives as four "sista" scholars studying higher education in the United States as perceived Black women. Sistahood means embodying an ethic of care to treat each other like sistas, centering love and spirit while helping each other with tangible information and resources (Adkins-Jackson et al., 2022; Dillard, 2000; Minnett et al., 2019). Our sistahood takes several different forms in the ways we retain each other, with each of us leaning into our strengths and receiving support in our growth edges. We use the term "sistahood" in this chapter, to describe the multiple facets of our peer relationships, which include bidirectional mentoring, mothering, and everything we need in that moment, especially when institutions, administrators, and faculty are ill-equipped to sustain and nurture our full selves, mainly due to compliance in global capitalism and cisheteropatriarchy (hooks, 2000b; Nzinga, 2020; Patton, 2016).

CRITICAL FRAMEWORK

Endarkened feminist epistemology helped frame this chapter, a worldview brought to us through the work of educator and scholar, Cynthia B. Dillard. As Black women scholars, we needed an epistemological lens that resonates with our spirit and intellect. Endarkened feminist epistemology is a worldview rooted in history, memory, and healing (Dillard, 2006; 2012). Embracing Dillard's (2012) endarkened feminist epistemology allows for a methodological design that "honors the wisdom, memory, spirituality, and critical interventions of Black women's ways of knowing and being" (p. 60). Scholarship corrupted by oppression relies on a false disconnection from our positionality and spirit. An endarkened feminist ethos asks us to center the spirit of who we are and what we bring to our work. Embodying deep consciousness, this epistemology makes sacred space for Black women scholars to embrace Black creativity in our work.

Six underlying tenets undergird endarkened feminist epistemology used to guide this chapter. First, inquiry arises from personally and culturally defined beliefs that render the scholar responsible for one's community's well-being, both inside and outside the academy (Dillard, 2006). Second, our work is "both an intellectual and spiritual pursuit, a pursuit of purpose" (p. 20), which means we come to this work bringing our full selves. Third, dialogue is necessary for both conducting scholarship and assessing knowledge claims. Dillard (2006) specifically mentioned, "Only within the context of the community does the individual appear and, through dialogue, continue to become" (p. 22). The fourth tenet stated, in "Black communities, what happens in people's daily lives is critical for making sense of actions, expressions, experiences, and community life" (p. 23). Fifth, "knowing and research are both historical (extending backward in time) and outward to the world: To approach them otherwise is to diminish their cultural and empirical meaningfulness" (p. 24). And lastly,

141

assumption six highlights that the tenet of intersectionality is rooted in the work of the Combahee River Collective (1986) and Kimberlé Crenshaw (1989). Black women marginalized at the intersections of race/ethnicity, class, gender, sexual expression, body type, and dis/ability face higher rates of targeted violence (de Heer & Jones, 2017). The above tenets of endarkened feminist epistemology and intersectionality acknowledge Black women's legitimate experiences and help us transform oppressive systems, particularly in academic spaces.

METHOD

Leaning into endarkened feminist epistemology, spirit, and intersectionality, we brought our whole selves to this process, sharing language, stories, songs, laughter, and tears across scholarship team meetings. To uplift our voices and provide a seat at our proverbial sista circle, we used narrative artistic expression in our chapter through an imagined conversation regarding how we retain each other in doctoral education. Narrative inquiry centers on detailed stories and the meaning-making experiences of individuals and communities (Clandinin & Connelly, 2000). Although narrative work can take many forms; our team used art, conversation, photography, poetry, journaling, and creative writing to capture our experience retaining each other through doctoral education (Figure 9.1). Utilizing narrative artistic expression through an imagined conversation allowed us to practice our framework and create a counter-hegemonic practice in higher education literature (Green & Bey, 2017).

Figure 9.1 Scholar selfie after healing session with Scholars Willis, Breeden, and Gyamfi (left to right)

Each of us met through the doctoral program in College Student Affairs Administration (CSAA-D). Although only two of us met in the same cohort, we developed our bond through shared courses and events held for Black doctoral students in our department. To begin this inquiry, we took two weeks to self-reflect on how we retained ourselves through our doctoral program. We left the type of reflection open-ended to honor our critical framework and the tenet of Black creativity. Our reflections resulted in data sources including personal narratives, poetry, research memos, text messages, and photographs which we shared with each other formally when we met in March 2021 (Figure 9.2). We began with sharing each of our personal narratives, leaving time for processing, tears, and laughter. Once everyone shared, we then analyzed our narrative data discussing the interconnected pieces across our experiences and focused on the experiences and themes that emerged most frequently or had the largest impact on our retention. Our process honored our critical framework, endarkened epistemology, focusing on our shared history, memory, healing, purpose, and community while allowing ourselves to "become" in our dialogue with one another. We chose to represent the findings in a way congruent with our intellectual and spiritual pursuit of purpose that closely mirrors our ways of being, knowing, and connecting. In the next section, we introduce ourselves using text from narrative expressions each scholar wrote describing her co-scholars and

Figure 9.2 Scholar grimes leading session on helping skills in student affairs

143

the impact we have on one another. We include these introductions to showcase our positionality as transformative qualitative scholars and as an example of the narratives we produced through our methodology.

Positioning Our Sistahood

To describe our positionality, we used an analogy to describe our mentoring relationship with each other. We think of mentorship like the relationship between a trainer and a workout. The mentor is the trainer and the mentee being trained. Your workout (mentorship) can leave you feeling euphoric and energized or sore and tired once the routine is done. One feeling keeps you coming back to your trainer each session and the other one makes you want to run away. The trainer is the one who is going to nurture and evaluate your workout to make sure you get the best results. They are going to challenge and motivate you. They are your biggest advocates in the journey. You can probably get results without them, but having the support and guidance of a trainer makes the process feel more organized and achievable.

Jenay Willis (JW)

Jenay is the trainer who is our inquirer and preacher. When conversing, Jenay inquires about experiences shared in this journey. Connecting with her Southern Baptist rural upbringing intersecting with her Black womanhood, it is without a doubt that her inquiries turn into a praise that is cause for a good faithful shout. Jenay is our old soul that embraces the beauty of her Blackness and being from the country, always offering us a thoughtful word that is sure to end in crying, laughing, dancing, and singing.

Konadu Gyamfi (KG)

Konadu is the trainer who will watch and listen; she takes in everything. You can literally see her processing in her mind before she spits it all back to you in the most profound yet comprehensible way. Konadu is witty, sharp, and carries her New York City sass seasoned by her Ghanaian heritage into every room she enters. Her deep roots in the Christian faith inform how Konadu empowers her sistas to be tempered radicals in the academe and beyond.

Roshaunda Breeden (RB)

Roshaunda is the trainer who asks us to reflect. If we ask Roshaunda a question, she'll give you deep thought instead of an answer. She'll ask us more questions to encourage us all to think deeply and question everything. As the othermother of the group, and someone who identifies as a Black, southern, fat-bodied person,

Roshaunda embodies home in how she creates space for us, checks in on us, while also lovingly snatching our edges.

Niah Grimes (NG)

Niah is the trainer who gets our spirit together. She unapologetically called out cis-heteronormative patriarchy, racism, ability, like it was her job. We learned more from her in our first year than we did from class assignments. In her scholarship, we notice that she always shows up authentically as herself – using storytelling, music, activities, and cultural wealth to express ideas. Most of the things we learn from Niah are not just from what she says but from what we watch her do. Niah is just going around being herself; she is laughing, yelling, crying, chatting, cussing, and just being free. When we watch Niah work, whether it be a presentation or her written work, we are in awe and fascinated because she is everything.

"NOW YOU KNOW WE HAVE TO TALK OUR SH*T!": THE SPIRITUALLY GUIDED AND INTERSECTIONAL NARRATIVES OF FOUR BLACK WOMEN DOCTORAL STUDENTS

From family cookouts at the CSAA-D House, Powerful Partner study sessions at Panera, to car rides to Kroger, hilarious voice notes/messages, among our many gatherings, we retain each other. Our conversations are a mix of good whole-body laughs, necessary cries, unrehearsed dance moves, and dropping knowledge – practical pedagogy for passing milestones that exist in the academy. Spiritually led and bonded in our sistahood, it is the powerful art of truth-telling that we show up in this work as our full selves in being Black women. To better illuminate what retention means to each of us and honor our distinct voices, we re-created a conversation that embraces the values of endarkened feminist epistemology and reflects a typical conversational style and meaning-making between our sistahood. We embedded in the re-created conversation the challenges and recommendations for how the academy impedes our success as well as ways to enhance the success of Black women doctoral students. The following is our recreation of that magic of collective, grounded in spirit based on the narrative data we collected.

RB: Heyyyyy y'all! Thanks for coming over to celebrate the end of the semester! We got bae on the grill and dranks in the fridge, so just kick back and enjoy yourselves. None of y'all are guests here, you are all family, so help yourselves.

NG: I brought the wine. Y'all know a bitch stay ready to entertain and shit. Any appetizers ready or...

JW: Iont know about no appetizers, but I brought fried chicken, macaroni and cheese, collard greens, and sweet tea…

KG: Y'all eat jollof rice?

NG: **hears jollof** There is a GOD!

JW: If Konadu made it, I'll eat it. But who trying to catch this L in Black Cards Revoked real quick?

RB: Bitch, what? Where did that come from? You know I'm the household reigning champ. You don't want to see me, Jenay!

JW: Y'all know I'm random as hell.

All of us looking at each other and laughing in agreement

NG: I hate to get sappy but y'all know I'm a Pisces sun and rising! I am just, so grateful spirit led us all to UGA, I was suffering without y'all.

RB: Then thanks to my three homegirls, Drs. Jemilia Davis, Jillian Martin, and Joan Collier because I wanted to stay home in North Carolina.

Dr. Breeden's partner, who is outside on the grill, cosigns

RB: Before applying, my homegirls sent me care packages, emails, messages, checked my application materials, and included me in conference presentations to enhance my curriculum vitae during the recruitment process. They were retaining me then. Once I got in, we had a conversation about responsibility. Without their sistahood and mentorship, rather guidance, I would not be sitting here, and bae would not be on the grill making barbeque. We miss North Carolina every day.

JW: After spending three years on the east coast, spirit led me home, back to the South where I belong. The South is home, and Georgia specifically raised me from childhood to adulthood. Embarking on my doctoral journey, I knew what family and having a close connection within reach to my support system meant. It meant having home-cooked meals by mama and daddy, good eating with Godmama and Godfather, and feeling endless love from my hometown family. The family feeling was it for me. I chose Georgia, and Georgia chose me in return through the family feeling I feel from this sistahood. It all started when Dr. Roshaunda Breeden started sending me apartment recommendations and sharing assistantship opportunities.

KG: I ain't wanna come here. Not to the South and especially not to Georgia. I wanted to be closer to home, in a city, and close to the airport. But I also knew I shouldn't apply to one program alone, so I did some research and saw that a sista scholar I admire got her doc degree from Georgia. That's literally what brought me to Georgia's website, and I eventually applied.

NG: After finishing my counseling degree so far from family, I knew when I was ready to return to school, I needed to be close to family. I applied to two schools near family. I realized during my visit to UGA that this degree would be challenging, and after talking to several Black women doc students and docs coming out of UGA, I thought, where Black women are, you go. Period.

Everyone in unison: PERIOD.

RB: During my first year, I was assigned the role of GA for the department and I made concerted efforts to recruit Black students, particularly Black women. When I got emails from Konadu and Jenay, I emailed them immediately making sure they knew I was one of their supports during this doctoral process. I even made sure Jenay had housing for her visit and requested that she receive my assistantship once I left! That's what Dr. Qua'Aisa Williams did for me.

NG: Black women will forever make it happen. Dr. Qua'Aisa Williams and Dr. Marvette Lacy were the first Black women I came into contact with before entering UGA. Although they were not in classes with me, they have held me down throughout this journey, and I wouldn't be here without them making space for me and mentoring me. I was the only Black femme who entered my year. After Ro arrived, I knew I was no longer alone. And then spirit brought Jenay and Konadu to us.

RB: Having each other in classes to lean on is a major key. Meeting frequently. Being able to ask questions that seem silly or forbidden to ask but mostly just hanging out with y'all retains me! Keeps me here when I want to pack my shit and leave.

KG: Scheduling classes together, sharing rides together, sitting in classes together, and processing all the microaggression and harm after classes together. Those practices have retained me as well.

RB: Processing after class served as the biggest stress reliever for me. In those conversations, I counted on my sistas to help unpack the violence faced in class, and it went unchecked all the time, leaving processing with y'all the only outlet sometimes.

NG: Retaining each other cannot happen if we aren't admitted and able to share space with one another. We face so much harm from all sides. You all are a large part of my coping through doctoral education. My informational interview for the program, with a Black woman.

The person who held me down while I was vomiting through prelims, a Black woman.

The person who gave us the gift of returning home to Ghana, a Black woman.

KG: Same. Oftentimes I'm in my head trying to solve my problems, shouldering the burden all alone, having this group of sista scholars meant I was no longer isolated.

JW: But you know I got to disrupt this shit! Why is the onus on us to retain each other?

NG: Seriously! Before you and Konadu came, in Spring 2019, I led a healing circle for Black grad students; we were mostly queer. When I thought about all we were carrying, I needed something actionable to lean on that would support not just me but us. Coming together like that was transformative

147

and it made me realize how much institutions lack. The following semester the counseling center started offering groups for Black women specifically. I wondered how my queer identity would have been accepted there or rendered invisible like many of my intersecting identities.

RB: I remember that group! It was my first year and I was so grateful to have an outlet to heal and process everything that was flooding me in that year transitioning into doctoral work.

KG: What baffles me is how we are doctoral students doing professional-level work...

NG: ...yet with undergraduate level resources

RB: ...make it make sense!

JW: If it made sense, it would be too easy, sis!

KG: Not even undergraduate-level resources. We can't get federal grants for this work. Federal aid is all loans. If we sound upset, that's because we are.

JW: A WHOLE WORD SIS!

NG: The lack of structural support for professional students like us is concerning. We barely make enough money through our assistantships and part-time work to cover our basic needs. The least institutions could do if they aren't going to adequately compensate is house us and feed us. NO! And we make too much for food stamps. We can't win fam.

RB: How they want us to produce and we can't heal? How we supposed to create theory when we can't eat? How we supposed to challenge systems of oppression when we can't sleep? If our basic needs aren't met, how can we expect Black women to thrive while carrying our whole families on our back?

NG: How can we learn when we don't feel safe? How can we heal when we are facing constant trauma? From the micro to the macro level! They love to gaslight and render our lives invisible. Well, we are here and we need better structural support. We need equitable change at the societal level, not just interpersonally. Nah, instead, the board of regents checkin' for who is teaching about race and making Christian white men feel singled out. You show us every day which students matter and which students don't.

JW: The angry Black woman has reason to be angry. Just because we bear it all doesn't mean it's not heavy. Just because we are unbreakable doesn't mean you have to test it. We are resilient and we are tired. And tired people should have the grace to be angry.

RB: I don't know if she wants me to say it, but one of my sistas offered to pay for me to attend a conference. Unprovoked. She just slid in my imessage and said I got you. Who does that? What grad student does that? We can't sleep good. We can't eat good but we out here making sure everyone gets the chance to learn good. Wow.

KG: Stop giving all the Students of Color to the one Faculty of Color! Stop piling Faculty of Color with so much! Lack of faculty support is directly related to retention. I find faculty support through Niah and Ro. It feels like when

I need support from other outlets, formal or informal, I end up mentoring and providing the support instead of receiving the support I need. When do I get to be centered?

JW: That's why I'm blessed to have my family to lean on during this time, especially during a global panoramic. Without support, it's hard to make ends meet, let alone learn scholarship, while conducting it, analyzing it, writing it up, and still attempting to maintain coursework and relationships. It's a hot ass mess! Meanwhile, my family has no reference for what I'm doing. They cannot understand why I would transfer and what it means to find faculty members who can mentor us and pour in.

NG: We need courses and spaces where we are free. Where we can cut up, laugh, cry, get loud, clap back, hold each other accountable, get uncomfortable towards growth.

JW: Academia says they want us to heal, but with capitalism running through its veins they can't envision what it means in practice. Ingrained in the fake, which they portray as real, like white supremacy, continuously puts our livelihood and wellness as Black women in occupying these spaces at stake. Nonetheless when we rise and bring to this work the spirit of favor from God and our ancestors, we will not let the act of white supremacists cause our faith to waiver.

KG: Jenay stay with a sermon am I right!

RB: Every squad needs a preacher!

Everyone: AMEN, ASHÈ!

NG: For me it's the cookouts, sista circles, writing groups, conference shenanigans, trips to the flea market, or just doing Black shit with our friends and talking trash that is what gets me through the moments of WTF are we doing!?

RB: Now we all know Niah don't write in writing groups.

Laughter

NG: Okay, I come for the fellowship you're right. I like writing alone. Let me have my process.

JW: Being in community with my sistas is how I know I am where I am supposed to be, which is in alignment with the presence of my ancestors and my spirit. Here, I am reminded that we must continue this work. However, in continuing I will say what I need from the academy – critical conversations and not throwing the word critical in front of work casually. Classes that provide honesty over performativity is a must in order to build and sustain a deep trust. We have no trust when the history of the institution is burying Black bodies on its campus and proclaiming it as myth. These institutions need to own their history and their harm.

149

NG: What use are we to students when we graduate if we are so beaten and bruised from trying to sustain ourselves? Do you know what it is like to feel a Black woman take her life on campus? I know that pain too well. No one should ever know that unimaginable pain.

RB: The day institutions start taking real accountability and atoning for their atrocities against what is sacred we can begin building structures to retain our most marginalized.

NG: We can start to erase the margins and honor peoples' differences as a gift to the whole.

IMPLICATIONS

"When we choose to love, we choose to move against fear, against alienation and separation. The choice to love is a choice to connect, to find ourselves in the other."

-bell hooks (2000a, p. 93)

Largely our findings showcase the context of our doctoral education is deeply entrenched in global capitalism and white supremacy which creates a bind for minoritized and Black women doctoral students like us. Often our strongest sources of retention, our faculty mentors, are not able to provide healing and sacred space because they are bogged down with courses, administrative tasks, scholarship, and battling structural and interpersonal violence (Chancellor, 2019; Comer et al., 2017; Nakamura, 2019; Nzinga, 2020), so we have to retain each other. Spirit and faith are rarely recognized in the academe yet are at the center of our retention practice. Black women have an unspoken agreement that we hold each other down. There are obviously exceptions to this unspoken rule, and there are a lot of novigender (gender that cannot be described by political social labels) Black women who are pushed out when white supremacy conflates our understanding of gender, kinship, and sistahood. Despite the pushout of gender fluid Black women in nearly every educational setting we have been in, there were Black women at all levels there supporting us. Feeding us, providing mentorship, offering hair tips, giving the low down on the community to avoid unspoken politics that hinder a lot of first-generation and low-income Black Indigenous graduate students of color. The labor of equity and retention cannot continuously be placed on those in the margins. We need academic gatekeepers and those with power in our institutions to practice love, spirit, and equity. Institutions champion diversity and equity as an act of interest convergence to hide behind their mainly neoliberal and capitalist agenda (Patton, 2016; Wright-Mair & Museus, 2021). No more.

Our narrative expressions showcased examples of retention with the intention to (1) illuminate our persistence, awareness, and advocacy skills, (2) provide ideas and inspiration for doctoral students facing similar barriers, and (3) challenge people with authoritative and capital power in the academy to reconsider their compliance in systems of domination that directly enact violence and harm against Black women doctoral students requiring us to retain ourselves. Our critical framework, endarkened epistemology, focuses on history, memory, and healing with the pursuit of purpose. Through our narratives, we garnered two homework assignments for institutional agents in higher education to consider.

Homework Assignment #1: Shift Campus Environments to Support Equity and Healing

The most immediate transformative change can happen if campus administrators and faculty create and maintain campus environments for doctoral students to heal, rest, and thrive in. Our narrative described the importance of physical places for us to act and be free. One immediate change administrators and faculty can make right away is creating spaces on campus to support communities of freedom. Students will naturally come together; administrators and faculty need to aid in that natural process and not hinder it. What does a doctoral student café with study rooms, whiteboards, free food for graduate students, and plenty of space for creation and fellowship look like on-campus? What would it mean to include free and safe housing near campus and a meal plan in each graduate assistantship package? Often when doctoral students complain about anxiety, stress, and depressive symptoms, we are told to see a counselor in an overworked counseling center with limited sessions. Have you ever tried processing your trauma while experiencing it? It is a very hard task for the mind, body, and soul to reconcile. What would more somatic therapies on-campus for doctoral students mean for our well-being? Somatic therapies, such as rapid eye movement therapy, have all been well studied in their impacts aiding in trauma management and decrease symptoms of post-traumatic stress disorder, anxiety, and depression (Shapiro & Brown, 2019).

Homework Assignment #2: Make Wellness the Standard, Not a Bonus

Institutions are directly responsible for our wellness and basic needs on-campus, such as food, water, shelter, and safety. The level of professional work such as teaching, scholarship, and administrative duties elevate and help maintain the mission of our institutions. The better institutions meet or exceed our needs, the more time we can dedicate to our professional studies and healing because we will no longer have to divert large amounts of our energy and time on eating, housing, and money. Departments need full-time staff dedicated to the needs of doctoral students, not doctoral students hired to support other doctoral students. Full-time graduate coordinators can hold space for each program's various needs and provide 1:1 advising regarding wellness and health and navigating campus resources for graduate students.

We imagine a world where doctoral students have all their needs not solely met but exceeded. We can thrive on-campus, and in return, we pour that same level of care and support back into our communities on- and off-campus. No policy changes or changes in practice that directly impact us, should be made without us (Combahee River Collective, 1986; Taylor, 2020). When decisions are being made regarding housing, parking, food, courses, faculty, pay, insurance, you name it, we should not be the last to hear about it. We can and need to be included at the onset. Lastly, our faculty, especially minoritized faculty need to be better supported, especially new faculty in the margins. The better supported minoritized faculty are at the institution, the better supported our institutions will be as a whole. Despite having to take on mentoring and retention as a labor of love, we welcome the mentorship offered from our faculty and administrators. We need the academy to create structures to support faculty well-being and incentives for our faculty to be able to pour into our hearts, not just our minds.

REFERENCES

Adkins-Jackson, P. B., Jackson Preston, P. A., & Hairston, T. (2023). 'The only way out': how self-care is conceptualized by Black women. *Ethnicity & health*, *28*(1), 29–45. https://doi.org/10.1080/13557858.2022.2027878

Boss, G., Porter, C., Davis, T., & Moore, C. (2021). Who cares?: (Re)visioning labor justice for Black women contingent faculty. *Journal of African American Women and Girls in Education*, *1*(1), 80–94.

Chancellor, R. L. (2019). Racial battle fatigue: The unspoken burden of Black women Faculty in LIS. *Journal of Education for Library and Information Science*, *60*(3), 182–189.

Clandinin, D. J., & Connelly, F. M. (2000). *Narrative Inquiry: Experience and Story in Qualitative Research*. Jossey-Bass.

Combahee River Collective. (1986). *The Combahee River Collective Statement: Black Feminist Organizing in the Seventies and Eighties*. Kitchen Table: Women of Color Press.

Comer, E. W., Medina, C. K., Negroni, L. K., & Thomas, R. L. (2017). Women faculty of color in a predominantly white institution: A natural support group. *Social Work with Groups (New York, 1978)*, *40*(1–2), 148–155.

Crenshaw, K. (1989). Demarginalizing the intersection of race and sex: A Black feminist critique of antidiscrimination doctrine, feminist theory, and antiracist politics. *University of Chicago Legal Forum, 1989*(1), 139–167.

de Heer, B., & Jones, L. (2017). Measuring sexual violence on campus: Climate surveys and vulnerable groups. *Journal of School Violence, 16*(2), 207–221.

Dillard, C. B. (2000). The substance of things hoped for, the evidence of things not seen: Examining an endarkened feminist epistemology in educational research and leadership. *International Journal of Qualitative Studies in Education, 13*(6), 661–681.

Dillard, C. B. (2006). *On Spiritual Strivings: Transforming an African American Woman's Academic Life*. State University of New York Press.

Dillard, C. B. (2012). *Learning to (re)Member the Things We've Learned to Forget: Endarkened Feminisms, Spirituality, & the Sacred Nature of Research and Teaching*. Peter Lang.

hooks, b. (2000a). *All about Love: New Visions*. William Morrow and Company, Inc.

hooks, b. (2000b). *Feminist Theory: From Margin to Center* (2nd ed.). South End Press.

Green, K. M., & Bey, M. (2017). Where Black feminist thought and trans* feminism meet: A conversation. *Souls, 19*(4), 438–454.

Love, B. L. (2016). Anti-Black state violence, classroom edition: The spirit murdering of Black children. *Journal of Curriculum and Pedagogy, 13*(1), 22–25.

Minnett, J. L., James-Gallaway, A. D., & Owens, D. R. (2019). Help a sista out: Black women doctoral students' use of peer mentorship as an act of resistance. *Mid-Western Educational Researcher, 31*(2), 210–238.

Nakamura, M. (2019). Working with faculty of color at a predominantly white institution: Challenging whiteness and model minority stereotypes. *New Directions for Teaching and Learning, 2019*(158), 49–58.

Nzinga, S. M. (2020). *Lean Semesters: How Higher Education Reproduces Inequity*. Johns Hopkins University Press.

Patton, L. D. (2016). Disrupting postsecondary prose: Toward a critical race theory of higher education. *Urban Education, 51*(3), 315–342.

Roland, E., Hughes, T. N., & Simmons, F. (2021). Imagine paying for a course, then you end up teaching: Black woman doctoral students in equity, social justice, and diversity courses. *Journal of Diversity in Higher Education*. Advance online publication. https://doi.org/10.1037/dhe0000368

Shapiro, R., & Brown L. (2019). Eye movement desensitization and reprocessing therapy and related treatments for trauma: An innovative, integrative trauma treatment. *Practice Innovations, 4*(3), 139–155.

Taylor, K. Y. (2020). *Until Black Women Are Free, None of Us Will Be Free*. New Yorker.

Wright-Mair, R., & Museus, S. D. (2023). Playing the game just enough: How racially minoritized faculty who advance equity conceptualize success in the neoliberal academy. *Journal of Diversity in Higher Education, 16*(1), 109–119.

Chapter 10

There Is Only So Much a Peer Can Do!

Sharon Fries-Britt and Bridget Turner Kelly

THE IMPORTANCE OF BUILDING A MULTIDIRECTIONAL APPROACH TO MENTORING

The BWNM is a multidirectional mentoring model of which peer mentorship reflects one of four major components including across rank mentoring, centering self through radical self-care and the power of community mentoring. We envision this model metaphorically working like a slinky. A slinky moves forward from collective action. Essentially, the propelling force of a slinky is a result of a wave of motion that goes back and forth as a slinky travels along. The energy that gets activated allows all of the connecting circles on the slinky to gain momentum. There are moments in the process when some circles in the slinky are helping to move the momentum forward more than others; however, in doing so they too are propelled.

As evidenced by the chapters in this book when a community of Black women is committed to work together, it creates a wave of energy that moves all women connected to the network forward. The commitments that the authors expressed to each other throughout this book served to advance them individually and collectively, illustrating how committed action leads to collective success. Peer mentors can provide the right balance of challenge and support when students individually find themselves isolated and struggling to succeed in the academy.

Our aim is to not leave any Black women behind; thus, we recognize the need for multiple circles of support and mentorship in our model. We are especially focused on reaching Black women who have faced significant gendered racism to the point that they begin to believe that they are not supposed to be in, or successfully graduate from, a doctoral program. Every day, somebody tries to kill Black women literally and figuratively. Yet we survive! We do not want the academy to continue to be one of those societal spaces where the murder of Black women's intellectual brilliance and ancestral wisdom is sanctioned by inaction and complacency.

DOI: 10.4324/9781003394648-14

Black women peers constantly remind each other that they are worthy of love and of being mentored. However, the development of academic mastery also comes from interaction with others who are in different stages of their career and life. The need for cross rank mentoring and community circles of support are essential. Peers cannot provide every aspect of the learning process. Black women should seek to expand their network to have access to a wide range of mentors who have navigated the academy beyond degree completion and who have access to support and wisdom garnered outside of the academy. Ultimately, one of the most important circles of mentorship is within Black women through radical self-care. Black women must believe in themselves enough to ask for a mentor and to believe that they are worthy of a community rooted in love. Whether that mentor is a peer in their program, a faculty member on another campus they met at a conference or online, Black women must ask for what they need. Moreover, they must know that they are valuable enough to give the gift of mentoring to themselves and others. Next, we turn to two key areas that must be addressed to amplify the success of Black women in doctoral programs: (1) access to Black women faculty and (2) increased support for Black women doctoral students.

ACCESS TO BLACK WOMEN FACULTY MENTORS

Finding Black women faculty mentors is easier said than done when you consider the overall low numbers of Black women faculty who are full time. According to the National Center for Education Statistics (NCES) of all full-time faculty in 2020, only 4% were Black women, and of the full-time faculty in degree-granting institutions, only 2% were full professors and associate professors, respectively, and 3% were assistant professors (NCES, 2022). These low numbers also point to some of the underlying challenges that Black women professors navigate including their own challenges with finding effective mentors and career direction (Stanley, 2006; Stanley & Lincoln, 2005). Several of the chapter authors discussed the complexity in having access to Black women faculty. Grimes, Breeden, Willis, and Gyamfi (Chapter 9) noted Black women faculty often cannot mentor or help retain Black women doctoral students in the ways they need to be mentored because Black women faculty are too few, often overworked and burdened by the same systems of capitalism, sexism, and racism the students face (Kelly & Fries-Britt, 2022). Similarly, Gayles and Smith (Chapter 2) described how few Black women faculty there are in certain disciplines, such as STEM. In the STEM disciplines, this is critical. I, Sharon, have for a long time studied the experiences of Black students in STEM-related fields, and the access to faculty shaped a number of research opportunities and access to other professionals in the field. Early exposure of Black women in STEM to faculty who look like them can go a long way to developing greater pathways of success. We concur with Johnson, Campbell, and Summerville's (Chapter 7) overall observation for the need to hire more Black women faculty and administrators. However as Bent, Stephens-Peace, and Smith (Chapter 4) observe, we need to have Black faculty who can teach about the Black diaspora, such as scholars who teach about Caribbean societies.

As Black women faculty and co-editors, we are certainly familiar with many of the challenges in the literature identified across this project. In our own lives, we have maintained a strategy that allows us to keep front and center the reasons why we were willing to take on this academic journey. We both serve as mentors from a place of consciousness of purpose knowing that we are gaining from the experience and able to make important contributions. For me, Bridget, the academy is where I met my partner of over 20 years. My life enables me to care for our two kids, care for my aging parents, be there for my sisters, and my friends. I feel blessed to have a job that pays me to think and be creative. I do not want to shut off faculty life for other Black women. I want them to know what it is like to be sought after because of their ideas, innovation, creativity, and wisdom. I mentor and serve in my faculty role because it is a way that I can help open the door for others who want to do the kind of research that excites them and teach in ways that lift people up, particularly those on the margins.

Across the chapter, the authors offered important recommendations when Black women faculty are hired, such as fully supporting them in their efforts to work with doctoral students. So much of the work of Black women professors goes unnoticed. Increasingly, there has been more recognition of the invisible labor of Black women (Kelly et al., 2019) that must be acknowledged and compensated. Young, Johnson, Douglass, and Turner (Chapter 8) and Gray, Hall, Andrews, and Clark (Chapter 6) submit that institutions should provide compensation for the unpaid labor of Black women faculty who overserve, advise, and mentor because the need is so great but who do not get recognized for this labor in formal promotion, tenure, and compensation packages. Expanding on faculty support, Grimes et al. recognize that even with reduced loads, minoritized faculty should not be the only ones mentoring and advising students of color. They recommend campuses hire full-time staff to support doctoral student advising, wellness, and health. Finally, it should not be assumed that faculty fully understand how to mentor and work with students in equity-minded ways; thus, Gayles et al. noted that all faculty and staff working with doctoral students should be engaged in equity-minded training and workshops that may help shift the environment to one that is more equitable, inclusive, and supportive.

INCREASED SUPPORT FOR BLACK WOMEN DOCTORAL STUDENTS

As educators we often write about the ability of students to successfully *navigate* the academy. The significant measure of successful navigation is degree completion. However, along the doctoral journey, there are important bench-marks that must be achieved prior to degree completion, such as course completion, proposal defense, data collection, among others. Support is necessary at every juncture; thus, a central theme across the chapters is increasing the amount, and type, of support that Black women doctoral students receive to enhance their navigation of the academy.

Institutional networking support. There are a host of resources and connections that doctoral students need that can be facilitated by institutional agents. Young et al. noted that graduate schools can work to create Black women doctoral students-listservs, affinity groups, and paid mentorship connections. They observe that these listservs could intentionally cut across programs, colleges, and the campus, particularly so Black women can connect with others they might never see on campus or in the classroom. Focusing on the need for affinity groups, Greene, Ogwo, and Newsome (Chapter 5) and Gray et al. submit that institutions need to create Black women-specific affinity groups, including affinity groups in Afro-Caribbean communities of women scholars to advance more opportunities for research collaboration and work (Bent et al., Chapter 4). Additional opportunities such as internships, increased funding, professional development opportunities, and access to training for aspiring faculty members would be beneficial. The McNair program is an example of a program that endeavors to provide many of these opportunities that prepare Black women for faculty or administrative roles. Other institutional support could come from the office of Study Abroad. Bent et al. specifically recommended institutions expand study abroad offerings to include the Caribbean and institutional agents work to form partnerships with institutions, such as the University of the West Indies.

Spirit and well-being. Talking about the importance of retention and the mentoring of Black women students, Grimes et al. observed that retention and mentoring are not enough to support Black women doctoral students. They argue for the need to support Black women doctoral students' spirit and wellness if the academy really wants to retain Black women. For many, the notion of supporting the spirit and well-being of Black women may seem ambiguous; however, we submit that the COVID-19 crisis and the racial unrest expanded our skills, knowledge, and understanding of what communities in and outside of higher education were dealing with as they encountered loss of life, jobs, and emotional instability. In the academy, we became more aware of the emotional needs of students and the desire that students had to focus on their well-being in the midst of global pandemics. Understanding the spiritual needs of Black women and the importance of soul work should be a space that we can hold in the academy especially if there is genuine collaboration and conversation with Black women to learn what resources are necessary for them to thrive and to be authentic in the academy.

Greene et al. echoed this sentiment-encouraging institutions to design mental health resources for Black women doctoral students and then marketing to them in various ways. While the need for mental health and supportive services is increasingly necessary, we acknowledge that these efforts will not resonate with every Black women doctoral student; thus, it will be important to remain open to finding solutions that offer alternatives that address the diversity of needs within the community of Black women graduate students. Gray et al. suggest talking to Black women doctoral students on your campus about their needs and not relying on students to have to figure it out only among peers. The authors point to the need to conduct mixed-method assessments and exit interviews with Black women scholars to learn more about their needs.

Representation in the Curriculum and Campus Space. The curriculum is a powerful tool for communicating what is valued in the academy. The importance that is conveyed of topics that are covered in class and whose voice is included matters. The readings and assignments that are selected offer insight into what the professor has identified as a problem worth exploring and one that she has evaluated as having merit. Representation matters in what is taught and who is given power and position in the teaching and learning exchange. The authors in this book call for Black women to be represented in the curriculum in all the diversity that exists within the community of Black women. Gray et al. buttressed this by pushing for a decentering of whiteness in higher education, calling on allies of Black women doctoral students to spend time in reflexivity and self-examination on anti-Blackness, power, and oppression. These practices allow allies to show up in constructive ways. Ideas of curriculum also extended to authors asking for seminars and professional development opportunities geared toward Black women. Gordon (Chapter 3) noted the importance of including queer Black women students. Gordon stated that cis-het Black women faculty, staff, and students need to assume there are queer women in doctoral spaces and use their power to invite them into those spaces. As cisgendered Black women faculty, we heed this advice and use our power to invite queer Black women into our programs. We have endeavored to create an empowering intellectual community where the needs of Black women can be centered and where Black women have access to informal and formal systems of power. One of the ways a community experiences freedom is through power, such as putting a system in place whereby Black women doctoral students are a part of any policy or program for doctoral students. Part of empowering Black women doctoral students is cultivating conscious cohorts of Black doctoral students within an academic context that can support their growth.

The University of Maryland: Case Example of Supporting Black Women Doctoral Students

Many of the calls for Black women faculty mentors and support for Black women doctoral students that the authors in this book described have been applied and are in the making at our own institution, The University of Maryland (UMD), College Park. UMD serves as a unique case to highlight because of the structural racial and gendered diversity within the faculty and students but also the current climate of intentional efforts to work on issues of systemic oppression and racism. We draw attention to it here to demonstrate how the calls from authors in this book are doable in higher education, even, or particularly, at historically white universities. In our case example, we focus on two concentrations that are within our Higher Education, Student Affairs and International Education (HESI) Program: (1) Higher Education and (2) Student Affairs.

For nearly two decades, the higher education concentration has had a majority racially diverse faculty. Recent and impending retirements resulted in a 2022 search process with two new hires that are also racially diverse, thus continuing our majority diverse faculty for the foreseeable future. The Student Affairs concentration boasts an all-women faculty of color for more than ten years. Of the five Black professors who work across our two concentrations, four identify as Black women, and four are UMD alums having earned at least one of their graduate degrees at the university many years ago. On one level, we believe that this is an important factor and recognition of our universities progress. I, Sharon, can recall a time in higher education where there was a huge debate about "growing your own talent", and hiring graduates from your program was viewed as less favorable in terms of rigor and academic standing of your program. Put differently, it was not fully accepted as the most successful strategy. At the UMD, we believe that it has significantly impacted our efforts to advance equity. Across both programs, the same is true for students who have enrolled and graduated from both programs. Each has had a critical mass of Black women doctoral students who create supportive, healthy communities and peer mentoring groups. Over the years, Black women doctoral students in our programs have submitted conference proposals and papers to discuss what it has meant to be studying and conducting research in a program with a critical mass of Black women professors. The changes in our programs have happened through considerable labor from Black women professors who have recruited, mentored, and supported the careers of Black women doctoral students for decades.

Some time ago, I, Sharon, was in a casual conversation about my tenure in higher education when a colleague from MIT asked me how long I had been at UMD. At that time, it was just over 30 years (now 38). Upon learning this, he commented, "oh you are a lifer". According to my colleague, a lifter is someone who has been at the same institution for 25 years or more. Lifer had an immediate negative connotation for me. The label did not reflect my years of experience at UMD which have resulted in deep roots and connection. It has been an opportunity to be a part of a long history of collective labor to improve access, retention, and success for Black, Indigenous, People of Color (BIPOC) communities for nearly four decades. For me personally, it has been a place where I have had opportunities to grow and expand my career initially as an administrator and then professor. As I have shared in this and other contexts, UMD has not been without its barriers (it is the academy after all). Despite the challenges, it has afforded me an opportunity to work collaboratively to build a legacy in our higher education program for mentoring students to academic success. It is a campus where a commitment to race, equity, and diversity research and practice is shared by many faculty, staff, and students across the campus. This is a characteristic I greatly value in a university community.

In addition to the campus commitment to racial and gender equity, the Dean of the College of Education has spent her career studying mentoring. Dean Kimberly Griffin is well known for her scholarship on enacting equitable communities, and she is bringing that research to bear in the college. I, Bridget, lead a group in the college called Council on Racial Equity and Justice (COREJ-pronounced courage). We conducted an Institutional Review Board (IRB)-approved study of the experiences of students of color in the college. The Dean is taking the recommendations from the study and putting them into practice. The main participants in the study were graduate students of color, many of them Black women, and they asked for (1) creation of community of color spaces, (2) staff and faculty professional development around racial equity, (3) interrupt pervasive whiteness throughout the college, (4) market the anti-bias policy in the college, and (5) create community. Many of these can find homes in the ideas the authors in this book laid out. While peers can support each other as the college works to implement these ideas, it is up to the Dean, Department Chairs, Program Coordinators, faculty, and staff to build a culture of transparency and trust but showing progress and action.

CONCLUSION

So much attention has been given to the large number of Black women pursuing doctoral degrees (Patterson-Stephens et al., 2017) compared to their Black male counterparts. Yet we know that the experiences of Black women in these programs have not always affirmed their intellectual capacity and well-being. This work reveals the importance of Black women being able to speak for themselves and having a space to tell their stories of collaboration and support that led to their success. Being with a community of Black women does not ensure that you will always be able to relate to your peers. The intersecting identities of Black women are complex and multifaceted. We hope that this book will inspire you to work strategically as you support Black women doctoral students. We believe that transparency and trust matter in collaborating with Black women. I, Sharon, try to always remind myself of how much I did not know when I began my doctoral program and the help that I needed to understand what it would take to complete the PhD. I try to demystify the process and yet prepare my students for the rigors of the work. As a professor, I believe that it humanizes me and opens the space for real learning and collaboration. As we are coming to spaces fully human, we invite our students to do the same. Institutions and institutional actors seeing Black women doctoral students as unique, wise, innovative human beings who are worthy to be fully supported in the academy would go a long way in peers not being the only support systems available to them.

REFERENCES

Kelly, B. T., & Fries-Britt, S. L. (2022). *Building Mentorship Networks to Support Black Women: A Guide to Succeeding in the Academy.* Routledge Press.

Kelly, B. T., Gardner, P. J., Stone, J., Hixson, A., & Dissassa, D.-T. (2019, December 19). Hidden in plain sight: Uncovering the emotional labor of Black women students at historically white colleges and universities. *Journal of Diversity in Higher Education.* Advance online publication. http://dx.doi.org/10.1037/dhe0000161

National Center for Education Statistics. (2022). *Characteristics of Postsecondary Faculty. Condition of Education. U.S. Department of Education, Institute of Education Sciences.* Retrieved May 31, 2022, from https://nces.ed.gov/programs/coe/indicators/sce.

Patterson-Stephens, S. M., Lane, T. B., & Vital, L. M. (2017) Black doctoral women: Exploring barriers and facilitators of success in graduate education. *Higher Education Politics & Economics, 3*(1), Article 5. Available at: https://digitalcommons.odu.edu/aphe/vol3/iss1/5

Stanley, C. A. (2006). Coloring the academic landscape: Faculty of color breaking the silence in predominantly White colleges and universities. *American Educational Research Journal, 43*(4), 701–706. http://www.jstor.org/stable/4121775

Stanley, C. A., & Lincoln, Y. S. (2005). Cross-race faculty mentoring. *Change, 37*(2), 44–50. https://doi.org/10.3200/CHNG.37.2.44-50

About the Book Editors

Sharon Fries-Britt is a Professor of Higher Education and University of Maryland Distinguished University Professor. Her research examines the experiences of high-achieving Black collegians, underrepresented minorities (URMs) in science, technology, engineering, and mathematics (STEM) fields and race, equity and diversity in higher education. She served as the faculty co-lead of a national case study of the University of Missouri recovery process following the campus racial unrest of 2015. This work is in collaboration with the American Council on Education (ACE) and has resulted in two national monographs. She was a member of the American Institutes of Physics (AIP) National Task Force to Elevate African-American Representation (TEAM-UP) in physics. She has published widely within peer-reviewed journals, and she has served on the editorial boards of the *Journal of College Student Development*, the *Journal of Diversity in Higher Education*, and the *College Student Affairs Journal*. Her research has been funded and supported by the Bill & Melinda Gates Foundation, National Science Foundation, Lumina Foundation and the National Society of Black Physicists.

Bridget Turner Kelly is an Associate Professor of Student Affairs at the University of Maryland, College Park. Her scholarship focuses on marginalized populations in higher education, such as women and faculty of color. She has authored over 40 publications, including two articles that have received over 200 citations each and two that have been cited in amicus (friend of the court legal brief to aid the court by providing extra relevant information or arguments) briefs for U.S. Supreme Court cases. She is an award-winning teacher of intergroup dialogue and presents nationally on the topic. She served on the editorial review board of the *Journal of College*

Student Development (JCSD), as Associate Editor for Media and Book Reviews for the *Journal of Student Affairs, Research and Practice* (JSARP), and now serves as the Executive Editor for JSARP. She is an author and co-editor of *Engaging Images for Research, Pedagogy and Practice: Utilizing Visuals to Understand and Promote College Student Development* (2017, Stylus).

About Book Chapter Contributors

Krystal E. Andrews is the Director for Student Success (School of Education) at Virginia Commonwealth University and a doctoral candidate at the University of Illinois at Urbana, Champaign. Her research centers on the experiences of Black women graduate students at HBCUs and the persistence of Black student populations across institutional types.

Stephanie Bent is a PhD candidate in the Higher Education, Student Affairs, and International Education Policy program at the University of Maryland, College Park. She conducts research about student affairs practice in the Caribbean and Caribbean universities' contributions to regional development. Her research also explores Caribbean tertiary students' identity development both in the region and in the diaspora.

Roshaunda L. Breeden is an Assistant Professor in Educational Leadership in the College of Education at East Carolina University. Her research addresses access and equity in the U.S. post-secondary educational system. She uses art-based and participatory research methodologies to center students, leaders, and communities in the margins of higher education.

Erica T. Campbell earned her PhD in May 2022 and currently works as a full-time faculty member. Her research centers Black women administrators in multicultural centers due to her former experience in student affairs. She is motivated to highlight Black women's experiences to shift how they are treated at historical white institutions.

Brianna C.J. Clark currently serves as the Director of Academic Programs within Marymount University's College of Business, Innovation, Leadership Technology. Her research examines HBCU athletics and gender and racial equity in sport. She is the second graduate of the Higher Education Leadership and Policy Studies Program at Howard University.

Tyanna A.E. Clayton-Mallett received her master's in Student Affairs in Higher Education from Marquette University. She is pursuing a doctorate at the University of Maryland, College Park. Her research interests include examining the racial and political identity development of Black higher education professionals across the diaspora.

Courtney A. Douglass, a doctoral student in Urban Education at the University of Maryland, is a birth worker and educator who centers Black families' liberatory and decolonizing parenting practices. Courtney investigates Black unschooling, homeschooling, and other approaches to self-directed education as current and historical forms of Black fugitivity and refusal.

Joy Gaston Gayles is an Alumni Association Distinguished Graduate Professor of Higher Education and Senior Advisor for the Advancement of Diversity, Equity, and Inclusion in the College of Education at North Carolina State University. Dr. Gayles is internationally recognized for her research and scholarship on women and people of color in STEM fields and her work in the area of intercollegiate athletics in higher education.

Liliana G. Gordon (she/her) is a social justice researcher and queer prison abolitionist. Her research interests include Black queer feminism and carceral justice. After her gap year in Nashville, she will attend Harvard College as a pre-law student in the fall of 2023. She plans to obtain a JD/PhD in Sociology.

Ashley L. Gray is the founder of ALG Consulting specializing in equity, diversity, and inclusion services and qualitative research in higher education. Her research focuses on equity and pathways to the college presidency. She is the first graduate of the Higher Education Leadership and Policy Studies Program at Howard University.

Patrice Greene is a PhD candidate in the Student Affairs concentration at the University of Maryland, College Park. Patrice's professional experience includes advising, residence life, and career services. Patrice's research interests include community and support for Black women, virtual learning, racial equity on college campuses, and Black youth activism.

Niah S. Grimes (she/her/hers) is an Assistant Professor of Higher Education and Student Affairs in the Department of Advanced Studies, Leadership, and Policy at Morgan State University. She focuses her scholarship on eradicating violence and systems of oppression in higher education through creative, narrative, healing, and spirit-based approaches.

Konadu Y. Gyamfi is a Clinical Assistant Professor in Sport Administration at Georgia State University. Although never an athlete, she describes herself as a sport enthusiast as well as an educator and social action advocate. Her scholarly work is centered on examining scholar activism and issues of social injustice through sport.

Candace N. Hall is an Assistant Professor at Southern Illinois University Edwardsville. Her research interests include the recruitment, retention, and support of Black faculty at historically white institutions. Hall aims to show the possibility of Black joy and foster community among Black faculty in the academy.

A.C. Johnson earned her PhD in 2021 and currently works with graduate students. Her experiences during her doctoral journey centered around family life and being a first-generation student. Therefore, her research aims to explore the nuances of first-generation Black women doctoral students' experiences with a focus on their perseverance.

Mary Johnson (MJ), a doctoral candidate in Urban Education at the University of Maryland, is a multisensory storyteller. She is passionate about documenting, expressing, and celebrating Black stories with integrity. Her work emphasizes how multisensory storytellers cultivate environments that are responsive to the depth and range of Black expression.

Antoinette Newsome is a PhD candidate in the Student Affairs Concentration program at the University of Maryland, College Park. Her professional experience includes housing and residence life, Greek life, and first-generation programming. Her research centers racial equity-based practices, support for Students of Color, and Women of Color peer-mentoring relationships.

Ashley Ogwo is a PhD candidate in the Higher Education program at the University of Maryland, College Park. Her professional experience includes diverse undergraduate and graduate college student success programs and mentorship programs. Her research centers on Black diasporic relationship dynamics and strengthening communication across diverse Black ethnic groups.

Blake O'Neal Turner is a critical mathematics scholar, educator, and doctoral candidate in Urban Education at the University of Maryland. Her scholarship, undergirded by the wholeness and humanity of Black doers and learners in mathematics, employs critical race method(ologies) to disrupt anti-Blackness in the education enterprise.

Abigail Smith holds a BA in Sociology from Randolph College and an MA in Higher Education and Student Affairs from the University of Connecticut. She currently works at the American University of Sharjah in the UAE within the Student Residential Life Department. She plans to enter an International Education PhD Program.

Chelsea Smith serves as the Assistant Dean at Fordham University in the Graduate School of Arts and Sciences. Her research interests include Black women in STEM, graduate education, diversity, and inclusion education. She completed her MEd and Graduate Certificate at Iowa State University and her BA at the University of Georgia. She will complete her PhD at North Carolina State.

Kat J. Stephens-Peace has a BA from Sarah Lawrence College and an EdM from Teachers College, Columbia University, in Higher and Postsecondary Education. Her PhD is from the University of Massachusetts Amherst in Higher Education. She is an Assistant Professor at Allegheny College in Community and Justice Studies.

Kiara S. Summerville earned her PhD in December 2020, and she currently works as a student success practitioner. Her research interests are situated on the experiences of Black college women. Informed by her own undergraduate experience, her award-winning dissertation research explored how undergraduate student leadership experiences shaped Black women's belongingness in college.

Jenay F. E. Willis is a doctoral candidate in Higher Education at the University of Pittsburgh. Her research agenda highlights college access among rural Black students. As a Southern rural Black woman, her lived experiences inform her scholarship. She centers the narratives of this student population through asset-based and critical approaches.

Alexis Morgan Young, a doctoral candidate in Urban Education at the University of Maryland, collaborates with preadolescent Black girls to co-create spaces that forefront their imaginative practices to foster environments to enrich their liberatory literacies, dream of otherwise worlds, and have their recommendations for the future recognized as valid knowledge.

For Product Safety Concerns and Information please contact our EU
representative GPSR@taylorandfrancis.com
Taylor & Francis Verlag GmbH, Kaufingerstraße 24, 80331 München, Germany